SHOCK

Edited
STEFAN JAW

TITAN BOOKS
LONDON

SHOCK
ISBN 1 85286 707 8

Published by
Titan Books
42-44 Dolben Street
London SE1 0UP

First edition September 1996
1 3 5 7 9 10 8 6 4 2

British Library Cataloguing-in-Publication data. A catalogue record for this book is
available from the British Library.

Printed and bound in Great Britain by Hillman Printers (Frome) Ltd,
Frome, Somerset.

Picture credits:
Amblin Entertainment, Anglo-Amalgamated Film Distributors Ltd, Artificial Eye,
Artists Releasing Corporation, AVR Entertainment, BBC Films, BFI Stills, Posters &
Designs, Best Video, Bizarre Video Productions, Boxoffice International Film
Distributors Inc, Jörg Buttgereit & Manfred O. Jelinski Productions, Cannon Film
Distributors, Columbia Pictures, Compton Cameo Films, Concorde, Contemporary
Films Ltd, Creative Artists Productions, Derann Film Services, First Independent, HBO
Showcase Productions, Hokushin Audio Visual Ltd, HVC, Independent International,
International Entertainment Corp, Jezebel Films, Manson International, George
Harrison Marks, Silke Mayer, Media Home Entertainemnt Inc, Medusa Home Video,
Merrick International, Miracle Films, MGM Inc, MGM/UA Home Video, Mountains
Films Ltd, National Film Archive, New World Pictures, Dennis Nyback, Pacemaker
Pictures, Palace Video, Paramount Pictures, Redemption Films, Something Weird
Video, Tigon Pictures, 20.20 Vision, Troma Inc, United Artists, Vipco Ltd, Virgin
Vision, Visual Entertainment Films, Warner Bros Inc, WVI Gold Productions.
Any omissions will be corrected in future editions.

Front cover photo:
The immortal Mickey Hargitay in *Bloody Pit of Horror* © 1965 M.B.S Cinematografica
(Rome).

Back cover photos:
Top: Traci Lords.
Middle: *Freaks* © 1932 MGM Inc.
Bottom: *Bloodlust* © 1976 Monarex.

CONTENTS

For Robert

ACKNOWLEDGEMENTS:

Mark Ashworth, Allan Bryce, Michael Farin/Belleville Publishing, Gary Graver, Piers Haggard, Mick Hamer, Dave Hyman, Alan Jones, Traci Lords, George Harrison Marks, Silke Mayer, Marc Morris, Prometheus Books, *Psychotronic* magazine, Massimo Pupillo, Steve Roe, *Shock Cinema*, Tamara Ustinov, *Video Watchdog*, Simon Williams, Nigel Wingrove and Robert Wynne-Simmons.

Special thanks to David Barraclough for keeping this project going, and to Jack Stevenson for his inspirational enthusiasm and dedication.

All Titan's film & TV titles are available through most good bookshops or direct from our mail order service. To order telephone 01536 763 631 with your credit card details or contact Titan Books Mail Order, PO Box 54, Desborough, Northants., NN14 2UH, quoting reference SHK/PB.

NEW AGE AQUARIAN MEDITATIONS

I'm humiliated. Something's gone terribly wrong. For the first time in my life I admit defeat. It's only the third volume of The Publication Formerly Known as *Shock Xpress* and I'm already incapable of thinking up an excuse for using the word 'fuck' in the first paragraph. Whether I'll recover from this mortifying lapse remains to be seen; let's just hope my malaise doesn't have a detrimental effect on the contributors...

But enough of this cheery banter — it wouldn't do to have anyone labouring under the misapprehension that I'm here under anything but the most agonising of sufferance...

There are now enough forms of Rage and Panic on the market to justify everything from defenestrating homosexuals who wink at you in gay bars to severing the vocal cords of next door's baby with a rusty can opener when its yowling sets off a speaking car alarm ("You're too close to the vehicle, please step away") at 4am... Naturally I subscribe to all of them. My latest addition (many of you are doubtless also victims) is Satellite Rage. It begins like this: you receive this month's worthless, incomprehensible listings magazine (and 'personal' letter, informing you that you're now the proud recipient of The Miasma Channel, The Defilement Channel and The Abhorrence Channel — free and fun for all the family! — for which your account is being debited by merely an extra zillion yen per minute) and scan it on the crapper, emitting howls of fury as you realise that yet another entire month's schedule comprises of emissions from Murdoch's satellite sphincter... "What the fuck is going on here? I can't take this shit any more! I didn't sign up for this crap! If I ever see another copy of this fucking magazine I'll tear it to pieces. I'm going to write and tell them to stuff their stinking Astra up their etc, etc, etc. (*Pause.*) Uh, well, maybe I'll give it another few months and see if it improves..."

The only person I know who had the courage of her convictions (stemming from, in her case, Cable Rage) is Anne Billson, who cancelled her sub when the engineers failed to arrive on time to repair a fault. She said it felt good, like a great weight had been lifted from her. Well, for all my monthly ranting and raving I've been incapable of even composing a suitably foaming letter; instead, I *added* over twenty channels by enlarging my dish to accept pointless transmissions from some Martian satellite capable only of beaming out useless, unintelligible gibberish. I've got Polish stations (even my father quickly made me turn them off in disgust), Italian, Spanish, French (these clowns have the gall to legislate against culturally impoverishing American garbage while subsisting on a diet of *Jeux sans Frontières*-style drivel where Mr Blobby-types dunk hooting merkins in vats of warm lard), Turkish, Arabic, continental MTV rip-offs brutal enough to force you to appreciate the Eternal Genius of Ray Cokes, and god knows what else...

The Turkish channel shows the crudest, most barbaric, ratty-looking soap operas conceivable. Imagine Andy Milligan, Ed Wood and Guy Maddin co-producing endless black and white variations on fat, ugly blockheads arguing in cardboard rooms, shot on pre-World War One recycled nitrate stock. The soundtracks crackle and pop, squiggly lines and Dadaist scribbles obscure the picture, gruesome slug-like human beings yammer forever... Occasionally they'll run a comedy programme (more revolting blockheads, this time in silly outfits — probably Turkish drag queens — sitting on rickety chairs talking in squeaky voices, for eternity), with sketches so astonishingly laboured and torturous that even the canned laughter — doubtless produced at gunpoint — sounds pained. The Arab channels are much more fun, with great, surreal adverts and good music videos. I watch them a lot.

The Polish stations incorporate many cheap-looking current affairs and chat shows (so inane my father thought they must be aimed at Polish retards in exile), cut-rate, sleazy-looking homegrown dramas (ugliness, cluelessness and garish fashions are a common denominator), and that peculiar-to-eastern-Europe phenomenon of the one-man, voice-overed foreign film: a rat-eaten print of a mouldy John Wayne turd with one miserable Pole slowly, monotonously mumbling the lines of every single person on screen *over* the original soundtrack...

(In Romania they interrupt the output of local stations [not that most Westerners would even recognise their transmissions as anything resembling 'TV programmes'] with current movies shot onto camcorder from the back of a cinema — people wander around, come in, leave or talk throughout, all captured on the video, naturally. The movies often begin randomly, maybe halfway in, stop, are obviously rewound and begin again. Quality is around that of a fifth generation bootleg, and the same deal of one loser translating all the parts applies. It's a viewing experience so deadening that I'd rather take my chances in one of Jack Stevenson's grindhouses where jizz drips from the ceiling...)

There are a bunch of other channels I can't even stand to think about right now, but no matter how intolerable and incomprehensible they are, they must be a more acceptable alternative to the demonic messages encoded in The Degradation Channel... So next time you're subject to an attack of Satellite Rage, forget your idle threats of cancelling the lot — simply add more, in languages you can't understand. The calming effect is miraculous...

Little to note otherwise apart from the slight confusion in 'The Periodical Formerly Known as *Shock Xpress*' department. 'Pathetic beyond description' seems to sum the situation up quite adequately, so you'll have to make do with that and use your imaginations to fill in the blanks...

And, although it seems impossible, as we hurtle headlong towards End Times, our worthless nation is sinking even further into the mire, caught between the crypto-fascist depravity of the Tories' death throes and the smirking hypocrisy of Tory Blair's 'acceptable' Conservatism... Rabid bats pour out of the Channel Tunnel in their thousands, BSE bounces round the empty skulls of the nation's *Sun* readers and E-guzzling teenagers metamorphose into 400lb monstrosities after glomming gallons of water every hour... Here at *Shock* our only noteworthy casualty is Alan Jones, hoist by his own global fabulousness and consequently too busy to contribute to this volume. He threatens to return next time with a cross-referenced inventory of Michele Soavi's laundry basket. Don't hold your breath. Or perhaps you should...

It seems appropriate to conclude with an excerpt from a little post-modernist, pseudo-Dadaist mani-festo, courtesy the Schimpfluch label of Switzerland: 'blasphemy, obscenity, charlatanism, sadistic excess, orgies and the aesthetics of the gutter, these are our moral expedients against stupidity, satiety, intolerance, provincialism, dullness, against the cowardice to bear responsibility, against the sack that eats at the front and shits at the back? Who could possibly take issue with such profound and touching sentiments...? ∎

Stefan Jaworzyn, January 1996

FIVE NIGHTS IN NOWHERE NICE

BY DAVID KEREKES

Monday, March 6

Eight o'clock sharp. The cable test card disappears and the Sky Radio music cuts off. A jingle starts to play, accompanied by a station logo (a hand reaching for the knob on a TV set). The certificate which precedes each film looks much like the BBFC certificate, but that's where the association ends. There is no voice-over introduction, no advertisements which play during the feature.

The first of the four movies this evening is *The Bees*, Alfredo Zacharias' eco-horror yarn starring John Saxon and John Carradine. South America, it would seem, is plagued by killer bees — a revelation which comes courtesy of a map, solemn narration and happy travelogue music. There are hiccups

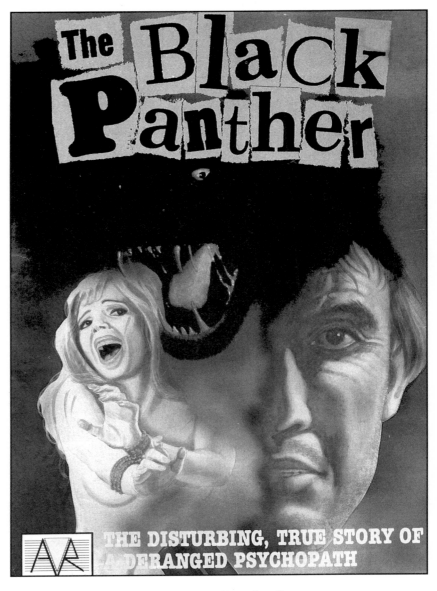

THE DISTURBING, TRUE STORY OF A DERANGED PSYCHOPATH

in the transmission. The sound cuts out momentarily. Carradine plays Uncle Ziggy, a scientist with a bad German accent: "Ya. I'll have a look at zem, later." The bees are antagonised by radiation from a satellite dish. Footage of Gerald Ford is intercut. Someone uncovers a capitalist plot — an organisation importing 'frozen bee sperm from Brazil' into the United States for purposes of making money out of honey. As the bee menace starts to spread across the US, John Saxon hits upon the idea of turning the "bees into homosexuals". Some nobody retorts, "That reminds me of a certain neighbourhood in LA." The Agricultural Department holds a meeting. It's down to Uncle Ziggy to try and find the solution to the bee menace. He sits in his lab attempting to communicate with the insects. "It's very much like translating an unknown language," he says, translating the unknown language. The sound cuts out with increasing regularity — there is no pattern to it. Fire-fighters are called in. Black bee clouds are superimposed on the film. Bees infiltrate the baby units of hospitals. Bees are in the drinks cabinet of the honey-making corporate pig's office. Ziggy uncovers embezzlement on a grand scale and deduces that assassins are out to nail him. John Saxon places a container of bees on a man's head. Stock footage of a controlled test plane crash is played with footage of bees over the top. "Are you mad," says someone. "You want us to ——- bugs?" The sound dropout is getting worse. Uncle Ziggy is communicating with the bees and they with him: "We haven't been ab——guage." The end.

A 'digital' countdown displays the minutes before the next feature commences, in this instance *Exit the Dragon, Enter the Tiger*. Another seventies production, released theatrically in Britain (but with cuts), it's of the type that tried to establish a kung fu star to take

the place of the recently deceased Bruce Lee. This film's contender is Bruce Li. *Exit the Dragon* perhaps tries harder than most by having Bruce Lee — played by an actor — actually hand over his legacy to Li in the opening moments of the movie, seconds before he suffers a headache and snuffs it. Actual footage of Lee's funeral follows, with numerous shots of him lying in state. Li is convinced that foul play is behind the master's death. The movie is a curious blend of factual and fictional characters set in a hypothetical situation (not unlike Larry Buchanan's *Down On Us*, shown earlier in the week). To drive home the fact that Li is destined to fill the late star's shoes, wherever he goes people mistake him for Lee. Posters of Lee adorn most every wall in most every shot of every room. In one scene, Li passes himself off as the dead star, saying that 'his' death was only a promotional gimmick. No concession has been made to adapt *Exit the Dragon* to the small screen. When a fight breaks out in a yard, Li runs to one side and fights for some minutes in and out of shot — the viewer gets to hear the blows and see the results of some particularly flighty fist work as men tumble into shot, but the actual conflict itself is largely obscured. "I have to find out how Bruce Lee died," is Li's oft heard call to his girlfriend, Suzie Young. She is kidnapped by a gangland boss called The Baron. Li infiltrates the warehouse where Suzie is being held by posing as a telephone repair man. They let him in and tell him to get on with it (repairing the telephone), regardless that the girl is tied up in the middle of the room. Lee *was* murdered, Li discovers. He refused to sell drugs through his internationally renowned kung fu schools. After the inevitable confrontation at the close of the picture, from which Li emerges victorious, a voice-over proclaims him to be Bruce's true successor.

Pieces, which follows, is a cut version of the J. P. Simon horror movie about a chainsaw maniac. "It seems some maniac's running lose," says a reporter to a policeman, "or something like that." The pot-bellied guy at the start of the last film of the evening is not about to embark on *Murder in the Orient*. That privilege belongs to an American kung fu instructor, searching for the men who killed his sister. He sorts out a bunch of bad guys with his kung fu prowess. The felled boss says he won't let him get away with it and calls for "Kang the butcher... the executioner." The instructor then teams up with an ex-Green Beret and together they go in search of treasure supposedly buried by the Japanese in World War Two. "Coral Beach?" queries the instructor, a finger upon his lips. "Mm?"

There is a hole in the TV time continuum. It is in my house.

Newcomers to satellite or cable television will recognise the affliction known as channel hopping. Bouncing through the stations, one after another, not really watching anything in particular. I turn on my newly acquired cable TV access and commence to channel hop — a woman gives birth, a lion jumps over a small wall and mauls several other animals, advertisement, advertisement, advertisement, Mountain play a song, a football match from 1987 is re-run, a shark rams the cage from which a diver observes... On station 35 I hesitate. A car is running out of control down a hillside road. A momentary respite, however, and it's back to the channel hop. Talk show, quiz show, Roald Dahl's *Tales of the Unexpected*... station 35, that swerving car. It's a white

They Prey on HUMAN FLESH!

the BEES

Starring JOHN SAXON · ANGEL TOMPKINS · JOHN CARRADINE
Music by RICHARD GILLIS · Director of Photography LEON SANCHEZ
Written, Directed and Produced by ALFREDO ZACHARIAS

car. There is a camera crew up in the hills filming from the back of the truck. A man has a rifle. On the director's signal he fires the rifle and the car crashes. The two men jump off the truck to go and investigate the crash, leaving two dope-smoking camera operatives to smoke their dope. The men have an ulterior motive. Once on the scene they admit to wanting the stunt to have backfired and the woman driver to be dead. Later, they eat her (holding a private banquet with limbs and organs set amongst a salad dressing). A female masochist enters the picture. She manipulates a scenario whereby the two men feel they must break into her apartment. She is waiting for them. Instead of calling the cops, however, she invites the cannibals to take a bite out of her. She craves the sensation of being eaten alive. The two guys drag her to her bedroom and tie her naked to the bed. With a knife, they slice the nipple off her right breast and eat it before her eyes. The woman groans in ecstasy, like she's about to come. They slice off the second nipple. Ends.

I consult my cable guide. *Feast* — starring Neil Delama and Chuck Gavoin — is a horror film. 'Two eligible bachelors,' it says, 'are actually flesh-hungry cannibals on the prowl.' That's followed by *Skinned Alive*, a movie in which 'Leather salesmen use an unusual source for their goods.' I quickly deduce that, not unlike *Feast*, *Skinned Alive* would find itself bouncing off Jimmy Ferman's toecap if ever submitted to the BBFC.

From eight o'clock every evening until about three in the morning, the horizontal and the vertical of my TV set fall into the hands of HVC. Station number 35 on my cable box. HVC isn't normal broadcasting, it isn't proper television. It's a highly temperamental movie channel, broadcasting films of such eclecticism and diversity that the viewer will think themselves dead and gone to heaven. The films are invariably low budget, of a kind that Vipco would have snapped up and released under a re-title several years ago (Vipco's *The Nostril Picker* has shown up on HVC under its original title *The Changer*, and *Zombie Nosh* as *Revenge of the Living Zombies*). Mix in a few Troma stinkers (*Rabid Grannies*, *The Toxic Avenger Part II*), some exploitation nuggets (*Ten Violent Women*, *Playgirl Killer*, *Death Trap*), some obscurities (*Sinthia the Devil's Doll*, *Pigs*), the occasional BBFC reject (Ted V. Mikels' *Angel of Vengeance*), ultra-gory horror movies (*Killer Dead*, *Robot Ninja*), uncut sleaze (*Fantasm*, *The Tormentors*), schlock sci-fi (*Battle for the Lost Planet*, *Steel and Lace*), reprehensible oddments (*The Black Panther*, *Parole Violators*) and you have the gist of the HVC schedule. HVC has screened all the above and more. And the downside? The transmission quality is often barely tolerable. On many occasions, the movie scheduled to play doesn't. Sometimes no movie plays at all, or it does but there's no sound. Other times the sound is intermittent. And the picture might on occasion flip from colour into black and white.

People are swinging a bright blue bag over their shoulders. Backwards and forwards, to and fro. Someone else indicates the muscles deployed in such activity. It looks like a fun thing to do and provides plenty of exercise. Blue bags half-filled with water. The name of the product — as with everything else the young man in the studio says — is lost to a horrible static hum. No sound but white noise. Cut to kids in the park, middle-aged executives in the office, pensioners on the lawn, individually and in groups,

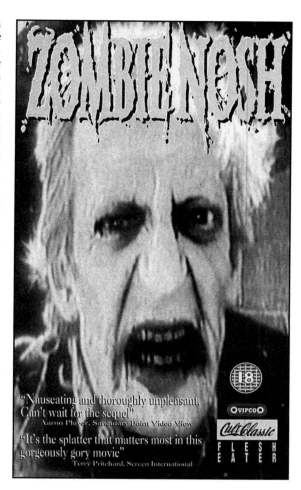

'Cult Classic' claims Vipco. We beg to differ.

swinging their bags. State of the art video technology has the scene fragment to reveal the words 'Regal Shop' — where we're at — then returns to a studio audience who silently applaud their own return.

Regal Shop — an American advertising feature set to look like a bona fide TV show — shows no sign of abating (they've taken the blue bag to the streets for some vox pop opinions), despite the fact there was a movie scheduled to start twenty minutes ago. And what of the horrible noise — will it disperse?

J. R. Bookwalter's *Robot Ninja* is notable only for several gore-sodden fight sequences, one of which has the hero sinking two Freddy Kreuger-like finger blades into an opponent's eyes and twisting them about awhile. But something peculiar about the soundtrack has me scratching my head for several long minutes. Something's wrong. I wasn't aware that video had two independent sound tracks, but now — after seeing *Robot Ninja* on HVC — I presume it does: The track with the music, background and incidental noises is playing; the track with the dialogue is not. You get to hear footfalls, face slaps, television sets being smashed, but no actual dialogue. Restaurant scene: a waitress fetches a bill, the conversation between the characters on table four is of zero audibility while the sound of their cutlery clattering is very loud. The couple get up to leave, STOMPING their way to their car. Outside in the car park, a van pulls up and they are kidnapped. A gun is drawn and shots RING OUT. A police SIREN. People look like they might be yelling. A cop mouths something into his walkie-talkie, but all that can be heard are the crickets CHIRPING. How long before the

(Above) Rubbish from Troma.

(Right) Another 'Cult Classic' for IQ-impaired twelve-year-olds to watch at snuff parties.

HVC controller figures something's amiss? Usually never. But then, suddenly, the *Robot Ninja* voice track returns. And then it goes again.

HVC is a premium channel, exclusive to cable — meaning there is a fee to pay if you wish to receive it. Subscribing to HVC automatically entitles you to receive the Adult Channel — soft porn hi-jinx on a nightly basis. The more I delve into it, the more I believe that the only hold HVC has on this package is that of a 'cover' for outwardly respectable Adult Channel enthusiasts. Presumably it's much easier to call the young, female cable operative and ask her about HVC than it is to request sex entertainment nightly.

The print of *Troma's War* which HVC played was cut, as were *Turkey Shoot* and *Sleepaway Camp* parts one, two and three. However, these aren't instances of HVC imposing censorship — the station really doesn't give a fuck what's in a movie — so long as it doesn't involve a hard-on or penetrative sex; nothing illegal by British law. The 'erotic' movies on HVC are invariably superior to those on the so-called Adult Channel. The Adult Channel is predominantly concerned with direct-to-video fare from the US, latter-day fuck pictures with plot factor zero. HVC, on the other hand, goes more for seventies product, the occasional dregs, which, to me, is by far the better option.

In either case, the pornography itself is excised. For new movies, such as John Leslie's *The Chameleon*, it seems two versions have been shot: one for the hardcore market, the other toned down for British sex channels. Where no alternative version exists, offending images tend to be 'panned out' or scenes are excised altogether. In some instances, films will mask the intercourse with a patch lifted from elsewhere (it looks as good as it sounds — men and women with alternate body parts pasted over their genitals, like Butthead in *Society*). More often than not, the soundtrack will continue to run normally, while an earlier, 'less offensive' sequence is played over the top to maintain a reasonable running time. Occasionally, such a sequence will be played two, three, maybe even four times in succession. (Think of the modern hardcore porn film. Think of the running time should all the scenes deemed obscene by British law be removed...) However, the most imaginative example of porno censorship came with HVC's screening of *I Want More*, starring Sharon Mitchell. Where the erect penis should have been, bottles and jars had been superimposed on the film — the impression being that a table 'is in the way'. Behind this earthenware assortment, a girl licks and masturbates the guy's unseen member. Whoever masterminded this neglected to take into account the 'payoff' — the bottles and jars are not tall enough and when the guy comes, blobs of the stuff can be seen clearly skipping over the bottle tops and into shot.

Part of the HVC 'regular' sex slot has included butchered versions of *Sex Boat* and Henri Pachard's *The Oddest Couple*. Far more entertaining, however, are the supposedly soft porn endeavours which have no recognisable names behind them. One such film is *Poor Cecily*, made in the early seventies by F.C. Parks. It follows Cecily, a seventeen year-old girl at the turn of the century who, after her uncle dies, is sent to stay with Lady Hamilton in France. As could be expected, this arrangement comes not without a little sexual congress. Within minutes of arriving in France, Cecily

flees her charges when Lady Hamilton tries to seduce her while her husband observes through a crack in the door. Fearing a scandal, Monsieur Hamilton sets out to kill the girl. It's an exceptionally long chase, concluding with perhaps the greatest cop-out in the history of cinema — just as he's about to catch his quarry, Cecily's pursuer suffers a stroke and falls down dead. (Cecily is doomed to wander the movie with a mortified expression from here on, regarding each act of simulated intercourse as "the most perverted thing I have ever seen.")

Better still is *The Captives* by Carl Borch, a particularly inspired piece of filth. A Rolls-Royce pulls up to offer a female hitch-hiker on a lonely stretch of road a lift. It's a trap, however, and a two-guy, two-girl gang jumps out from behind a bush, drag the driver from the car and beat him up. His wife can do nothing to help. Unconscious, the man is unceremoniously bundled back into his car, and the hippie-thugs drive off with their newly acquired captives. One of the girls says that watching the fight has made her "wet". To further oblige her, when the guy starts to come round he gets punched unconscious again. Two of the hippies make out on the back seat of the Roller. (It might be softcore, but it's exceptionally down-and-dirty and squalid.) The gang happen upon a deserted cabin and park up for the night. The captors bind 'Mr and Mrs Establishment' — as they come to be known — to chairs. There is a hippie sex-in-a-shower sequence followed by a brief shot of the log fire and more sex. "Why are you doing this to us?" cries Mrs Establishment. "Because we hate you!" comes the reply. The gang force the woman to take a 'special' pill and, to ensure that she swallows it, punch her in the stomach. One of the chicks tries to arouse the bound Mr Establishment. "Bitch!" he splutters. "You disgusting little bitch!" A wide-angled lens zooming in and out of his wife's face suggests that the special pill is kicking in. So begins an impressive — and very long — trip sequence. In her dream, Mrs Establishment sits at the end of a very large black room. In reality, she is being touched-up by the gang members. Her husband gets punched a few more times. Mrs Establishment is walking down a long hall, the walls of which are comprised of loose fabric, gently billowing. There is an unflattering close-up of her nose. Different coloured lenses. A distant wind howls and laughter fills the soundtrack. There's a door at the end of the corridor, behind it her husband sits at a desk in an office. She takes off her clothes. (The sequence has been going on for several minutes at this point.) She is in the car. It's a snow scene. Flowers. Blue. Back in reality, one of the guys exclaims, "Introducing Mrs Edith Cog into a world of depravity." They take advantage of the stoned woman. Seating Mr Establishment in a prime position, the two men take his wife successively and then together. Then the girls join in, each sucking on a nipple. On all fours, Mrs Establishment stares blankly into the face of her husband. One of the hippie chicks moves to the edge of the bed and starts to masturbate in front of him. The following morning, the gang and the wife leave in the Rolls-Royce. "So long, Mr Establishment!" they call as they go.

I have good reason to believe that no one watches HVC but me.

The extensive roadwork, which marked the encroachment of cable television in the town where I live, finally manifested itself at the door of my house one autumn evening. There stood sales representative

Nigel, come to sell me on the idea of cable. Everyone I know was so pissed off by the digging and inconvenience created by this company, I didn't expect anyone would give Nigel the time of day, let alone allow him in. But one by one, house by house, the neighbours crumbled. Not me, I was having none of it. I didn't want more TV stations. I didn't want MTV. I couldn't afford £12.99 a month. Lesley said "Don't let him in." I let him in. "I'm going upstairs," she said. "I don't want to even be here." (She closes the door in the faces of children collecting Penny for the Guy.)

Nigel told me about MTV. I told him I wasn't interested. He told me about the vast and exciting range of programmes — everything from re-runs of *Dr Who* to tips on gardening and *Top of the Pops* from the seventies. I told him I wasn't interested. He told me how he had been in a motorcycle accident and showed me the scars on each arm where he had metal pins and was in traction for almost a year. I wasn't interested. He used to play bass guitar but couldn't anymore, because of the accident, and now worked as a sales rep. He told me how I could save on my phone bills by switching from BT to cable. He casually mentioned the Adult Channel in passing. Then casually mentioned it again later. I told him I wasn't interested. He showed me the free cable TV guide that would be delivered to my door, free of charge, every month. It cost £1.50 to buy in the shops. Look at all the channels, he said, as I flicked through the pages. Crap, is all I thought. Then my eye caught something called the Home Video Channel. He exploited my hesitancy to the max. Home Video Channel, HVC — action, horror, sci fi, comedy and violence. The Horror and Violence Channel, he called it.

As Nigel was making his way out the door, he

Neville Brand's performance is so naturalistic that **Death Trap** could easily be mistaken for a documentary. Better censor it! Quick!

stopped and shook my hand. "I hope you enjoy it," he said, much louder than I would have liked.

Came a muted cry from somewhere upstairs: "Enjoy what?"

Not only had I signed my soul away, but they were coming for it the very next day. At least that's how my 'spouse' viewed it. After an engineer had laid a trail from the nearest junction box to my house, and another representative had been and shown me how to work the remote, I was on the phone requesting a young female to fit me up with HVC. Which, of course, sounded like a cover for something else. On top of the standard cable rate, HVC pushed the price up an extra £5.49. I soon discovered that most of the general programme details in my free guide were incorrect. The 'details' for HVC were even worse, offering nothing beyond the titles of the movies showing. The first movie that August night was to be *Blood Orgy of the She Devils*, followed by something I'd never heard of, followed by something else I'd never heard of, followed by *Trauma*. It didn't take many minutes of viewing HVC to realise that, whatever it was the station was offering, Dario Argento's latest movie — as I believed *Trauma* to be — wasn't about to be a part of it. *Blood Orgy of the She Devils* was the Ted V. Mikels thing; *Trauma* starred none other than Howard Vernon. Not, it would be correct to surmise, of the Argento stable.

Things had already started to look 'off' when the film prior to *Trauma*, a really cheap T&A movie set on a California beach, stopped suddenly and started to go backwards, then stopped altogether, replaced by the last five minutes of something starring Donald Pleasence. The credits on that began to roll and then the same few minutes of footage starring Pleasence played again.

Three months later the fees went up. Some months after that, the free cable guide was no longer free.

Tuesday, March 7

The first film of the evening comes with a sound akin to that of an overworked projector. *The Ultimate Challenge* has a 15-rating. It has music by Hold That Thought ("...") and a lot of Dan Quayle jokes. For much of its running time it looks to be a 'comedy' of a type one might associate with the word 'zany'. It has commercials for bogus products and news flashes which 'complement' the narrative. An ambassador's daughter is kidnapped. A new initiative for office workers sees a group of bimbos interred in a backwoods training camp. Some rogue FBI agents and a paramilitary group have got some arms deal going. About two-thirds of the way through the picture, it becomes apparent that somewhere down the line the film-makers have forgotten to administer the jokes and the commercials have stopped. In a hitherto unprecedented moment of nastiness, the main protagonists determine that the office girls have become a threat to their operation and set out to terminate them. One man throws a blindfolded girl onto the floor, kneels on top of her and shoots her point blank in the back of the head. The three remaining bimbos — afraid to break their nails — looking extremely uncomfortable with big guns — somehow manage to infiltrate the bad guys' camp, kill them all and rescue the ambassador's daughter.

Fatal Justice is from Fred Olen Ray's American Independent Pictures group (of which there is a lot on

HVC). Directed by Gerald Cain, it concerns a mercenary agent by the name of Diana working for the CIA. Her latest target for a hit turns out to be her father (Joe Estevez, another HVC favourite). Johnny Vik, a war veteran, mentally crippled by the 'Nam, is hounded in *The Hunted*. The film uses people with real physical disabilities, images of which keep coming back to haunt Vik. Supposedly based on a true story, there is a precredit note that states *The Hunted* was made where the legend actually happened.

The last film of the evening is advertised as *Deadly Rivals*, but the title which comes up on the print is *Krishna Shah's Rivals*. (The HVC guide often seems to be presenting alternate titles for movies shown.) The earliest childhood memory of a boy called Jamie has him sitting on a toilet taking a piss as his dad shaves in the mirror and his mother takes a shower. The camera closes in on the infant urinating. His father dies in some skiing accident and his mother, while making moussaka, encourages the boy to play 8mm films of the family in happier times. At age six, Jamie is said to possess an IQ of 142. Whilst in his early teens, Jamie's mother, Christine, meets a new man-friend by the name of Peter. At first she's afraid to bring Peter home for fear of what Jamie might think. When eventually she does, the precocious brat tries to make a fool out of him. A Jamie flashback has his mom and dad sitting in bed, trying to decide between making love and playing Scrabble. Scrabble wins through. Jamie has a black and white nightmare. Folk move in a circle around his room, while outside Jamie attempts to take a leak against a tree but is unable to because of his baby-sitter watching. The boy wakes up screaming. The rivalism of the title is altruistic — Jamie believes Peter is taking his mother's love away from him. After one argument, Peter — who looks like Neil Young — packs his case and leaves. He comes back. One evening, Jamie's baby-sitter — not much older than he — suddenly notices how hard her breasts have become. She turns to Jamie and asks, "What else do you do to make someone excited?" They both get naked. A lingering pubescent breast shot. "Do you want me to lie down?" she asks. "I don't know," Jamie replies. "Mary, maybe we'd better stop. I don't know what to do." After this non-event, the boy wanders around with images of the naked Mary coming toward him. Jamie formulates an elaborate plan, intending to murder Peter, but succeeds only in burning his mother to death. Impossible as it sounds, the overall impression is that director Krishna Shah wants Jamie to be seen as a victim, a sympathetic figure. What a cunt.

Pressured into buying my own copy of the cable TV guide, I opt not for Brand Ecch but one with some proviso on what to expect from HVC. The best of these offers a brief — and frequently wrong — synopsis of each feature. *Spanish Harlem* is down as 'drugs drama.' (A Spanish connection, presumably.) *Tie You Up* is 'misfits get involved with a religious cult.' *Cognac* is an 'adult drama.' And *Exit the Dragon, Enter the Tiger* is 'an action-packed documentary about the life and heady times of Bruce Lee.'

Another 'documentary' is *The Sexiest Animal*, which the guide claims is based on Dr Alex Comfort's book, *The Joy of Sex*. It is said to examine contemporary sexual trends in every corner of the world, from French Polynesia to the streets of New York. Anything with doctors and sex has got to be worth a look, so I tune in. The minutes leading up to the screening are without sound — just the awful white noise. A compilation of eighties music on CD is advertised in silence. Things looking decidedly grim, the HVC logo then suddenly bursts into life, sound and all. A godsend. But then, the wrong film is played. American New Wave Pictures present not *The Sexiest Animal* but *Taxi Dancers*. I double check the guide. *Taxi Dancers* — an 'erotic thriller' — is actually scheduled to play tomorrow night. Perhaps the programme has inadvertently been switched around, as is sometimes the case... I tune in the following evening. The swinging blue bag Regal Shop is on. Followed by the eighties music CD collection. Then the HVC logo bursts into life and American New Wave Pictures introduce, for the second consecutive night, *Taxi Dancers*.

Similar was *Innocent Prey*, starring P. J. Soles. That was mistakenly screened three times in a single week.

Most recently HVC have scheduled *The Toxic Avenger* parts one and two and managed to play only the latter, twice.

Wednesday, March 8

A courtroom drama set in Cape Town, 1937, *The Native Who Caused All the Trouble* intercuts its magisterial proceedings with flashbacks showing how the defendant came to be in the dock. A native wishing to build a church ignores the fact that the land on which he wishes to build it doesn't belong to him; there already exists a house on the spot, currently occupied by another native. The police are called in and a stand-off ensues. It's very much a moralistic and anti-colonial piece, with the native forcing the white police officers to deliberate on what exactly it is they're doing in Africa. "If your country is so great," asks the native, "why did you come here?" To which the officer-in-charge responds, "You evil smelling wog."

Carjack is directed by Maximo T. Bird (also responsible for *Queen of Lost Island*) and purports to be the Grand Prize Winner of the Winnetka Film Festival. A big fat long-haired guy with plenty of tattoos kidnaps a blonde girl. For a long time they converse in a very peculiar position — he looking over his shoulder in the driving seat, she lying down on the back seat. The camera begins a jerky, syncopated effect in mid-conversation for no discernible reason (and continues to do so indiscriminately throughout the picture — looks like an HVC fault, but isn't). She eventually admits that she isn't a top model but works on a telephone sex line. "Where are you taking me?" she asks. "Nowhere nice," replies the Fat Guy, pulling into a clearing and shooting her dead. Elsewhere, in a totally unrelated incident, another girl is kidnapped. "Where are we going?" this one asks. "Just relax," replies her captor. Ernie — jumping parole — insists that he's not actually kidnapping the girl, only "trying to get out of town." He and Bobbie formulate a love-hate relationship. In the desert they decide to take some magic mushrooms. Before they even eat them, the camera starts to swirl and the couple laugh. Later, whilst driving along a desert road, Bobbie says something to upset Ernie and he tells her to get out of the car. This she does. Ernie decides, a little further down the road, that he may have acted hastily and turns back to get the girl. But the other kidnapper — the Fat Guy from the beginning of the movie — suddenly happens upon the scene. A shoot-out leaves both men dead. Alas, it's all a waking dream. Bobbie is in the middle of nowhere nice, stranded without gas.

The last two features of the evening set an interesting precedent for HVC — the nearest the station has gotten to 'continuity' — scheduling *Fantasm* and *Fantasm Comes Again* back-to-back. However, any cheer is quickly dissipated by the insufferable audio interference during the latter.

More rubbish from Troma.

Fantasm is the relatively infamous 1976 porn comedy from Australia, directed by Richard Bruce (aka Richard Franklin). It was truncated by as much as sixteen minutes on British theatrical release. This version is complete. Case studies collected by an eminent professor make up the vignettes comprising the film. Though the doctor plays it for laughs, the sexual episodes are themselves pretty squalid. *Fantasm* opens to a dreamy female playing with herself. Close-ups of her nipples, her pubis and the sound of her sighs accompany the credits. The professor walks into shot — much to the girl's bemusement — and explains the nature of fantasy-thinking. 'Anxiety' is represented in a fantasy episode titled 'Beauty Parlour.' A woman imagines that her hairdresser is blow-drying her hair, while other men paint her nails, tweak her nipples and shave her pubes. 'Card Game' centres on a poker game in which the winner(s) get to have sex with 'the wife'. A role reversal fantasy ('Wearing the Pants') has a woman espying a transvestite trying to steal underwear from her clothes-line. She forces the man to put the garments on, before dragging him whimpering into the house. She pushes him across the kitchen table and proceeds to administer a flogging, then straps on a dildo and buggers him. Of course, there is nothing approximating actual penetration on the screen, but it's fairly safe to assume that here lie several minutes of the contentious footage excised by the BBFC. Other case studies include 'Mother's Darling', which incorporates an incest theme as a mother succumbs to the desire she feels for her soldier son home on leave; 'After School' has a schoolgirl sexually tormenting the teacher she feels has been victimising her in class; and 'Blood Orgy', wherein a girl, victim of a strict religious background, imagines herself at a Black Mass with a lighted candle being extinguished on her pubic region. *Fantasm Comes Again* transposes the linking device from that of the professor to that of an Agony Aunt working on a daily newspaper's problem pages. The film tends to dip into the same themes — group sex, underage sex, religious sex, lesbianism — but without the persuasion of the former entry.

Several weeks after its installation, I wrote the first of several letters to the cable company.

24 September

I have a complaint to make. I subscribe to cable. In addition to the standard service, however, I also pay to receive the Adult and HVC Channels. Indeed, the latter channel being unique to cable was one of the deciding factors in my choosing cable over satellite. My complaint is with regard to the erratic and seemingly shoddy nature of the way the programmes on HVC are broadcast. I had this premium service added on 20 August this year and in this short space of time, on at least four evenings, the programmes broadcast have not been those scheduled in the listings magazines. Worse still, on another night, the programming was without sound entirely. This itself ruined a film I had specifically tuned in to watch (Guess What Happened to Count Dracula, if it makes a difference). When, last night, 23 September, I tuned into HVC again to catch the repeat of this same film and found that it was being broadcast not with the original soundtrack, but the sound of Sky Radio, I felt I had to write this letter. (Furthermore, this same night, none of the other three films were screened at all. That is, nothing but the test card came on... well, one picture did commence broadcasting when it was already three-quarters of the way through, but that had a Sky Radio soundtrack.)

The odd break-down in transmission I could appreciate. But this is ridiculous. Granted that the sometimes awful picture quality on HVC — that blue tinting — appears to have been improved upon of late, but you must remember that I am paying extra for this service. More to the point, I'm paying in advance for something I am not getting.

21 October

You may recall that I wrote to your office on 24 September with a technical complaint with regard the HVC Channel to which I subscribe. I thank you for your prompt acknowledgement of my letter and the unexpected — but welcome — personal visit from one of your area representatives. The gentleman who called (at the beginning of this month) went through several points in my letter and, as to the irregular/non- broadcasting of HVC during several nights throughout September, concluded that I would be refunded my payment of £5.49 for HVC that month. It isn't a lot of money and I wasn't expecting it, but it was a nice recompense and one I appreciated. However...

I received my cable bill earlier this week. On it there is no deduction of the sum as I was told and, seeing as no money has been refunded in the post, I called Customer Services to check out the matter. My call of 20 October was met with no record of such a refund and I had to explain the situation over again. Because I didn't know the name of the rep who came round, I was told I would get a call back later that day after the rep in question had been traced and the authority to make such a refund consulted. Needless to say, I received no return call and, upon ringing Customer Services myself again the following afternoon, had to relay the whole sorry story once more.

I've now been told that my bill has indeed been amended and the £5.49 will be deducted from my Direct Debit payment next month. The bottom line is, as you must appreciate, I don't have absolute faith that I will see this amended bill when it comes to my next Direct Debit payment. Should that be the case, then I will cancel my Direct Debit.

It was a bluff, of course. I wasn't about to cancel cable because cable gave me HVC and to that I was hopelessly addicted. It had planted a signal in my frontal lobe. I asked the representative who called — whose name I did not know — if they had received many complaints about HVC. He said no, I had been the only one. I had visions of people all over the country sitting in front of their sets, tuned to HVC and watching nothing. They couldn't have been watching anything because nothing was on that could be watched. For several weeks the transmission quality was either of supremely poor quality or completely blank. It was then I realised that no one was watching HVC but me. They couldn't be.

As to the reimbursement, it did eventually arrive — after several months of my bill being in topsy-turvy land, crediting me the £5.49 one month and then billing me again the following for twice that amount. Though not clear of faults, the transmission itself had improved. The rep with no name told me that the films on HVC were broadcast from videocassette — sometimes the tapes themselves were of poor quality, more often than not, the machines which played them were at fault. "The play heads get dirty." I began to see a pattern. The broadcast quality would start off 'reasonable' and over the weeks would deteriorate until, eventually, I imagine, someone made the decision to clean the heads. Then the whole sorry process would start over again. It might have seemed a dumb question, but why didn't HVC maintain a

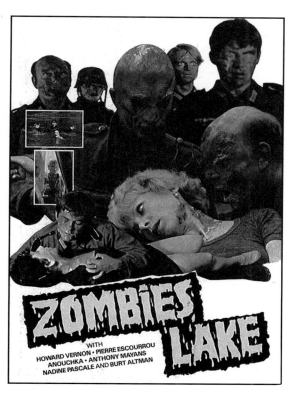

ZOMBIES LAKE

WITH
HOWARD VERNON · PIERRE ESCOURROU
ANOUCHKA · ANTHONY MAYANS
NADINE PASCALE AND BURT ALTMAN

(Left) **Zombies Lake** — heard the one about the video jacket that was more interesting than the film? Of course you have...

system of regular checks? Was the set-up the responsibility of one man, surrounded by a bank of video players awaiting authorisation for head cleaner? That began to look a very distinct possibility when, several months after my meeting with the nameless one I had reason to contact the company again.

Thursday, March 9

All other movies this day are overshadowed by Ken Dixon's *Zombiethon*. As with the S&M cannibal picture *Feast* and *Angel of Vengeance* — Ted V. Mikels' survivalist romp which the BBFC rejected outright — the screening of *Zombiethon* would seem to be audacity bordering on self-destruct. A compilation of clips from zombie movies, it included in its miscellany — in its entirety, uncut — the splinter-in-the-eye sequence from Lucio Fulci's *Zombie Flesh Eaters*. That's British television, uncut. The rest of the picture proffered 'gory' moments from *Zombies Lake*, *Oasis of the Zombies*, *The Invisible Dead*, *Virgin Among the Living Dead*, *The Astro-Zombies* and something possibly called *Fear (actually a Riccardo Freda film...Ed.)* Dixon's framing device proved itself a very astute approximation of European transcendental horror — schoolgirls and bathing beauties with heavily reverbed voice-overs abstractly contemplating life while being pursued by undead assailants. In the sunshine.

I had almost resigned myself to the faults on HVC as being par for the course. But not quite. Although the quality failed to sink quite as low as it had in the early weeks of my subscription, it nevertheless did go bad. More of a subtle, irritating, Chinese water torture kind of bad. I wrote again and this time got a telephone call from John, who worked in the HVC monitoring department. The trouble, he said, was that he had no way of monitoring the transmission at his end and thanked me for bringing the matter to his attention. He was going to sort the matter out at once and even gave me the telephone number to call should I experience any further difficulties. An HVC hot line. On this number I could reach John any time up until 10.30pm, at which point he went home.

That night, when a post-apocalyptic tale by the name of *Mutant Men Want Pretty Women* stopped midway through its climactic laser battle to be replaced by the premature commencement of the next programme, I had visions of John setting off for home, but stumbling on his way out and catching the 'play' button on the second VCR with his lunchbox.

Friday, March 10

Memorial Day. Someone is murdered and everyone thinks a biker gang is responsible. In his attempts to find the real killers, Bird, a white guy, dons an afro wig, paints his face black, assumes the name 'Leroy' and heads off to Zodiac's, a black nightclub. He talks like Huggy Bear and looks like Stevie Wonder. This is not a comedy — Bird is a master of disguise. The film is pretty mixed-up, but does include an impressive head exploding scene when Sludge, one of the lead gorillas, plows a cement truck into a stoolie (though why this should cause his head to explode is a mystery). Bird disguises himself as a telephone repairman to get into Joey Piretti's office. Joey's bodyguards are all at least two feet taller than Joey himself. *Scandal* comes over like a blue version of a *Carry On* film, the story being that the employees at Quebec's Ministry of Culture try to earn extra cash by making and appearing in their own porno film. In an attempt to inflame their imaginations they go to a sleazy bar, sitting through several burlesque acts. Of these, one act features a lesbian punk couple who frolic with a pair of scissors, running the blades over their breasts and between their legs.

Dirty Leather opens with a passage (in writing) from Steppenwolf's 'Born to be Wild'. It's a biker film with very little biker action but a lengthy skinny dipping sequence. Following some altercation, the gang go in search of Mark. They manage to extract his current whereabouts from a guy by pushing his groin into the wheel of his motorcycle and revving it up. No director is credited. *Pools of Anger* features Cody, a Vietnam vet, who takes a stand against the evil in his community after finding his 'Nam buddy dead — a victim of suicide upon discovering his daughter hanging around with the local pusher. When Cody finds the girl, she is desperately — randomly and cluelessly — stabbing a hypo into her arm. Cody gives a speech at the local PTA on the subject of teenage suicides. He receives a standing ovation. At the end, in a bar where all the characters from the movie are gathered together holding hands, Cody takes out his guitar and sings a song called 'Children of the World'.

I called the number John the monitoring man had left. It turned out to be the number for the cable operatives. I asked to speak to John. "John who?" said the female voice on the other end. "John in the monitoring department". "What extension is that?" she queried. "There is no monitoring department."

After relating the story of John and the fact that I ought to be able to call him any time up until 10.30pm, the girl on the line said someone would get back to me in half an hour. They did. It was Bill. He was going to send one of his men round to look at my TV. I said I was certain that it wasn't my TV at fault. He said he didn't think so either, but had to eliminate the possibility anyway.

L'ABIME DES MORTS VIVANTS
avec
MANUEL GÉLIN
et FRANCE JORDAN
INTERDIT AUX MOINS DE 13 ANS
Visa censure nº 9379

Another bomb from Jesús 'talent is not my middle name' Franco.

A few minutes before 9am on Saturday, a cable representative called, checked my TV and said he would relay his findings to head office first thing Monday.

Maybe he did. Perhaps John took the message. ∎

AN HVC TOP TEN

A personal selection of the station's more 'outstanding' presentations, in no particular order...

Dead End. 1992. Dir: Robert Tiffe. With: Martin King, Robert Restaino, Carrie Stevens.

"Fourteen dollars thirty-six — does it look like we carry that kind of cash?" Two hoods bring bad medicine upon themselves when they rob and kill an old Indian storekeeper before heading off for LA, taking a short cut through an Indian reservation. The journey turns into a hallucinogenic bad trip where nothing is what it seems. And they both die.

Death Penalty. 19??. Dir: Stephen Calamari. With: Steve Sayre, Billy Franklin, James Westbrook.

A detective's tolerance for low-lives drops to minus-zero when his fiancée is murdered by the Satanic Slayer. Any punk in his path he shoots. The killer — a big guy with a motorcycle — spills a cripple's drink in a bar. A girl tells him that he ought to apologise so he smashes a bottle over the cripple's head.

Zero in and Scream. 19??. Dir: ?

A soft porn outing in which a killer by the name of Mike stalks and shoots go-go dancers. "Don't use that language around me!" Mike yells when one girl says "crap." The police warn everyone to stay indoors. Mike goes into the Hollywood Hills and trains his rifle sight on a potential victim sitting by a pool. He pans away from the girl to a pair of feet. The feet belong to guy holding a rifle pointing directly back at him. A puff of smoke and The End comes up. The soundtrack is reminiscent of Zappa's *Hot Rats*.

Boat People. 199?. Dir: Guy Lee Thys. With: Bruce Baron, Jessie Elmido.

Illegal emigrants fleeing Vietnam, crowded in a small boat, are attacked by Thai pirates. All the men are killed and the women raped and sold into prostitution.

Road-Kill. 19??. Dir: Tony Elwood. With: Andrew Porter, Sean Bridgers, Deanna Perry.

Josh, a young hitch-hiker, is picked up by a seemingly pleasant couple. But Clint turns out to be a psychopath who kills one man by tying him to a chair and sealing his mouth and nostrils shut with super glue.

Hell Hole aka Guardian Angels. 19??. Dir: Cirio H. Santiago. With: Ingrid Greer, Nanette Martin, Kerry Nichols.

"If that's what you call help, don't do me any favours." 'Beautiful' girls are being kidnapped and interred in a hell hole for reasons never satisfactorily defined. A stripper shakes her breasts in a club and gets a standing ovation. A woman, sick of it all, sticks a revolver in her mouth and her head explodes.

Sweet Sugar. 1972. Dir: Don Levesque. With: Phyllis Davis, Ella Edwards, Timothy Brown.

SEE! BERSERK HUMAN TRANSPLANTS

SEE! ASTRO SPACE LABORATORY

SEE! CRAZED CORPSE STEALERS

ASTRO ZOMBIES

A Mountain VIDEO Presentation VHS COLOUR 78mins

Sugar is sent to a jungle prison for two years when marijuana is found in her possession. Here the inmates suffer drug-crazed cats being thrown at them (in slow motion) and are strung up in the sun while lecherous wardens stick pistols down their knickers.

To Make a Killing. 1988. Dir: Karl Zwicky. With: Tamblyn Lord, Craig Pearce, John Godden.

Damon is a good kid gone bad gone good again. Trying to impress some outlaws, he fabricates a story of how a local kitchen magnate has a safe full of money in his house. Too late, he finds that the gang intend to rob the place at gun point. Nobody stops screaming in a scenario that has 'the king of kitchens... the king of shit' and his family being beaten and blasted.

Blindside. 1987. Dir: Paul Lynch. With: Harvey Keitel, Lori Hallier, Lolita David.

Keitel plays the owner of a motel, inadvertently caught between two warring drug cartels when one gang member takes some time out in Room 203. Not much of a story, but for Keitel — commanding from start to finish as per usual — a departure.

Down On Us. 1984. Dir: Larry Buchanan. With: Gregory Allen Chatman as Jimi Hendrix, Riba Meryl as Janis Joplin, Bryan Wolf as Jim Morrison.

The deaths of these three rock icons was no accident but a government conspiracy, says Buchanan. While the actors playing Hendrix, Joplin and Morrison come off surprisingly well, the songs stink. The story is related in flashback, courtesy of recently discovered notes left by the CIA hitman responsible for the murders, himself killed in a pre-credit hunting 'accident'. Says the assassin in this instance, "I know I didn't need that second barrel, but who counts birdshot in a man's chest. Rock 'n' roll is dead. Long live rock 'n' roll."

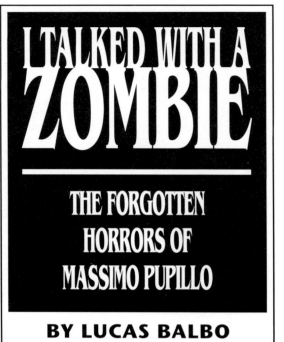

I TALKED WITH A ZOMBIE

THE FORGOTTEN HORRORS OF MASSIMO PUPILLO

BY LUCAS BALBO

"I am *the* Scarlet Executioner"...

Those who have seen *Bloody Pit of Horror* will never forget those words and the crazy gaze in the eyes of Mickey Hargitay as he hams it up at the top of the medieval staircase — in a remote part of Rome's Cinecittà studios. This sick piece of sixties schlock still stands at number one for many Italian horror fans, but very little is known of its director, 'Max Hunter', and his career. Even Alan Upchurch in his excellent and informative *Video Watchdog* article

couldn't verify if 'Max' had directed another Italian horror classic *Terror Creatures from the Grave*, signed by 'Ralph Zucker'. So, because of the various pseudonyms used on his films, we could never confirm if Massimo Pupillo had directed those masterpieces... All hope of discovering the truth seemed lost when I read in an Italian directors filmography that he had died in 1982... But on 20 July 1994, I happily discovered that our director was still alive and well in eternal Rome.

He was puzzled that the pseudo-historians who wrote the book didn't even check in the *Annuario del Cinema Italiano*, which is updated yearly and still prints his bio with his address and phone number, and couldn't understand why he was supposed to be dead. The confusion probably originates from his first feature film, *Terror Creatures from the Grave*. He explained: "Because I didn't care about the film, I let the producer, Ralph Zucker, take the credit. Also we made a deal with MBC for two films — *Terror Creatures* and *Bloody Pit of Horror* — and we didn't want to have the same name on both films. So to please him, I let him sign *Terror Creatures* and put my name on *Bloody Pit*... I didn't give a fuck."

Well perhaps he should have; when Ralph Zucker died in 1982, some idiots thought he was Massimo Pupillo and assumed *he* had died! The following interview was conducted in his apartment in Rome...

LB: Were those films the first you directed?

MP: Before those two films I shot about 250 shorts, mostly documentaries, and one dramatic feature about Italian youth called *Gli Amici dell'isola*. One of the films even won a prize in the Oberhausen Film Festival. Most of them were done with a very small budget, so I had to find a different trick every day, it was a constant challenge. I also made a documentary for Walt Disney Productions on the white donkeys of Sardinia, a unique breed which only live on that island.

But I started in the cinema industry as an assistant director to Marcel Pagnol, in France...

LB: Did you have larger budgets for your full feature films?

MP: Not really. The two first films, although one was in black and white and the other one in colour, had an equal cost. The difference mainly came because of the film's sensitivity. For *Bloody Pit* we had 100 ASA film stock which needed a lot of light — which requires electric generators, floods and a lot of equipment. But we didn't need those for the black and white film because I used 1100 ASA Ilford film stock, which was scarce and expensive at that time. It gave excellent results, like the final night scene in the garden for *Terror Creatures*.

LB: What about special effects? Did you have a budget? Who was in charge?

MP: For *Bloody Pit* I worked with Carlo Rambaldi, who won an Oscar for special effects in *E.T.* In my film he made a fake spider, but it didn't work at all! In *Terror Creatures*, when I needed a thumping heart, I prepared the effect myself without the aid of any specialist. First I bought a pig's heart and a Japanese toy for a dollar. It was a little doll with a rubber ball hand-pump connected to it. When you squeezed the rubber ball, the doll jumped. I inserted this mechanism into the pig heart and it worked perfectly. *Thump, thump, thump.* The heart would beat as soon as you squeezed the pump.

But the key special effects scene featured six severed hands which had to move at a precise time. They were on display in glass jars inside a cabinet. I had the cabinet designed so that six people wearing latex hands could sit behind and protrude their hands though holes. The effect was very successful, and the six people had a lot of fun asking each other to scratch their heads. That's the part of creativity I like in those films. You had to invent a new trick every day.

To check if the effects were working, I attended a screening in a very popular movie theatre in Rome on Via Prenestina. I sat behind a big guy who was almost bald, and I waited for the thumping heart scene. As the scene progressed, I could see drops of sweat slowly dripping from this guy's head and he mumbled to himself, "Fucking son of a bitch"... To me that was the best compliment!

LB: For *Terror Creatures* there are two different versions, one more violent than the other. Was it planned like this?

MP: Yes, at that time it was usual to make a stronger version for export and it was originally planned like this for *Terror Creatures*, but I was never very interested in those details. The Italian censorship at that time was very strict so we had to be very careful, but in foreign countries it would work more easily.

For example, one of my other films, *L'Amore, Questo Sconosciuto* — I saw it abroad and it included fellatio scenes I never shot! They weren't even additional scenes I would have shot for an export version. Those scenes were shot by Angelo Fillippini's brother who made them in Switzerland and they were added to my film.

LB: How was it to work with Barbara Steele?

MP: Although she saw her contract and knew we had a small budget, she showed up on the first day of the shoot, acting like a diva, demanding everything. We had a big fight and I laid down the law. After that, everything went very smoothly.

LB: I've seen photos of a nude bathing sequence with Barbara Steele. Was that a scene you actually shot or were those just publicity stills?

MP: No, this scene was shot but maybe not kept in

(Previous page) Moa Tahi menaced by hyper-realistic Carlo Rambaldi spider – no wonder Pupillo took to using $1 Japanese squeezy dolls.

(Above) A Terror Creature finally emerges, too late to rouse Barbara Steele (below) or the viewer...

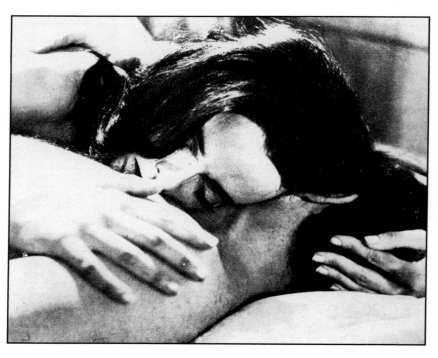

the final editing.

LB: Did you have problems with the cast for _Bloody Pit of Horror_ ?

MP: It was very hard to get anything out of Rita Klein, one of the actresses. In one scene she was supposed to express fear, but she couldn't do it. So, with my cameraman, Carlo Di Palma, I agreed on a code to signal when he was supposed to shoot the scene for real. I prepared a long stick connected to a battery, and we started to rehearse the scene again and again, then I gave her a small electrical shock. She did the most expressive fear I've seen on screen... She also didn't speak to me for the next two days! But when she saw the result on screen she kissed me. Another problem we had — actually, it was the continuity girl's problem — had to do with Rita's bra: she was constantly putting wool in her bra to make her chest bigger day by day. The continuity girl had a hell of a time — you could say she had her hands full!

Then there was Mickey Hargitay. Like most Americans, he was professional, really correct. But I had to show him everything he was supposed to do for this film, I really had to play every part during the rehearsals. But Mickey and I were accustomed to each other from previous work together, like a documentary I was doing which expanded into a dramatic feature thanks to the involvement of he and his wife, Jayne Mansfield. It eventually became the film, _Primitive Love_. But some of the other girls who played models were pretty good. There was the Yugoslavian girl, Femi Benussi, it was her first big part in Italy; and Moa-Tahi, a real Hawaiian girl, was also good.

LB: _La Vendetta di Lady Morgan_ was your last horror film?

MP: Well, I wasn't interested in making any more horror films and I had turned down a lot of propositions. I started in the horror genre because I wanted to get out of documentaries, I wanted to enter the commercial market. In Italy, when you do a certain type of film, you become labelled and you can't do anything else. I remember one day, a producer called me to do a film only because the other

producers told him he had to get either Mario Bava or me. When I understood this, I felt dead...

LB: How did you come to direct the western, _Bill il Taciturno_? Was it a difficult transition?

MP: I was interested in a change of style when this screenplay came along, but it was so ordinary that I decided to locate the action in a ghost town to give another dimension to this tedious Western. After the first two weeks of shooting I was having dinner with the producer, a rich Neapolitan, when he said, "You had a wonderful idea, but now we must absolutely include a brawl scene." I was shocked! How do you justify a fighting crowd in a supposedly deserted town? As an answer, he took out his cheque book and said, "Here is five million lira if you add this brawl scene". What was I supposed to say...? I took the cheque!

Another night, his composer, Umberto Pisani, came to pay me a visit, accompanied by a tall guy and an insipid looking girl, totally vacant. Despite the late hour, they forced me to go to the recording studios under the pretence of presenting me the score. Once we arrived he said, "You see this girl? Well, you have to get her a part in the film. I give you a million lira for that". Once more, I did it to please him. I added a scene where a dance hall girl appears in a saloon. This joke must have cost him six million lira!

To make up for these extravagances I created a scene where a stagecoach rides down rocky mountains along a river, loaded down with luggage and driven by cowboys. I bought the cowboys for $10 in a toy store and a miniature stagecoach for $4. I stuck those on a strip of velvet. The rocky mountains were large stones and the river was a small canal that the set dresser built me. To hide the immobility of the model kits, I added falling snow made of shredded straw. The effect worked perfectly and the scene only cost about $14!

LB: Your last film to date, _Sa Jana_, is ignored in most references..

MP: I shot that in 1981, and I also wrote the screenplay. It's a drama shot in _ciné vérité_ style with non-professional actors, mostly fishermen. The story is an allegorical fairy tale; in fact, 'Sa Jana' means fairy in Sardinian dialect. It's the story of a young fisherman whom we follow through life, and it won an award as 'Best Cultural Quality Film' and I was to receive a grant. There was just one problem; nobody wanted to release it, and in order to receive the grant I had to have a public screening. So to cash in, I organised a public screening. Apart from this one screening the film was never released...

It's a very beautiful story, without any violence or sex. I wrote it in Sardinian dialect and it was corrected by a university professor, then I explained to the fishermen who acted in it the concept I wanted on screen. It begins in front of caves, called 'Casa Delle Fate', where a grandfather explains to his grandson that those caves are the houses of fairies. He explains that, in exchange for their respect, the fairies give the fishermen a boat full of fish. In reality, this legend is a cover for illegal fishing. When the boy's father dies suddenly, he becomes head of the household and must provide for the whole family. So, believing his grandfather's story, the boy goes into the caves begging the fairies to help him. Meanwhile, all the fishermen who knew his father put their catch of the day into the boy's net, and when he finds the fish he really believes the fairies put it there. For that scene, this non-professional actor cried for twelve minutes — real tears, without any glycerin or artificial means. I

An inspired, startling representation of something or other from **Terror Creatures...**

made that film in fifteen days for two million lira. As acknowledgement, Cinecittà never called me again...

LB: Weren't you originally scheduled to direct *King of Kong Island*?

MP: No, I never heard about that film, but I did start a war film. All the aerial fighting sequences were shot, those were performed by professional pilots of the Italian army in two different airports. It was co-produced by Achille Lauro, who was ruined because of the Christian Democratic Party, and a Bulgarian producer named Peter Ziaparof.

It told the story of an Italian pilot fighting against the British forces in the Baleares islands, during the last war. The main character is not a very good looking guy, but a real hero, the ace of his squadron. His plane is shot down and he is hospitalised in Spain, where they change his face. Although it is a beautiful face he is not the same, it is like he becomes someone else.

When he goes home his dog recognises him and licks his hands, but his wife doesn't. He decides not to tell who he really is and pretends to be a friend of her husband and falls in love with his wife again. It is the drama of a man who loves the same woman twice and is forced to betray himself, a story which explains that love has nothing to do with beauty or ugliness.

More recently I was working on a new kind of musical film with the poet and singer Georges Moustaki, about a man who travels alone on a rowing boat with his guitar, a sort of river hobo who sings. He meets up with a kid who escaped from an orphanage, and they decide they'll row to Venice because the kid has dreamed about it since seeing posters calling it 'the city on water.' But soon the kid is arrested and taken back to the orphanage. During his desperate search, the vagabond remembers a song that he and the boy made up and sings it outside every orphanage he can find. Through the walls, the kid recognises the tune and signals to his friend that he is trapped there. We then find out he's not really a vagabond at all, he's a millionaire from Piacenza who abandoned his 'bourgeois wife' and children who are now grown-up. So he goes back to the orphanage in a big limousine and rescues the boy.

Moustaki was very interested in working with me, but the Italian TV wanted it as a mini-series of three episodes and wanted to introduce other writers. So I abandoned the project in 1987 and haven't made anything since. I'm really disappointed by the Italian cinema industry.

Pupillo also talked about his activities as a member of the film rating board and his work on restoring the re-release of Carmine Gallone's *Scipio Africanus*, and much more. So in short, I want to apologise for cutting this interview... Thanks to Stefano Galanti and Massimo Pupillo Jr for their help in setting up this instructive evening. ■

FILMOGRAPHY

1938: LA FEMME DU BOULANGER/THE BAKER'S WIFE.
Dir: Marcel Pagnol. MP: assistant director.
1940: LA FILLE DU PUISATIER/THE WELL-DIGGER'S DAUGHTER.
Dir: Marcel Pagnol. MP: assistant director.
1961: GLI AMICI DELL'ISOLA.
Colour feature with non-professional actors, set in Sardinia.

1963: L'AMORE PRIMITIVO/PRIMITIVE LOVE.
Dir: Luigi Scattini. MP: co-story, with Scattini. With: Jayne Mansfield, Mickey Hargitay and others...
'A student of anthropology, absorbed in prayer, shows material relating to sexual customs amongst primitive people, to her teacher... Sacred ceremonies and cruel rituals that explain the initiation into life and love to prove their masculinity and become warriors.' 'Film obviously shot in two parts, one with Jayne Mansfield (mostly shot in France and Italy), which was also used in *The Wild Wild World of Jayne Mansfield* and used in Super-8 mini-features sold by mail, and the other shot in Cannes and Italy with Ciccio and Franco. All of this intercut with stock shots of primitive wedding rites and animal copulation.'
I TABU/TABOOS OF THE WORLD.
Dir: Romolo Marcellini. MP: co-script, uncredited.
Another mondo, narrated by Vincent Price.
1965: CINQUE TOMBE PER UN MEDIUM/TERROR CREATURES FROM THE GRAVE/CEMETERY OF THE LIVING DEAD.

Alfredo Rizzo is overawed by Mickey Hargitay's codpiece.

Pre-production title: Tombs of Terror. Italy/USA. B&W. Running time: Fr 86m, USA 82m, It 87m.

Production company: M.B.S. Cinematografica (Rome) & G.I.A. Cinematografica (Rome) in collaboration with Ralph Zucker/International Entertainment Corp (USA). Assistant producer: Frank Merle [Francesco Merli]. Dir: Ralph Zucker [actually Massimo Pupillo]. Scr: Roberto Natale & Romano Migliorini [with M. Pupillo, uncredited]. Photography: Charles Brown [Carlo Di Palma]. Music: Aldo Piga. Art director: Frank Small. Editor: Robert Ardis [Mariano Arditi]. Assistant director: Nick Berger [Ignazio Dolce]. Sound: Geoffrey Sellers [Goffredo Salvatori]. Special effects: Bud Dexter. With: Barbara Steele (*Clio Hauff*), Walter Brandt [W. Brandi] (*Albert Kovaks*), Marilyn Mitchell [Mirella Maravidi] (*Corinne Hauff*), Alfred Rice [Alfredo Rizzo] (*Docteur Nemek*), Richard Garret [Riccardo Garrone] (*Maître Josef Morgan*), Alan Collins [Luciano Pigozzi] (*Kurt*), Tilde Till (*Louise*), Edward Bell [Ennio Balbo] (*Oscar Stinel*).

IL BOIA SCARLATTO/BLOODY PIT OF HORROR/THE SCARLET HANGMAN/THE CRIMSON EXECUTIONER/THE RED HANGMAN.
Shooting title: Il Castello di Artena.
Re-release (1972): Io... Il Marchese De Sade Nel il Boia Scarlatto.
Italy/USA. Colour. Running tim: It 90m, USA 74m. In 'Psychovision'.
Prod: Francesco Merlin [F. Merli] for M.B.S.

Cinematografica (Rome) & Ralph Zucker/International Entertainment Corp (USA).
Dir: Max Hunter [Massimo Pupillo]. Scr: Robert Nathan [R. Natale] & Robin McLorin [R. Migliorini] (with M. Pupillo, uncredited). Photography: John Collins [Luciano Trassati]. Music: Gino Peguri. Art director: Frank F. Arnold. Sets: Richard Goldbert. Editor: Robert Ardis [Mariano Arditi]. Special effects: Alan Trevor. Assistant director: Henry Castle. Sound: Geoffrey Sellers [Goffredo Salvatori]. With: Mickey Hargitay (*John Stuart/Travis Anderson*), Walter Brandt [W. Brandi] (*Rick*), Louise Barrett [Luisa Baratto] (*Edith*), Alfred Rice [Alfredo Rizzo] (*Daniel Parks*), Rita Klein (*Nancy*), Ralph Zucker (*photographer*), Moa-Tahi (*Kinojo*), Femi Martin [Eufemia/Femi Benussi] (*Annie*), Barbara Nelly [B. Nelli] (*Suzy*). The most complete version is that on Something Weird video, part of Frank Henenlotter's 'Out of the Vault' series. Alas, as usual with most public domain American prints, it's poorly transferred and washed out.

1966: LA VENDETTA DI LADY MORGAN.
Italy. B&W. Running time: 88m.
Prod: Peter Jordan for Morgan Film. Dir: Max Hunter [Massimo Pupillo]. Scr: Jean Grimaud [Gianni Grimaldi] from an idea by Edward Duncan. Photography: Dan Troy [Oberdan Trojani]. Music: Peter O'Milian [Piero Umiliani]. Art director/costumes: Hugh Danger. Editor: Robert Ardis [Mariano Arditi]. Special effects: Max Justice [Massimo Giustini]. Assistant director: Dean Swey. Sound: Alex Durby. With: Gordon Mitchell (*Roger*), Erika Blanc (*Lilian*), Paul Muller (*Lord Harold Morgan*), Barbara Nelly [B. Nelli] (*Lady Susan Morgan*), Michel Forain (*Pierre Brissac*), Carlo Kechler (*Sir Neville Blackhouse*), Edith McGoven (*Terry*).
The story takes place at the turn of the last century. After the accidental death of her fiancé, a young heiress marries Lord Harold Morgan. With the help of his governess and his majordomo, Lord Harold murders his wife in order to inherit her estate. But the ghost of Lady Morgan returns for revenge...
Only released theatrically in Italy, this is one of Pupillo's hardest films to see...

1967: BILL IL TACITURNO.
Dir: Max Hunter [Massimo Pupillo]. Prod: Alberto Puccini. Scr: Renato Polselli. With: George Eastman, Liana Orfei, Edwin G. Ross.
SVEZIA, INFERNO E PARADISO/SWEDEN — HEAVEN AND HELL.
Dir: Luigi Scattini. MP: co-scr (uncredited). Mondo movie on sex swap clubs, lesbians, drug addiction, bikers, saunas and porn, narrated by Enrico Maria Salerno in Italy and Edmund Purdom in the English language prints.
1969: L'AMORE, QUESTO SCONOSCIUTO.
Dir, story & script: Max Hunter [Massimo Pupillo].
"Documentary investigation into sexual deviation, illustrating various aspects of voyeurism, sadism and homosexuality, through sex in the cinema and advertising."
1982: SA JANA.

Rita Klein in **Bloody Pit of Horror**... *Yes? Yes!*

THE DAY THEY TURNED THE LIGHTS UP

A TRIBUTE TO THE LATE GREAT AMERICAN PORNO THEATRE

BY JACK STEVENSON

The American hardcore porno theatre of the 1970s was largely a parasitic creature, taking root in decaying, crime-plagued inner city districts, where store-fronts could be rented cheaply and old theatre buildings either rotted away, were boarded up, or lingered in irreversible decline.

Hardcore porn was one cactus that could flourish in this desert.

The birth of the hardcore porno theatre, or 'Pornie', was hardly a force of hope and renewal in the community; once converted for the exhibition of porn, the average vacated theatre or storefront acquired an even more palpable atmosphere of abandonment, with a sinister edge thrown into the bargain. The porno theatre operator never upgraded or repaired anything on the premises: broken chairs were left where they collapsed; even projectors were never maintained. This attitude of radical *laissez faire* gave the average Pornie a feel of timelessness akin to Pompeii — making it easy to believe that the lights hadn't been turned on since 1970 and — the overpowering smell of disinfectant notwithstanding — that the floors hadn't been cleaned since then either. There was a certain frozen-in-time ambience about these joints, though it wasn't a sudden wave of volcanic lava that had preserved them but a sudden wave of hardcore porn, a wave that struck the country broadside in 1969.

Until the Pussycat chain of theatres arrived to provide viewers with a more sterilised and controlled viewing environment, porno theatres were perceived by the public as absolute hell holes. Respectable citizens might more easily be persuaded to gatecrash a leper colony than push through their battered doors and clanking turnstiles and shuffle into the smelly,

(Above) The Playpen, a typical 'off-Strip' sleaze pit, now converted to live shows and video booths. (ph: Dennis Nyback)

(Below) 'The Strip' by night – presumably Julie Andrews' 'victorious' return to Broadway involved a different kind of live show from The Playpen's... (ph: Silke Mayer)

alien darkness wherein all manner of urban misfits sought sexual solace in theory and practice...

As depicted in mainstream movies like *Midnight Cowboy*, *Taxi Driver* and *Hardcore*, inner city porno theatres were dark dens of menace, criminality and unspeakable perversion. In *Midnight Cowboy* — where a twenty-four hour 42nd Street grindhouse doubles for the real XXX article, which wouldn't appear for another year or two — protagonist Joe Buck gets a blow-job while an outer space horror movie plays, metaphorically representing the 'alien' nature of these all-night theatres to mainstream movie audiences. Joe Buck: space traveller.

In all three of these films, the atmosphere of the porno theatre is characterised by a strong focus on the flickering beam of the movie projector and the small, close-packed audiences staring ahead in almost petrified silence; zombies or hollow pod-people posed by the beam of light, paralysed except for an occasional slow-moving hand reaching over for a neighbouring knee. The set-up reflected the tragic duality of big city living at large: an awkward intimacy superimposed with faceless anonymity. Porno theatre was therefore rendered a cultish, forbidden, urban experience on the evidence of viewing environment alone, since we never get to see the actual films (or if so only in the briefest of glimpses). Viewing environment was the key element. In fact, it often surpassed the actual films in importance.

In the San Francisco gay underground feature *The Meat Rack*, produced in 1968 (and often referred to as 'the poor man's *Midnight Cowboy*'), our bisexual protagonist flees to the sanctuary of a porn theatre where, again, the projector beam is given prominent play. He finds no safe refuge here, however, and, as if in a surrealist nightmare, is groped and savaged by five pairs of disembodied arms before bolting out onto a fire escape. Even a more sophisticated underground take on porn theatres couldn't resist a clichéd and over-dramatic interpretation. It seemed to be everybody's nightmare...

The proverbial porn theatre acquired an evil, almost mythical aura, and was blamed for a staggering assortment of social ills. In the public consciousness it came to epitomise 'sleaze' on a par with the subway toilet, the back alley and other dark corners of big cities that good people looked away from in fear and revulsion. If, by the end of the 1960s, our inner cities were being laid waste by a ravaging disease, the porno theatre was the visible pox.

It was hardly the type of urban neighbourhood institution to attract serious study by sociologists. Politicians and civic officials would not mourn the disappearance of the ignoble Pornie. And the new breed of film scholar, so eager to connect the dots between cinema and its socio-cultural manifestations, wouldn't touch the Pornie with a ten-foot pole — although they'd willingly tackle subjects like vampires and blood cultists with gusto. Such sociologically minded film scholars with a taste for the fringe would have to be dragged kicking and screaming to an admission that the reviled porno theatre possessed any significance beyond a rotting pile of lumber.

But of course it did.

They were institutions of urban street culture that personified the reckless excesses of the seventies. They existed within a specific time frame to exhibit a specific type of movie, and they came to fulfil a certain social function. They are like drive-in theatres:

outmoded relics of movie history that became economically and socially obsolete with the passing of time. Unlike the endlessly eulogised-over drive-in, which we look back on with nostalgia, the Pornie is more akin to a terminally ill plague victim refusing to die. Equal parts flophouse, bordello and bus station waiting room, the Pornie was a remedy of the last resort for the last in line, and in its more extreme incarnations it functioned as an anarchic 'free zone' that seemed to exist outside the laws and social codes of its host country. They were bottom-of-the-barrel bonanzas of public sexuality catering to a faceless urban clientele variously profiled in novels like *Junky*, *City of Night* and *The Sexual Outlaw*, but otherwise existing below the radar scope...

Finally, and perhaps most subversively, porno theatres were cheap places to spend time: a clutch of empty beer cans turned in for deposit could buy an all-day ticket. To modern urban real estate developers, reshaping inner cities for the pleasures of the moneyed classes, this was the ultimate subversion.

It's Alive!... Or Something: Birth of the Pornie

The first hardcore porn theatres to spring up — as opposed to the twenty-four hour grindhouses that had traditionally fulfilled their social function — were 'mini-theatres' and 'shoebox' rooms that often occupied store fronts. These tiny theatres were the descendants of the private back room peep-shows that had always existed; in fact, Pornies were often considered 'public' or wide-screen peep-shows, and often referred to as such in an effort to shield themselves from undue police attention. These theatres first appeared in San Francisco and Los Angeles, and soon after in New York City. They initially screened plotless 16mm shorts accompanied by wildly inappropriate music from tapes or record players. Classical, easy-listening and anything uncopyrighted were favourites, though many projectionists would simply play anything handy.

Theatre managers often dealt directly with the hippies, bikers and drug addicts who made the films, and a glut of generally appalling product followed. Film labs were happy to print the stuff. The business worked on a very basic level of supply and demand that any Republican capitalist could admire, and money was made all round. There was a gold rush mentality at work. You were constantly dodging the law, but it was well worth it. And you could start a porno theatre in any building that still had electricity and most of its roof. (At least one theatre in San Francisco was built slapdash in the ruins of a fire-gutted bar.) These, then, were the Wild West days of the dawn of hardcore pornography.

Around 1972, an 'industry' of sorts developed, largely run by mobsters, and a star system was also born. The blockbuster effect of *Deep Throat* introduced the element of major league money into the business and turned many a declining art house into porn theatres out of economic necessity. By the end of the seventies, many old 'legitimate' movie theatres and even the occasional grand opera house had succumbed to this ultimate defilement. Horrors!

In the late eighties, many porno theatres were forced out of business by urban developers riding the crest of the inner city 'rebirth' wave that turned out to be largely a mirage. Other theatres were forcibly shuttered by public health authorities in reaction to

the AIDS crisis. It has also been said that the growing popularity of home video took porno out of the public arena and into the living room, where many thought it belonged, but this overlooks the bedrock core audience of the classic Pornie; people who couldn't afford a video player or who, for one reason or another, didn't savour the idea of sitting at home alone, jerking off to a TV screen. In fact, conveying hardcore porn on the screen was one of the lesser functions of the Pornie. It could be *so* much more!

Although most of the few remaining Pornies have now converted to video projection, a handful of film-projected theatres survive in all their original glory, some still showing the same movies they were playing in the early seventies.

We now turn our gaze back to several specific theatres that operated in the seventies and eighties, which serve as a cross-section of the most notorious specimens.

You approach a grimy marquee that reads 'COLLEGE ORGY XXX' in broken letters, plop down three bucks for a ticket and pass through the turnstile as a fleshy, balding ticket-taker in a stained white T-shirt eyes you without a trace of human emotion. You push open a door grubby with the grease of ages, brush past a mouldy curtain into the pitch black... You're entering a time and place now past... You've wandered down a dirty, forbidden back alley of cinema. You've walked smack into the heart of everything decent people fear about big cities...

Fall of the House of Sleaze: The Variety Photo Plays

Located on 110 Third Avenue near 13th Street was The Variety Photo Plays, an old vaudeville house planted between a basement tavern called The Dug Out and a building that by the mid-eighties had become a Christian mission. The Variety was a rare surviving artefact of old New York City burlesque/B-movie culture that had been largely obliterated by the eighties. Refuge for generations of drunken shore-leave sailors and down on their luck *Midnight Cowboy*-style transients, the place maintained its forties B-joint atmosphere purely through a spirit of neglect, and the reek of an ancient karma oozed through it. Clearly it had served in other capacities in decades past, and its incarnation as a porno movie theatre was merely a modern economic expediency. The Variety was cosy in a beat way and was more brightly lit than most porno theatres. It had a single modest balcony where patrons (including underground film star Jack Smith) wandered in search of sex.

When this writer visited The Variety in the steamy hot summer of 1984, he entered to find the movie playing upside down. This lasted a good fifteen minutes. Nobody complained (or perhaps even noticed). Quiet, nearly invisible queers in starched white shirts, who looked like they were out of a fifties pulp paperback, moved around from seat to seat, while old floor fans clanged noisily away up front and prostitutes trolled the aisles. Other habitués of The Variety included trashy drag queens, the old and the overweight — what William Burroughs refers to in *Junky* as 'roominghouse flesh'. There was a preponderance of unshaven, overweight men dressed in dirty wool caps and multiple layers of T-shirts and coats, and I even saw a couple of them on that hot afternoon dressed as if it were the middle of winter.

The films featured were generally straight XXX hardcore porno titles, with the occasional old black and white sexploiter making an appearance. While the films were straight, the sex was generally otherwise. The movement of the patrons around the theatre was constant, with the toilets down front serving as a frequent destination. The place was filled with continual rustlings and creakings.

Thanks largely to the efforts of local gutter-beat writers like Bill Landis and Jimmy McDonough, The Variety Photo Plays achieved something akin to underground cult status, and acquired a reputation as arguably the sleaziest Pornie in the rotten Big Apple.

The curtain came crashing down on The Variety in 1989 after two undercover health inspectors reported 'omnipresent' unsafe sex between male patrons, sometimes while a young child of approximately eight years of age — apparently a theatre employee's kid — was present. At 3pm on 8 February, a troop of cops and public health officials rousted all the customers out of the theatre, into the cold New York City afternoon, and padlocked the doors. It remained boarded up for many months after.

The Variety was eventually divested of its old atmosphere, refurbished and successfully converted to live Off-Broadway theatre. And it wasn't cheap anymore...

It Came from 14th Street: The Metropolitan

For years Manhattan's Metropolitan theatre stood lowering on 14th Street just east of Third Avenue, its huge sooty, battered marquee seeming to blight the entire block as it provided refuge from the rain for a mob of loitering drug dealers and crazies. An historic, once grand 'legitimate' theatre, it had by the eighties become an unholy abomination, drawing like a giant magnet every pervert, pickpocket, bum, mark,

outpatient and junkie on notorious 14th Street. The Met's enormous twin balconies had long side aisles extending almost down to the screen, which were invariably lined with old geezers leering hideously with salacious intent down at the milling crowds below. 'The sound of constant rustling so peculiar to The Variety's ambience is amplified here to an unbearable noise,' noted Landis and McDonough after a visit to The Metropolitan in the mid-eighties, 'like a million bats walking in a cave.' While by this point the two were 'regulars' at The Variety, it had taken them years to work up the courage to go into The Met!

The Met's reputation always preceded it — it was a veritable wellspring of evil myths. Old projectionists told hair-raising stories of having to fight off groping hands in dark stairwells on their way to the projection booth, while tales of muggings and violence abounded. However, according to Mike Black, a student of Metropolitan mystique, there was, on the contrary, hardly any violence in the place at all.

Like many urban porno houses, the movies were heterosexual, but the quick and dirty sex action was of the other variety, and the theatre became everyone's worst AIDS nightmare come to life.

The bathrooms were a 'filth addict's wet dream,' Black noted in his magazine *Gutter Trash*, 'reeking of piss, grunge and body odour.' The urinals were perpetually flooded with rivers of piss, overflowing onto the floors to create a sea of 'green and orange slime.' Black recalled witnessing sixteen ounce beer cans standing in the urinals, filling up with piss. He once saw a man shake one to see if it was full yet, then place it back in the urinal...

Sex was everywhere, especially in the two toilets. Black once observed two drunken bums, one black and one Hispanic, dallying on one of the long benches in the lounge adjoining a bathroom, blowing each other. One after the other, two bottles of Thunderbird

'The Deuce' – Once the Camelot of sleaze, now a habitat for transient peddlers. (ph: Silke Mayer)

slipped from the folds of their drunken clinch and they immediately began to fight over who was the owner of the fuller bottle.

On another occasion Black saw a 300lb-plus Negro man who needed to relieve himself but couldn't because the toilet stalls were occupied with sex action. The obese patron simply went out to the lounge, pulled down his pants, squatted his fat ass over a trash can and took a dump. The unimaginably horrible stench sent people running for the exits and fresh air...

The Metropolitan was closed in 1987, but its marquee continued to haunt the neighbourhood until the building was demolished a couple of years later. Other stories have it that the structure was reconverted into a state home for the deaf. In any case, all traces of The Met were removed from the face of the earth.

The Gay, the Bad and the Ugly: Other New York City Theatres

Further up Manhattan were the famed 42nd Street theatres between Seventh and Eighth Avenues, a strip known as 'the Deuce'. These once 'legit' theatres had formed the core of 'The Movie Capital of the World', but by the early seventies were, like so many other American inner city cinemas, screening hardcore porno and violent exploitation. These theatres offered squalid but seemingly indestructible interiors and long ominous staircases leading down into ramshackle subterranean rooms ideal for muggings. The theatres of the Deuce, built in the twenties and thirties, had undergone many booking policy changes over the decades, from old westerns playing twenty-four hours a day to musicals and first run movies, but as New York took a crash dive in the seventies, managers started to book films with the kind of ghastly, lurid titles that all too well confirmed everyone's worst fears about the city. By the early nineties, all the theatres on the strip had been vacated, while everyone waited for the stalled redevelopment plans to take effect. After several false starts the Deuce is about to undergo a facelift engineered by the Walt Disney Corporation which, amongst other things, plans to sprinkle pedestrians with pixie dust...

But the real deal in terms of mid-Manhattan hardcore Pornie ambience was to be found in now defunct theatres like The Big Apple, The Harem (with its balcony 'for couples only'), The Cameo, The Mermaid, The Odd, The Doll and other unsung, under-appreciated dens of vice that lurked on the side streets and intersections outside the Deuce. Each theatre had its own individual style, born from appalling neglect. The Venus, at 45th and Eighth, proffered titles like *Sex Deal* and *Virgin Flesh*, and offered up an interior that was, as Landis and McDonough would note, so pitch black that you couldn't see your watch on your wrist, and smelled of 'lavender mothballs'.

Gay male XXX theatres abounded off the Deuce along Eighth Avenue, often favouring Greek names like Eros and Adonis, and offered more premeditated interior design. The Adonis represented the classic gay Pornie, with its kitschy reproductions of ancient Greek and Roman sculptures highlighted against a general background of opulent tackiness. The colour scheme consisted of red, red and more red. The Jewel, a gay Pornie of greater renown, lurking over on Third Avenue towards 12th Street, had preceded The Adonis

in its reliance on tacky ornamentation like Greek pillars and its obsessive fondness for whorehouse red. But while the gay Pornies differentiated themselves by their exhibition of *gay* hardcore films and by an attention to interior design that was non-existent in so-called 'straight' Pornies, it was all pretty much academic, since almost all the sex was gay and the movies were, for the most part, ignored altogether.

The essence of the twenty-four hour New York City Pornie was bound up in a joint off Times Square called The Night Shift. (By the summer of 1984 it had been renovated and renamed The Omega.) The interior design was a horror unto itself, 'vivid as a nightmare' noted Bill Landis, requiring a mind 'loosened by mental retardation' to tolerate the place for more than five

'The world's greatest movie center' presumably meant something else when this mural first appeared. (ph: Silke Mayer)

minutes. Positioned on the ground floor was a big video screen proffering out-of-focus hardcore for patrons who parked themselves among several rows of folding chairs. Off to the side were some busted lockers and a line of fake trees — a pathetic attempt to evoke the atmosphere of the Central Park Ramble, an infamous outdoors gay rendezvous. Another odd theatresque prop was a painted subway car. A slow 'mugger's paradise' elevator led to the second floor and the actual 'cinema', where low-paid projectionists ran choppy, scratched gay hardcore porn films from a projection booth resembling a treehouse shack. Old candy counters on both floors had been converted into sex goods concession stands. An adjoining pool room had been converted into a garbage-littered flophouse, servicing night owl pickpockets, drag queens and pale, streetwise teenage 'chickens' who swarmed the cinema in the wee hours and mingled with businessmen marks, Haymarket hustlers, naïve, drunk tourists and various unclassifiable urban flotsam.

Lairs like The Night Shift were havens for a special breed of pickpocket that frequented the all-male theatres: black and Puerto Rican hustlers who cut the pockets of dozing patrons with a razor blade and fled with their wallets. Sometimes they cut too deep and you'd see the unlucky victim run screaming through the lobby, his rear end covered in blood. Some pickpockets were adept at lifting wallets while giving blow-jobs; others tired of the formality and favoured quick toilet muggings — the preferred victim being a slight Oriental.

Phantoms in Paradise: The Pilgrim

While New York City had the right atmosphere and a crushing quantitative edge over any other town, Boston had The Pilgrim. A once-grand picture palace on Washington Street, it had hosted historic runs and premières (including William Castle's *The Tingler*), and had a proud history of movie exhibition behind it. By the early seventies the neighbourhood in which it stood, dubbed 'The Combat Zone', had degenerated into a classic urban red light district, and The Pilgrim had tumbled along with it. Instead of the showbiz glitz and ballyhoo that animated the old house in its heyday, it was now possessed by an eerie, impenetrable darkness.

Handing over five bucks and pushing through the turnstile, you're immediately hit by the damp smell of pine-sol disinfectant that ironically suggests a place swarming with germs rather than a place recently cleaned. You walk up a long, dim ramp sided by battered vending machines around which old men cluster silently. To the left is the entrance to a long, endless stairway that appears to lead down to the earth's core (but actually leads to the toilet). Walls are covered with obscene graffiti, while crudely hand-lettered cardboard signs confront you as you ascend the ramp: 'No sexual activity or exhibitionism! You can be arrested for this! It has happened here!!!' The signs have a desperate, almost pleading tone.

You walk into the main room, once a grand showpiece marvel, now too dimly lit to reveal even traces of its rich past. Two steeply descending balconies swirl off at the sides into eight curved, bulbous, private boxes. The domed ceiling is seemingly sky-high, and most of the luxurious drapery which once festooned the theatre still waits there patiently for a match tossed by a careless crackhead. This writer has experienced many different sensations in many different porn theatres, but only at The Pilgrim did I fear I might be burned to death in a great fire.

Indistinct forms float along the wide back aisle of the lodge in the almost impenetrable darkness, seemingly without moving their feet, to disappear and appear elsewhere.

The place is in glorious ruin: chairs completely wrecked or missing altogether; paint peels from the walls and ceilings. An ancient air-conditioning system blasts away to little effect.

Coming up the ramp you'd notice that all the stairways were chained off with defiant 'Balcony Closed' signs, yet as you reclined awkwardly in your broken chair, leaning slightly sideways, butt almost to the floor, you'd notice that the balconies were absolutely *full* of people. They are seen first as pale, transparent spectres, sexless wavering forms watching the screen from a box or doorway far above. You have to stare a long time to convince yourself you're not seeing reflections or mirages in the flickering shadows of the theatre, whose dimensions and mysterious recesses are never quite certain. In this strange light *nobody* looks genuinely human or real, not even the people sitting near you... Not even the old man who lurches into you as he staggers up the aisle. The place is full of old men — like, eighty-five or ninety — a larger concentration of old men than anywhere else except perhaps the mountaintop monasteries of the Himalayas.

Some of the human apparitions constantly walk the balconies. It's impossible to tell who is an usher and who is just wandering around. At one point, someone rattles a padlocked side door, probably just mistaking it for a functioning fire exit which by law it should be. Instantly out of the balcony three separate flashlight beams are trained on the door! No one there. The show goes on. Either The Pilgrim has the largest (and least efficient) troop of ushers in the world or the regular customers bring their own torches. Whatever the situation, the least of their problems is someone trying to get in for free.

The longer you're there, the more it becomes clear that the place is a veritable hive of activity — even if it never becomes quite visible. Faceless shadows restlessly and aimlessly wander the aisles, the stairways, the balconies... constantly changing seats. Yet the place is so dark that it takes almost a full hour for your eyes to adjust and hence most of the audience wanders in a state of virtual blindness — bumping into seats, bumping into each other... groping around like an army of helpless idiots. There's a pervasive, constant, low muffled background noise of shuffling feet, creaking chairs and floorboards, which is never pierced by the sound of a human voice.

And far above, seemingly miles above, the projector's beam slices through the smoky darkness.

In 1988, The Pilgrim converted to video projection and the aesthetic quality of its viewing experience plummeted even further. The image was now unbelievably blurry and the sound quality was even worse. The dim light of video projection consequently made the place even darker and you had to stand for an extra hour (two hours in total) stock still — for fear of falling on top of a seated customer or gashing yourself on a broken chair — before the interior began to vaguely suggest itself and phantom forms began to emerge.

Little Shop of Horrors: The Green Parrot

Located on First Avenue's 'Sleaze Row' and adjoining the historic Pike Place Market on its southern slope, The Green Parrot, built around 1915, was one of the oldest theatres in Seattle. Like many old theatres that end their days in a state of premature burial (via hardcore porno), The Green Parrot had, over the decades, served in a variety of 'legitimate' capacities.

By the early seventies that was all over. It converted to 16mm hardcore porno and opened on a twenty-four hour basis. It now doubled as a flophouse for patrons who during cold spells would sometimes stay for days at a time. It closed once a week on Monday morning from 5am to 9am to be cleaned by an Hispanic kid who, ex-projectionist Dennis Nyback recalls, pocketed the under-the-table $25 and subcontracted the actual cleaning to one of an endless supply of Spanish-speaking teenage girlfriends whom he paid $10.

The Green Parrot owner, Roger Forbes, was king of Seattle porno, owning at least twenty theatres around the north-west. His mansion, built by a bootlegger in the twenties, was a big old place nestled in a secluded area of Capital Hill, and some black and white sex flicks that played at The Parrot were filmed in its huge basement. It was later bought by the Wilson sisters of the rock group Heart, who still reside there.

The Green Parrot never had more than one employee on the premises, a union projectionist who could sit at either the ticket counter or in the projection booth, since he was responsible for both. If he sat behind the counter he could see the screen in a mirror. He couldn't really make out what was happening in the movie, but could tell when the film had tailed out of the projector and the screen went white. If he happened to be reading a book or was otherwise diverted, it could be quite a while before he happened to notice the movie had ended. No one ever came out of the theatre to complain. Porno theatre patrons are renowned for their silent acceptance of any sort of fuck up. If you were in the projection booth, you could sleep on a sofa — when the film tailed out of the projector it would flap until you woke up and started the next movie.

There was a double feature change every Friday — actually just two different 16mm reels grabbed from a supply of hundreds stacked in the back room. One reel was an actual sound and colour feature, while the other was a black and white silent reel shot in Forbes' basement starring local talent. All the films had previously flapped endlessly on unattended projectors, and all their opening and closing footage had been beaten off — hence the movies lacked titles and credits, beginnings and endings.

There was a battered, beaten-up old eight-track tape deck to provide music for the silent films, and anything played on it came out wowing and fluttering all over the place. The tape selection was not wide, most of it being easy-listening garbage. Nyback recalls his favourite tape was some sort of 'A Thousand Strings Play Broadway Show Tunes' type of thing that offered a deliriously distorted version of 'Old Man River', providing bizarre accompaniment to the on-screen porno. The advantage of screening a silent film was that you could play it at the slower sixteen-frames-per-second 'silent' speed, resulting in slow-motion porno and fewer reel changes. Often the projectionist would play the sound reel at the slow speed too, using the tape deck for music. This would give longer amounts of free time to be spent sleeping on the sofa.

A buzzer indicated when the front door was open. If you heard the buzzer and went downstairs and found no one there, it meant that someone had snuck in. For the conscientious, duty-bound projectionist (there were a few; Nyback was certainly not one), this meant returning to the projection booth, where the movie was stopped and the janitor lights turned up. These lights were so bright that the regular customers, trying to sleep or give a blow job, would be really pissed off and would gladly point out the guilty party so they could get back to being in the dark.

The dreaded balcony was 'no go' territory that even the janitors refused to enter — though they were no doubt motivated more by laziness than fear. During operating hours it was always pitch black up there, and if anyone bothered putting a bulb in the aisle light it would soon disappear. Nyback, for his part, lived by a strict code: always try to avoid entering the

(*Above*) *The infamous Variety Photoplays, cleaned up for 'legitimate' theatre (ugh).*

(*Below*) *'The Strip' on 42nd St, awaiting a sprinkling of Disney's pixie dust. (ph: Silke Mayer)*

(Above) 42nd St's Empire Theatre, boarded up and awaiting Julie Andrews. (ph: Silke Mayer)

(Below) The Mini Adult, San Francisco. Mini Adult???

effort to guarantee seclusion, thus further reducing the stock of usable seats and prompting retaliation in kind from Les. The projectionists were occasionally and unwillingly caught in the middle of these squabbles. Another regular customer was a nameless, well-dressed businessman-type, who always came in at noon and would stay less than an hour. When given his ticket he would keep it in his hand until he got to the trash can, where he would deposit it. He also wore a wedding ring and was no doubt eager to keep his wife ignorant of his lunchtime activities.

The regular customer of greatest renown was a plain-looking small man in his thirties, who never said hello or goodbye. His *modus operandi* was unique: he would unscrew the lightbulb in the bathroom, strip naked and sit in the urinal, so that anyone who came to piss would have to piss on him.

Violence would erupt, although infrequently considering all the combustible raw material. The balcony was actually bombed once by a right wing terrorist group that was into targeting porno theatres. The explosion blasted through the projection portals of the booth and sent the projector flying, embedding it solidly into the old wood door. It would certainly have killed the projectionist had he not wandered out of the room moments before.

Once, Mike Copner, one of the projectionists, had fallen asleep on the sofa without locking the projection booth door. He was awakened by a drunken Indian with a big knife sitting on his chest, demanding money. Mike told him the money was downstairs. The Indian started down the stairs first; Mike shoved him the rest of the way and fled back to the booth, where he crawled out of the window onto the marquee and began screaming for the police.

When the police arrived they discovered that the Indian had dropped the knife after slashing himself as he tumbled down the stairs. An ID card had also fallen out of his pocket — from which the cops recognised him and had no trouble finding him. The other projectionists, who'd just as soon grow another head as leave the door unlocked, speculated that perhaps Copner had fallen victim to his own grade-Z porno fantasy and hadn't locked the door in the hope that a woman would walk in looking for sex.

In the early eighties, The Green Parrot was gutted by a fire that many suspected Forbes himself had set, and the building was demolished. Fire was the only way out since, as it was part of the historic Pike Place Market, heavy building restrictions were in effect. Perhaps The Green Parrot had become too much of a hell hole even for Forbes, and suicide was the only way out (or at least the only way to get fire insurance out of it).

The Theatre That Time Forgot: The Mini-Adult

While most of the hardcore porno theatres that infested inner cities have been demolished or reclaimed for 'legitimate' use, San Francisco's Mini-Adult theatre continues, in time capsule fashion, to spin in its own orbit; a lost, lonesome relic from the days when the town was considered an open air whorehouse.

The Mini-Adult survives as an embodiment of all that was low-down, lawless and excessive about the proverbial Pornie. It supplies the classic product in spades: an endless glut of scratchy, splicy, choppy, early seventies 16mm XXX hetero hardcore porn films served up in appalling viewing conditions to a monumentally uncomplaining and usually otherwise engaged audience.

auditorium and *never* enter the balcony.

At least a third of the chairs in the theatre were broken. One customer had become enraged when he sat in a chair and it broke: he ripped the chair out of the floor and hurled it at the screen, leaving a gash that was noticeable even after half-assed attempts had been made to repair it. The ripped screen became a trademark symbol of the ultra-shitty Green Parrot viewing experience.

Despite efforts to the contrary, the projectionists became familiar with the parade of regulars. Especially well known was a circle of older gay men, one of whom was nicknamed 'Free Today', since that was what he unfailingly asked every day when he came to buy his ticket. Free Today was at least seventy years old and considered giving blow jobs the ideal retirement plan. Another old regular was Les, a very nice, effeminate man with pure white hair done up in a marvellous pompadour. Les had worked as a drag queen in vaudeville, and after that he'd been a dress designer for burlesque dancers. There was also an old Negro fellow named Joe, short for Black Joe. At one point he urinated on all the seats surrounding his favourite spot in an

Long-time favoured haunt of local gay film-maker and *enfant terrible* Curt McDowell (RIP 1987), The Mini-Adult is about nothing if not atmosphere. In contrast to previously profiled theatres like The Met, The Variety Photo Plays and The Pilgrim, which pervaded with constant rustling sounds, The Mini-Adult is a veritable sanctum of deathly silence — all the better to hear the clatter of the junky 16mm Bell and Howell projectors and the bang of the occasional empty beer can tossed onto the grungey concrete floor by a drunk patron who couldn't possibly care less.

The projectors are the key to the ambience. Placed behind portals crudely cut into the back wall, their light beams pierce a darkness laced with reefer and tobacco smoke at around head level. This guarantees that about every two minutes the blank, glassy-eyed mug of a wandering patron will throw a silhouette on the screen that no one ever complains about. Patrons wander and stand in front of the screen with a frequency and obliviousness that suggests brain damage, while behind them loom lurid, grainy images of greasy bearded guys with long sideburns screwing skinny hippie chicks in unappetising close-up. Ugh!

It's hard to think of The Mini-Adult as a movie theatre at all. There is no hint of a theatrical past to the interior. It looks slapdash, home-made, and has the cultish feel of a club, or of something illegal and temporarily set up in an abandoned building — which it arguably is (an abandoned building). The flickering projector beam dominates the atmosphere and suggests a vague intimacy and camaraderie, as if it were a group of school kids watching a movie in a darkened classroom, or a large family gathered to watch old home movies. And there is a home movie atmosphere here — impregnated with all sorts of other influences of a darker nature.

The Mini-Adult seems like the frailest of business enterprises: in five minutes the place could be completely cleared out and the room could return to being what it probably was before, a mouse-infested storage room for sacks of rice or boxes of stolen car parts. There are large, empty floor spaces in this irregularly shaped room, distant unexplored reaches cloaked in darkness, smelling of urine and disinfectant. You could die in one of the far back corners

and your body might never be found.

Viewing conditions here are the worst ever observed *anywhere*. Giant, bobbing, hairy insect shapes attack the on-screen fornicators as gobs of crud and hair work their way through the never-cleaned rat's nest projectors and jam in the gate. The screen itself is nothing more than a busted-up sheet of plywood, while seating consists of rows of old-fashioned hard wooden movie chairs that are more like church pews. The dialogue of the films is absolutely incomprehensible, and the easy-listening music that predominates is distorted and wobbly beyond belief, like something coming from underwater. Splices often break, followed by long stretches of total darkness. Films start and end without any warning, logic or continuity.

All of this combines to make you doubt your own senses in a style somewhat similar to The Pilgrim, but without its spatial extremes. These joints are sensory twilight zones to be sure; they control the horizontal, they control the vertical — but no one is in control!

Crude hand-drawn posters of early seventies porn films adorn the grubby entrance, announcing films to be screened and harkening back to hardcore's zero budget, home-made origins. The atmosphere *and* the films themselves are straight out of the early seventies. Here time stands still.

The Mini-Adult is a classic one-man operation similar to The Green Parrot, but even more spartan. It shares similarities with other Pornies, as well: ceaseless darkness, the predominance of elderly men, open drug use and sex activity, the absence of anyone apparently employed there. Over a series of visits, this writer never observed anyone who might be even remotely 'in charge', except once when I witnessed a black guy dragging around a plastic garbage bag full of empties. He would fish out empty beer cans between the seats, loudly crush them and then toss them into the bag. Approaching two musky forms engaged in a sex act, he simply looked around them for empties and continued on without a word.

There are no start times, there are no intermissions. There is no beginning, there is no end. There is no one in charge, there is no one at the wheel. The darkness is absolute, it is eternal. People fear only one thing: the day they turn the lights up at The Mini-Adult. ■

(Above & left) More of the Mini Adult, located in one of SF's less salubrious locales.

THE PRETERNATURAL FILMS OF JEAN PAINLEVE

BY JANE GILES

Fear of nature is a key inspiration for the fantastic imagination and horror genres, as the unknown depths of forests, deserts, space and sea are popularly thought to contain inhuman life forms of unpredictable behaviour and probably malevolent intent. Visualising these (real or imaginary) forms is part of the process of conquering dark forces, whether symbolically in fiction or actually through scientific research. The intimate factual investigation of plants and animals was massively advanced by the advent of cinema and advancements in stop-motion, slow-motion, macro-enlargement, infra-red and zoom

That most famous of contemporary French exports – the rabid bat...

photography. The natural history documentary is a compelling and strange species in its own right, but probably few films of this genre are more bizarre than the pioneering work of the maverick Jean Painlevé (1902-89).

A failed physician, Painlevé was studying the morphology of cells in Paris when he came across a customised film camera in which the crank was disengaged so that it could take single frame photographs rather than turning at sixteen frames per second. With this Painlevé made his first film in 1925, *The Stickleback's Egg*, to accompany an academic report. One frame was shot every three minutes to trace the development of the fertilised egg and, in Painlevé's own words, 'the film showed phenomena which, although not new in themselves, highlighted useful precisions and unsuspected sequences of events.' Some more unsuspected than others, as Painlevé later told how he first presented the film to the Académie des Sciences with one sequence hurriedly inserted upside down: 'the embryonic heart, spread on the nutritional ball, rejected the blood corpuscles instead of attracting them... I was horrified, but said nothing.' Early trick photography, such as the films of Georges Méliès, had characterised cinema as a sham and Painlevé suspected that had he owned up to the mistake in editing, rather than quietly rectifying it before the film could be seen again, then the medium could have been forbidden in laboratories and universities. Working with his life-long companion and assistant, Geneviève Hamon, Painlevé was to make around 200 short films. Favouring the lower life forms of crustaceans, sea mosses, diatoms and the like, his visually entrancing films tend towards anthropomorphism and the eroticisation of the subject. The films are also peppered with offbeat observations and unexpected connections. Painlevé's ethos was committed and meticulous, but also irreverent, ironic and humorous. Above all, he refused to take himself too seriously.

In addition to being a scientist, Painlevé was involved in avant-garde arts and it is the interaction of these two disciplines which is the key to his work. Painlevé was influenced by the films of Louis Feuillade, F.W. Murnau, Fritz Lang and Luis Buñuel; he applied the emotional response of German expressionism to clinical subject matter and created meaning through juxtapositions inspired by surrealism and Dada. Painlevé wrote under a number of pseudonyms, such as P.J. Alpin, Ben Levy and Yann O'Bara (as whom he published a collection of sixty short plays entitled *The Theatre of Derision*). Painlevé's writings are idiosyncratic, terse and poetic, full of word-play and reckless declarations, such as "'The foulest kind of trash': that is real distinction..." Having acted alongside Michel Simon in René Sti's (abandoned?) film *The Unknown at the Six Day Races*, Painlevé directed *Mathusalem*, a short made for projection during Ivan Goll's theatre play. He was particularly proud of the scene in which a black woman dances frenziedly on Hamlet's grave, but regretted his failure to capture on film the actor Antonin Artaud, dressed as a cardinal, verbally abusing a passing group of nuns with cries of "Stand back, you daughters of Satan!" Painlevé shot the starfish sequences for Man Ray's film *L'Etoile de Mer* and his work was revered by the surrealists. To a point. Although Buñuel admired the marine documentaries, he was horrified to watch a film that Painlevé had dedicated to Buñuel 'with love' which contained autopsy footage of an eighty-year old woman having her nose torn off with pliers to show the veins and bones of the organ. Buñuel responded, 'Do you really believe, just because I cut out an eye in a film, that I like this sort of thing? I do it for ideological reasons, but operations horrify me. I can't stand the sight of blood.' ['Don't Lean In', 1986].

Painlevé's scientific curiosity meant that there was no aesthetic turning away, but there's also no doubt that he cheerfully revelled in the grislier aspects of his subjects. Documenting the success of Normet's polycitrate serum in *Experimental Treatment of a Haemorrhage in a Dog*, Painlevé filmed not just one but two total bleedings of the unfortunate animal. His 1930 film *Dr Claoué* is a portrait of the man who invented plastic surgery but was also prosecuted for illegal practice of medicine. Claoué died following a car crash, having refused all medical assistance because of his hatred for doctors. In accompanying catalogue notes for this film, Painlevé reminisces fondly about his childhood mathematics teacher, 'his face in shreds, a graft of pubic skin adorning his upper lip with a thin moustache', and about his own attempts to carry an intractable corpse for Claoué on the Paris Métro. In *The Vampire*, Painlevé considers the bat: 'jolly companions in blood-soaked drinking bouts, his dumb grimaces call the jungle to arms. He lurches around on his cripple's legs, with a well-filled paunch... His visiting card reads: Home Service — rabies, paralysis and sleeping sickness.' He was particularly tickled that this film showed in the newsreel cinema of a Copenhagen railway station for two full years. In what is probably his most famous film, the dream-like *L'Hippocampe*, Painlevé is particularly fascinated by the fact that it is the male seahorse which gives birth rather than the female. He notes that this is 'a painful delivery, rich in suffering and agonising labour. If only all ended there! But the damned secretion of gases continue in the pouch after the last born has been expelled. Sometimes the lips of the orifice get stuck together, the pouch swells up and leaves the male floating with his head upside down, which is no enviable position'. With equal enthusiasm, Painlevé described the octopus ('the creature of horror') as a woman: 'draped in her skin of changing colours, the amorous lady has closed her eyes... Between the lids, heavy with knowing sensuality, an ever alert glance nevertheless filters through... It sees far, aims well and whoosh!! How can anything escape such a repeated embrace?'

Painlevé divided his oeuvre into three categories: specialist or academic research films ('films des recherche'), popular entertainment ('films de vulgarisation') and newsreels ('films d'actualité'). Although he claimed a dissonance with popular taste, he used jazz soundtracks in the public versions of his films with the intention of making the curious images 'more accessible'. However, the effect is probably more disconcerting than comforting, particularly in *The Vampire*, which uses Duke Ellington's perky 'Black & Tan Fantasy' as backing music to the image of a bat feeding from the face of a surprised-looking live guinea pig. Rather than creating an atmosphere of mystery or threat, Painlevé's jaunty soundtracks express hilarity in their celebration of the subject matter; he maintained that this eccentric juxtaposition of sound and image underlined his 'scandalous approach to science'. Painlevé was able to break the rules of both scientific and artistic film-making to

A seahorse.

realise his own unique vision because he had a considerable private income from his wealthy father. Paul Painlevé was an illustrious mathematician who established the formula of the resistance of the air (which is the main scientific foundation of aeroplane construction); he also became the French War Minister in 1917 and Prime Minister in 1925. In 1926, Jean Painlevé took the used ink blotters from the Meeting of the State Council and handed these to André Breton for publication in *La Révolution Surréaliste* alongside an article by Louis Aragon.

Politically nonconformist, Jean Painlevé was expelled from the League of Communist Students and became a committed freedom fighter. In 1934, he travelled to Austria as part of the Study Commission set up by the World Committee Against War and Fascism, and in 1936 was part of a commission investigating the pogroms in Poland. He was active in the French Resistance during World War Two; his speciality was dynamiting rail sheds and aircraft hangars. After the *Libération* he was appointed Director-General of French Cinema under the Provisional Government, but was relieved of his duties the following year and returned to film-making.

Painlevé worked painstakingly to the limits of his technology and subject matter. Filming underwater, he used an aqualung and a Debrie Parvo 35mm camera in a waterproof box, although this was complicated by the reels only lasting twenty seconds. Film reels became longer in later years, although ten minutes of 35mm weighed around 25kg and would not sink without weights. (It wasn't until 1947 that Jacques Cousteau, no less, invented a more practical underwater camera.) However, having been loaned a lightweight camera in a shoulder holster customised by Geneviève Hamon to shoot *Breathless*, Jean-Luc Godard later quipped, 'Without Jean Painlevé and his unsinkable camera there would have been no New Wave.' *The Love Life of the Octopus* lasts just thirteen minutes but took ten years (1955-65) to shoot, during the course of which Painlevé would wait forty-eight hours at a stretch for octopus

activity, only to fall asleep at key moments. Having waited years for the octopus to lay its egg, he was alarmed to see it devoured by the mother. He later related with relish how the short-sighted narrator of this film read the script standing so close to the microphone that the audience can hear his emphysema punctuating the doom-laden voice-over. In 1949, Painlevé achieved the distinction of becoming the first person to link a microscope with a (live) television camera to show the beating heart of a tiny water flea. His fascination for the microcosmic secret life of minute forms was endless. Exploring the globular, turd-like molluscs known as 'sea witches' in *Acera*, Painlevé marvels at their balletic performances whilst engaged in a chain of copulation. On the other hand, he conceded that *The Strange World of Axel Henrichsen*, a newsreel about a family living near Copenhagen, was 'of interest to nobody'.

Damning the state of film-making in 1933, Artaud hailed the documentary as the last refuge of cinema's partisans. Having established L'Institut de Cinéma Scientifique in 1930, Painlevé co-founded the World Union of Documentalists in 1947 and the 'Groupe des 30' in 1953. The French documentary tradition of the 1920s-1950s was technically superb, poetic and imaginative, but also unsentimental to the point of brutality; Painlevé's films fit well alongside the cinematically better-known work of Jean Epstein, Jean Vigo (*A Propos de Nice*; *Taris*), Buñuel (*Land Without Bread*), Georges Franju (*Le Sang des Bêtes*) and Alain Resnais (*Night and Fog*). Painlevé continued film-making up until the death of Geneviève Hamon in 1987, after which he wrote prolifically for the last two years of his life. In addition to his legacy of films, literature and freedom fighting, he left a reputation as a motor racing champion. But that's another story... ■

The British Film Institute is acquiring new prints of several Painlevé films. Selected titles are available on sell-thru from Connoisseur Video.

PULSATING POSTERIORS AND MASOCHISTIC MISSES

OR STRAPPED FOR CASH

BY RAMSEY CAMPBELL

'Sent home from school, Jenny is put over her mother's knee for a spanking. After a few wallops her tight navy blue knickers are taken down. The tawse is then produced and the strapping plus the further spanking that Jenny receives in front of her school chum, Jane, leave us in no doubt that this naughty young miss will feel her punishment for some time to come!'

Blurb for *Fighting in School* (Janus, c1981)

'A sixteen-year-old orphan, Sylvie, is sent as a boarder to a special school where the *malaise Anglaise* is the rule and every misdemeanour is the excuse for baring female rumps and administering a sound spanking.'

Blurb for *Education Anglaise* (1982, released by Jezebel, 1995)

'Drive a spanking new Citroen ZX and get three of the best.'
Full-page Citroen advertisement,
The Observer, 14 May 1995

"Where do they get actors who can do this?"
Max Renn watching a 'Videodrome' tape

At first sight the certification for video by the BBFC of *Education Anglaise* looks like a precedent, and perhaps it is. Ever since the Video Recordings Act came into force, near-anonymous British production companies have been submitting videos of this description for scrutiny, but every one proved too much for our censor. Not that chastisement as an element in films appears to have been frowned upon; indeed, it has been celebrated in such places as the poster for *McLintock!* and the trailer for Channel 4's recent Elvis season, which enshrined a severe encounter from *Blue Hawaii* (of which more later). But the idea of films whose bare-, ah, faced appeal is to those viewers who enjoy watching the administration of discipline appears to have deeply offended the BBFC, and so the casual buyer of *Education Anglaise* may not recognise it as a Gallic homage to a British film genre far livelier than the National Trust school of literary adaptation, or Ken Loach's propaganda-laden boomerangs, or even horror movies these days. So here are some notes and observations towards a history of the English schoolgirl chastisement film.

Before video there was 8mm, and the famed Harrison Marks. What appears to have been his earliest essay in this field, *Late for School* (Janus Publications, 1977), is represented in *Spanking Special* number 2 ('A martinet photo fantasy special beautifully illustrated plus articals [*sic*] and readers letters,' the magazine describes itself breathlessly, and no wonder, on the cover). I say represented rather than simply illustrated, since these are production stills involving a young woman whose single-minded look isn't quite able to conceal some amusement as she raises the school skirt of the plumpish girl draped across her lap. In the film itself, exhibited for a while in a viewing cupboard at the rear of a Soho bookshop, had there been a soundtrack it would no doubt have included the pleas of the director to the plumpish girl to show some emotion. As I remember, several seconds elapsed before she obliged with a series of grimaces while the

woman delivered some would-be hefty pats to her bare buttocks.

While *Late for School* must await revival by the National Film Archive, other examples from this late dawn of cinema were preserved on video as soon as that medium became popular. Harrison Marks was the auteur of a trio released on a single cassette. In *The School Lesson*, two rather senior schoolgirls are surprised at some mild mutual fondling by an apoplectic headmaster, who canes or at least mimes caning them; in *The Riding Lesson*, a squire discovers his daughter caressing her supposedly teenage friend, whom he spanks with more effort than conviction before a riding crop, and by the look of it some displaced lipstick between shots, is applied to the older girl's rear. Both men, as is often the case with male authority figures in these pantomimes, appear to be in grave danger of a heart attack. Not so the mistress in *The Gym Lesson*, who seems to devote most of her energy to not quite touching with a cane the behind of a pea-shooting girl, though she may give the accomplice a couple of actual smacks: hard to tell without a soundtrack.

Then, in 1981, came the advent of sound, and Harrison Marks was there. *The Prefect's Lesson* even boasts a voice-over by an unnamed narrator with a country accent, describing as we watch it how "Jane and I" throw Jackie Parsons, like them sporting a gym-slip and straw hat, on the school field and pummel her for her part in losing a hockey match. Enter the not especially fearsome Miss Clegginthorpe, who bustles them to the bearded Scottish headmaster and has, to put it mildly, improvised words with him. "Er, excuse me, er, headmaster, do you think I could see you for a mo, few moments..." Clearly this film, like many of its ilk, is of the school of One-Take Ed Wood. As the girls wait outside, the voice-over laments "Blimey, that meant a whacking... I'd never had one before, but I'd heard from the other girls what was in store from Mr Granger... It was going to be awful... My bottom was already beginning to tingle with anticipation." By this line the culprits have been summoned to the office while Miss Clegginthorpe departs, Pinterishly muttering. The voice-over then goes in for an alienation device if ever I heard one, whereby it explains what the dialogue it isn't quite covering up is saying, which means that the girl can protest in two ways simultaneously about having to lower her knickers. "Then suddenly I was draped over his fat repulsive knees. Was it a dream?" It might well be, since the headmaster rants at her without moving his lips and then moves them in a vain attempt to catch up with his lines while spanking her (though perhaps not her, or anybody, on the soundtrack). After not much of all this he canes her friend to the strains of the 'Ride of the Valkyries,' an accompaniment perhaps intended to distract the audience from the unsynchronised quality of the sound effects. The caned girl has assumed control of the voice-over, but it's left to her friend to tell us that they leave the office silently, which they don't. As the headmaster lights up a fag she confides that to her surprise she later finds herself looking forward to the next session of punishment.

Which is very unusual in this most English of sub-genres. The notion of the victim who begins by resisting but ends up wanting more (a staple of rape fantasies, I understand) seems to be commoner in the American equivalent, which tends to insist that the

(Previous page) After years of kicking Commie ass, John Wayne discovers a lucrative sideline in paddling film star ass. Unbeknownst to his fans, he starred in over 200 early Spankarama shorts...

(Right) The quintessence of spanking film naffness...

discipline has an erotic significance for at least one of the participants. By contrast, the British shorts are founded on the principle that some of us find the chastisement of girls dressed in school uniforms sexy, and I quite see that a few of my readers must be offended or enraged by now, or (if they should criticise this essay for, say, *Sight and Sound* — I have in mind the review which appeared there of the first volume of this annual [*Annual! Time obviously passes at a different speed in the parallel universe of Merseyside... Ed.*] will undoubtedly purport to be. Let's at least be clear that we're not talking about appeals to paedophilia. The films and magazines habitually declare that all those involved are over eighteen years old, and I mean no disrespect to the long-suffering actresses when I assure my readers that the evidence is there for all to see and, I believe, is intended to be seen. (When the age of any of the schoolgirl characters is referred to, it's never younger than seventeen.) Nor is the advertising nearly as misogynistic as the kind of description I remember outside the hard-core viewing booths in 42nd Street, where women were routinely described as 'bitch'. But isn't the subject of this essay (I hear myself asked) a genre which encourages violence against women?

That surely depends on whom the audience identifies with, and it's my observation that this is more complicated than it might seem. Back in the early eighties, a sex-shop back-room booth multiplied and eventually became a short-lived basement cinema club, the Spankarama, where my bladder one day urged me to the single toilet, effectively the Gents, since the audience packed into the small auditorium was almost entirely male. The toilet walls were covered with graffiti displaying the phone numbers of victims who were willing to be treated like the girls in the films and who, so far as I could tell, were as predominantly male as the audience outside. I cite this to share my confusion rather than to make a case, since (unless there's another group of films in circulation to a different specialist audience) very few indeed of the victims in chastisement videos are male. (By contrast, most commercially released overtly sadomasochist films — the turgid *Exit to Eden* will do as an example — concentrate on male victims, perhaps these days so as not to be accused of political incorrectness.) I note, however, that in his survey of Soho sex cinemas in the Winter 1982/83 *Sight and Sound*, Nick Roddick found that all the audiences were ninety-nine per cent male. Letters to the chastisement magazines suggest that the audiences for the home videos are more evenly distributed between the genders.

There remains, perhaps most importantly, the issue of consent. If we're to argue (as I suspect many of the readers of this publication feel) that the verdict in the Spanner case was wrong — that it isn't the business of the law to interfere in whatever sexual activity people choose to share — then it seems unreasonable to change the argument if the recipients of the treatment are female. I should have thought that films and magazines as specialist as these appeal to those consumers who already swing that way and who either have found a partner to share their tastes or take their pleasure in solitude. I'm more concerned about the young actresses, whose consent to (on occasion) pretty severe discipline I have to assume. That some of the most severely chastised come back for another film I take to be evidence of this rather than of their having

no choice. It also seems likely that they would watch examples of what they're letting themselves in for before they sign up. If only some of them would tell us!

Enough speculation for the nonce, and back to the films. Nick Roddick found that this genre suffered from the worst technical quality of any in his survey, and in the early days of video the budget was certainly all there on the screen. *Fighting in School*, whose advertising can be found at the head of this essay, is typical in not even being able to afford credits. The camera, whose whirring adheres to the soundtrack, frames a sofa and the actresses and occasionally goes in for a closer shot. Whatever charms the film has derive from the performances of the actresses, who appear to have established some rapport. "You don't like me," the daughter protests from across her mother's lap, to which the mother retorts, "No I don't. You're an unpleasant little brat." There's a heartfelt quality to this response which suggests either the Method or some derivation from the lady's own experience. "Ow, ooh, that's not fair" and "Ow, it really hurts" complains Jenny, with scant effect on her mother but perhaps intentionally more on the viewer. Her friend Jane watches the latter stages with some

fascination before departing to figure in her own dimly filmed sequel, *Cane for Jane*.

By now films were appearing with considerable frequency, and it may be that Janus decided to devote some of their profits to upgrading at least their production values. One result was the St Winifred's trilogy (or St Winnifred's, if we're to believe the name on a blackboard upon which a different bare-bottomed actress chalks the title of each episode). The films take place in a more capacious office than hitherto, sufficient to accommodate a bench occupied by the mortarboarded headmaster and Colonel Forbes, a school governor, and Norton, the head prefect, wearing black stockings with a suspender belt and kneesocks. (Nothing like trying to please every member of the audience.) "Young girls actually benefit from a good flogging," the Colonel declares in *The Athletes' Lesson*. "It's good for them." Norton announces two miscreants, at which five troop in, apparently confusing the headmaster into warning them to "adjust yourselves intelligently and in a civilised manner." Blissett and Beddoes are accused of writing bad essays and wearing erotic underwear. Norton duly spanks them and is told by the head that "the punishment has been executed with great decorum and artistic style." It's the conviction with which he pronounces his lines which suggests they must mean something. The Criswell of chastisement, he tells Beddoes, "I think you should be punished thoroughly, with anticipation and arrogance."

Words seem to fail him in *The Sixth Formers' Lesson*. It's left to Norton to tell off Lovat and Green, whom the zoom manages to locate after some stumbling about, for participating in a sit-in and reading *Playboy*, no less. "By gad, sir, if you'd put them in the army they'd have been shot," Colonel Forbes says. "Insubordinate young wenches." The historical interest of this short is its introduction of the slow-motion replay, slowed-down underwater sound and all.

Back comes the head, his lines in more disarray than ever, for *The Head Girl's Lesson*. "Little barnyard hussies behaving like tomcats" is his description of Slocum, the deputy head girl, and Norton, both of whom are found guilty of dallying in the woods with boys. "Your heinous crime has to be seen to be believed, Head Prefect Slocum, Deputy Prefect Slocum," he says without pausing, a man who knows what he's about even if nobody else does. "I see you're tattooed like an ancient bacon." I assume he can't really say that, but I challenge anyone familiar with the film to tell me what the actual phrase is. There was an utter lack of mirth at any of the dialogue of the whole trilogy in the Spankarama auditorium. All three shorts use as their soundtrack theme the 'Sanctus' from the *Missa Luba*, by the way, and this isn't the only resemblance to Lindsay Anderson's *If...* I'll have reason to cite.

Up to this point Janus seem to have had the field pretty well to themselves, but then along came Roué (a title which makes me feel old) to challenge them — indeed, it may even be that the St Winifred's trilogy was a response on the part of the Janus bunch. Not that Roué's *Jane and the Tutor* had much going for it technically: gloomy photography, a wobbly video camera, jump-cuts where the camera operator stopped filming too soon... What it does display is a new insistence on convincing the audience that the rather sweet inoffensive young woman has invited the

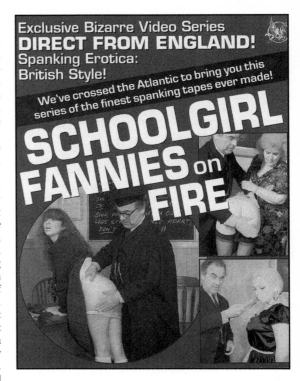

treatment she receives, by getting her under-rehearsed lessons wrong and by having written a letter mocking her convincingly humourless tutor. This is usually a stratagem of commercial mainstream movies; for instance, it's my recollection that the young teenager in *Blue Hawaii* falls foul of Presley by wishing that someone in the world would demonstrate they care about her. Indeed, *Jane and the Tutor* isn't unlike *Blue Hawaii* either in reducing the unfortunate girl to sobs on screen.

The next few Roué films seem to be the work of real film-makers. *Rebel at St Angela's* gives head prefect Norton her revenge as a teacher, Miss Paget, who canes Jennifer, a slim blonde girl, at considerable length. The editing and selection of angles, and in particular the timing, are almost too professional; there's even, as a build-up to the main action, a series of flashbacks to a spanking by the headmaster whose face, sinisterly enough, we never see. *Room 2D* introduces a baby-faced young woman for even more of a caning, preceded by her encounter with a master whose English accent and general behaviour are, to say the least, theatrical. Even the most realistically performed chastisement shorts include some such unrealistic detail, and I'm inclined to wonder if these are intended to reassure those viewers who need it that the spectacle is still to some extent acted.

The baby-faced actress playing Lucy Palmer (see *After Hours*) is featured as Carol Ellis in *First Week of Term*. (I have to refer to her in this unwieldy way because almost none of the performers are ever credited. I do recall Linzi Drew reducing the narrator of *The Prefect's Lesson* to a display of hysterics with a few strokes of a cane and a great deal more anticipation of them in a short whose name escapes me, and we'll come to Lindsay Honey later.) She and her friend Brooks are variously punished by an unpleasant bearded fellow who has made something of a career in this material. Brooks whines annoyingly, I have to say, and wails "It weren't me." The film (released in two parts) exemplifies a frequent ploy by which, if there are two girls, one is treated much more severely than the other. Brooks receives not much of a caning before she succeeds in weeping copiously, while her accomplice in drawing a phallic symbol on the Lord Mayor's car is severely spanked at length (some of it admittedly made up of repeated footage, in one case not cut off soon enough to conceal repeated dialogue.) She confines herself mainly to cries of "Ow" and "No", which soon becomes a bit dull — sorry, kid, after all that work.

Four O'Clock Report is another matter. Jennifer the rebel reappears, having perfected a screech of protest at the indignities visited upon her, as Virginia the hockey captain. She and Charlotte Lawson and Brenda, a Scottish new girl, wait uneasily outside the headmaster's office in a scene not unreminiscent in its mixture of bravado and apprehension of the equivalent episode in *If....* From the dialogue which he (not entirely accurately) quotes, I take this to be the film Nick Roddick cites as typical of the Spankarama programme, 'a series of playlets in which young girls, generally dressed in gym-slips and sensible knickers... are placed across the knees of middle-aged men and spanked, or made to bend over a table and whipped... The camera remains in fixed medium shot of the girl's bare bottom as it turns pink beneath the spanking (a colour rendered all the more lurid by the quality of the video).' Well, not quite or only all that, as I trust I've demonstrated already. Charlotte gets slippered for running down the corridor, and the new girl is caned for it hardly matters what — maybe her awkward reading of her lines. A fourth girl trudges into the office, but that's the end, whether to appeal to the imagination or betraying that the celluloid ran out we can only speculate.

The latter girl does fall foul of Uncle George, who is played by the bearded authoritarian from *First Week*. She's bent over a desk to have a ruler applied to the seat of her white knickers, a sexy image similar to one which survived the British censor to appear in *Education Anglaise*. She crops up again in *The Girls of Effingham Hall* (not, I think, a Roué film, and an oddly titled one insofar as no more effing takes place than in any others of these pieces), along with Lucy Palmer and a young woman who played a spanked secretary in a Roué production called *After Hours*. (Personally, I wouldn't dare to pinch a title from Martin Scorsese.) This is a mild example of its kind, which (like *Jane and the Tutor*) signals its status as a fantasy by having the young women dress up onscreen as schoolgirls, but the BBFC would doubtless have had none of it. Sympathisers with Lucy Palmer may find it comforting to see her being, for once, quite gently spanked and putting on a good show nonetheless.

As for the whiny Brooks, she was *The Tutor's New Pupil* before appearing in surely the most minimalist film in the entire genre, Roué's *Caned After School*. She plays an unnamed schoolgirl who is variously chastised by a master who keeps himself unidentifiable (though isn't that the bored voice of the former Uncle George?). There is virtually no dialogue: in the first five minutes he says only "Stand up" and "Get ready for the cane." Maybe the intention is to involve the viewer as directly as possible, but I don't think it works quite like that. The actress begins to whinge before the action starts and continues throughout, a performance which, I fear, becomes horribly irritating. Perhaps that's why this appears to have been the end of her movie career.

Alongside some of this, Janus returned to the competition with *Moral Welfare*, parts one and two. Of the three young women in these, the schoolgirl character, Jassi Hafeez, is Asian. Uniquely for the genre, she stays fully dressed throughout. Perhaps more significantly, a still of the third girl (a punk) being spanked by a middle-aged man was included by the Feminist Anti-Censorship Taskforce in *Caught Looking*, their anthology of images they found erotic.

Compared with the heartless efficiency of this film and the best-made of its competitors, the next Roué video is rather endearingly ramshackle. This is *Schoolgirl Nieces* starring a previously and subsequently unknown blonde girl and a brunette who talks like an understudy for some Southern comedienne. For a while it seems they're both called Jane, but the brunette proves belatedly to be called Sue. The budget runs to a pillow-fight in a bedroom as the first punishable offence, but not to more than one copy of the *The Sun*, which is still being read by the aunt THE FOLLOWING EVENING, as a rare intertitle has it — maybe the film-makers are too delighted at having found a front-page headline saying simply WHACKED. A squabble in the front room gives the uncle a reason to slipper the girls mildly while they wriggle a great deal, a scene which illustrates the generic ploy whereby one character is lenient so that their partner has an excuse to be less so. THE NEXT DAY announces a curious shot of the aunt in her underwear bending over a table while she talks to the girls' school on the phone, and THAT AFTERNOON shows up the budget again, when a dull thud offscreen prompts aunt and uncle to assure each other "There's the doorbell." The girls act being spanked harder than is the case by their uncle, who leaves the real chastisement to his wife. By the end, the film has more than delivered the goods,

John Wayne stars as Kurtz in the suppressed fifties version of **Heart of Darkness.**

and no doubt caused its admirers to do so.

Soon Roué went into decline as a video production company. I recall being told by a young woman at the Roué number that one of the "two nice girls" in *Private Tuition* was "a bit plumper than usual". More than a bit, I fear. From the same period, *Private Lessons* is shot in hideous shades of orange and green and involves an alarmingly beaky schoolgirl. No doubt it was time for some more competition, which *Blushes* magazine set out to produce ('the greatest C. P. videos in the world, featuring the most nubile young girls'). All of these films which I've seen feature the authoritarian who was Uncle George. In *Half-Term Punishments* he invites some friends around to his suburban house to spend an unlikely weekend disciplining several girls, rather like De Sade restaged in Milton Keynes or wherever. In *Big Girls Do Cry* he has just one niece to stay. *Sally's First Lesson* is, I think, the first example of the genre to film an actress in school uniform in the street before she arrives at the indoor location. In one scene (a caning filmed in a take as long as any of Hitchcock's) Sally makes such a convincing fuss that her soundtrack is reused over shots of a different actress in *The Detention Room*. This was the last *Blushes* video, and a description of the filming appeared in the magazine. 'The young ladies involved (both eighteen years old) were only given outline direction of the story line with no script. They didn't know what was coming next and the words and yelps are theirs. The result is very realistic, it must be, because it is real.'

Perhaps after that there seemed to be nowhere to go for a while; years appear to have passed before the genre was revived in Britain. I believe it was in 1989 that Vexfilms appeared, advertising to the *cognoscenti Punishment PT* with 'lots of navy blue knicker shots'. No purchaser on that basis is likely to be disappointed, and others may be charmed by 'Fawcett', a young woman with her blonde hair in bunches who grins while she tells her friend Johnson how nervous of their imminent treatment she is. "I thought you were looking forward to it," says her friend. Both wear high

heels with their kneesocks. After failing to impress their gym master they end up in the traditional position. While Johnson confines herself mostly to protests of "Ouch" and "Sir, not so hard", Fawcett giggles while being spanked and says "Oh, sir" and much else with great conviction. She's a star, and wriggles so much when she's about to be caned that the actor calls her Johnson by mistake. The second half-hour sees the girls strip off. "But why, sir?" Johnson asks, to be told "Orders are orders." Maybe, but it doesn't do much for those members of the audience whose interest in the material partakes of fetishism.

Lisa Must Be Caned (perhaps from the same source) is unusual in naming its actress, Sophie Fennington, at least in the advertising. She takes three minutes of screen time to play tennis and walk to the house of Uncle Brian, a *Janus* reader who delivers a singularly unconvincing lecture in a strangled Monty Pythonesque voice, for which spectacle Sophie Fennington may have felt the need to compensate. "Uncle Brian, please don't smack me... I don't want you to smack me on my bottom, please... Not my bottom, Uncle Brian." This might be more appealing if it weren't uttered in an accent very reminiscent of Alison Steadman's in *Abigail's Party*. Perhaps my essay will encourage someone to write a thesis considering the influence of Mike Leigh on the genre under discussion. As for *Lisa Must Be Caned*, it's vigorous but (apart from a recherché use of a table-tennis bat) not very distinguished.

College Classics is a continuing series, not all of which I've been able to see. In *College Classics 1* (A Vexfilm Production for Tallion, © 1989), both the gym master and one of the two girls (French, a blonde) seem somewhat bored — she even jokes while being spanked. Another PT session, this one in the nude. "Take all your clothes off, otherwise you're expelled." The camera operator hardly bothers to frame shots, except for the occasional one centred on a pubic area, an image not exactly abhorred by the genre but mostly treated as beside the point. The colour borders on the emetic, particularly in shots which use a purple curtain as a backdrop. A trailer for *Punishment PT* is appended, including several mysterious shots of wriggly Fawcett brandishing a letter which doesn't figure in the film itself — perhaps the scrap of paper contains the whole of the written script.

College Classics 2 is a good deal more efficient than its predecessor. In an untypically serious and fully acted setting-up scene, Elizabeth Jenkins, ex-head girl, returns to school to persuade the headmaster to chastise her because the rules forbid his doing so to her errant younger sister. "You're a very determined young lady," he eventually declares. "You've persuaded me." The film has established an unusual amount of sympathy for her, which lingers through several pretty relentless disciplinary scenes, during each of which she tries to escape punishment. For some reason the headmaster dons a mortarboard to perform the final caning. Elizabeth has to count the strokes and say "Thank you, sir" after each, perhaps another echo of *If....* "Twelve, sir, you bastard," she understandably cries at the last. There's a touching shot of her composing herself afterwards in her car to the strains of the 'Moonlight Sonata'. This is another Vexfilm, and indeed her number-plate contains the letters VEX.

The 'Moonlight Sonata' can also be heard over the

(Below) If... "This is going to hurt you more than it hurts me..."

opening shots of *College Classics 3*, which is, however, more fun. French from the first one returns as Saunders, a brunette. Blonde Jenkins isn't the same actress as the one in the intervening film. They write insults on a blackboard and mess up table settings for ten minutes in what appears to be a restaurant, until a master arrives to find the evidence of their behaviour and babbles to himself in a Birmingham accent. "Good gracious me, I can't believe this. I don't believe this at all. They've just got no respect for me whatsoever. I'm just going to have to sort these girls out. What am I going to do? Where are these girls?" is just some of what he says. "Good Lord!" he cries, much as characters in EC comics used to greet corpses on the move, on espying the girls from the window. Some interesting narrative disarray ensues, as French jumps out of a lawn chair to elude him only to reappear in it, and complains about leaving her shoes behind, at which they magically return to her feet. The anticipated spanking is enlivened by the odd line — "Let's get these down now, good Lord!" he says — and by bare-bottomed Jenkins' grin of pained surprise at an especially fierce series of slaps. It's Saunders, however, who can't contain a broad smile just before the end of being caned. This is a Tallion Video, and has as a tailpiece a trailer for *Tales of the Rod*, in which two young women hold out for £300 each to be disciplined. Is this documentary realism?

Around 1990 other production companies seem to have got in on the act. Lord knows who's responsible for *Headmaster's Study 1*, among the more static examples of the genre. A headmaster stumbles through his script and even looks past the camera for direction, apparently to have it confirmed that he should carry on spanking. The camera staggers about in search of angles while he chastises two Oriental girls, Ling and Jane. This average headmaster's study contains a birch. Ling (as Susie) makes the fun she's having more apparent in *Blakey's 7*, where Lindsay Honey, playing pop star Blakey Sputnik, gives her a lift in the street and takes her home to spank. He's better at ad-libbing than she is, but helps her past her fluffs; he even throws in what I take to be an in-joke about being famous for his pancakes. Huh? In the midst of being spanked she murmurs, "I'd rather have you [inaudible] me than spank me now." "Fuck you rather than spank you? We don't want any of that messy nonsense," he responds, neatly summing up the underlying bias of the genre. Halfway through, the story turns unusually explicitly sadomasochistic when Susie agrees to be his slave. "Can I do anything I want to you?" he asks, to which she responds, "Whatever you want" with an amorous look. Whatever proves to be a caning, more than halfway through which she admits "I do quite like it" with every appearance of conviction. For all the severity of the action, there's a sense of affection between the performers.

Sixth Form College is a Cheek to Cheek Production, beginning with a credit sequence in which a young woman walks away in slow motion, swaying her bottom, to a soundtrack unfortunately reminiscent of the tramp of the tyrannosaurus in *Jurassic Park*. The credits actually name the actresses: Nicky van Kiel, Sara Wilton, Emma Moore. Emma is threatened with a caning but by appealing direct to the audience for "anything else" gets let off with a mild spanking. "Ow," she says repeatedly with very little interest, a protest which sounds in the slow-motion replay not at all unlike a prehistoric roar. Her episode ends with an

inset showing her on the cover of *Razzle* number 11. Somewhat at odds with the title of the video, Sara plays either a stewardess or an employee of a stockbroker. Nicola hoists her school skirt and bends over for the camera and says direct to the audience, "Are you happy with that? I mean, is that the position you want me in now?" That's foregrounding the nature of the fantasy with a vengeance. "Do I have to have the slipper as well?" she later pleads with us, with about as much chance of a negative response as William Castle expected when offering to leave Mr Sardonicus in his toothy state. The film ends with out-takes of her getting her speech for the trailer wrong.

Several more scenarios take place in gymnasiums. *Condemned to the Cane* offers an actress who squirms energetically and protests "Don't do it hard" while being spanked, but otherwise fades from the mind. Trust *College Classics* to have more to offer — an interminable physical education session, or so it appears for the first ten minutes of the seventh film in the series. Blonde Simpson and brunette Jenkins then rebel against Mr Adams and are duly bent over a vaulting horse to be spanked, Simpson emitting an impressive squawk which is amplified by the acoustics of what appears to be an actual gymnasium. Cue the headmaster, an actor I could swear I've glimpsed playing a minor role in some commercial movie, who sends the abashed master off before spanking the girls himself. Neither teacher nor pupil at this school appears to learn much, since halfway through the

Jack Straw gets tough on a squeegee person... (If...)

video Mr Adams is at it with Tompkins, a brunette ill-advised enough to let fall a packet of cigarettes while trampolining. This time it's Miss Gibbons, an unsmiling sports mistress, who catches him spanking his victim and remarking conversationally "Ha, ha, ha." He flees, leaving Tompkins to her mercies, hardly likely to be tender when the girl has pinched money from the mistress' car and secreted it about herself to be discovered. You might say the film displays a formal structure — you might, if you've seen as many of these movies as I have. It's a Spanking for Pleasure Production.

I take virtually all the films I'm discussing to have been shot around London, but *Class of '94* appears to want the audience to think it was filmed in Liverpool. There's a reference to that city, and two of the three girls display its accent. One plays an unlikely head girl who sits on the edge of Mr Bruiser's desk and swings her legs while doing her best to get Parker and Jackson into worse trouble. Eventually they take a spanking revenge in a cat-fight so lacking in conviction that the head girl doesn't even bother trying to escape when the others let go of her to change places. She's delegated by Mr Bruiser to punish Parker, which she does with a will, though her announcement that she's going to cane her sounds about as fierce as a supermarket checkout clerk reading out a total. I don't mean to denigrate her lack of acting; in *Teacher's Torment* it's part of her charm. Here she's long-legged short-skirted Penny, who discovers Sir's collection of spanking videos while spending a weekend with him. Having been forbidden to watch one, she drops it in order to get the action moving. "Are you going to give me a spanking?" she pleads, apparently unable not to smile while attempting to look apprehensive, and it's

A horrible old man wallops a 'schoolgirl'...

impossible to tell whether she's acting or how much actual emotion she's trying to hide. "Please, sir, not on my bare bottom. Not my bare bottom, please." Who could resist such an appeal? The resulting scene has some of the lingering quality of the rubber-stamp episode in *Closely Observed Trains* (in which the provocative young woman was originally reminded, as I recall, "I told you I would spank you" but who in the recent BBC showing is warned "I told you I would mark your bottom"). Red-bottomed Penny eventually climbs the stairs and announces from the top, "I was just enjoying that, sir." After all this it seems mean of the teacher to use her having led him on as a reason to punish her again; after all, she only did it on behalf of the audience.

Two late examples of the genre conveniently take the question of acting further. In *Burning Ambition*, a Red Stripe Production, blonde Dobson is so resentful of her A-level results that she conspires with brunette Hills to set fire to the school. We gather this much despite the camera, whose zooms rise to new heights of shakiness and which at the end of a scene fades up from black halfway through more dialogue than it anticipated. Dobson has to vow twice to get her own back on Mr Pearson, Mr Bruiser that was, before the camera can find the lighter in her hand for a close-up. We next see Mr Bruiser-Pearson receiving with mild annoyance on the phone the news that the school has burned down. I appreciate this event couldn't have been staged, but might a couple of stock shots have improved matters? Still, by now it must be clear to the reader that the preamble hardly counts — only the action does. Mr B-P receives the girls in his office, or at least in a room with a sound keyboard in the background, and the difference between the actresses swiftly becomes clear. The more Hills is spanked, the more she acts, pouting and adopting a progressively more girlish penitent voice. Dobson, by contrast, gives a naturalistic performance unsettling enough for the next blunder in the staging to come as something of a reassurance, as Hills is sent into the next room to fetch a hairbrush only to walk not quite off camera and produce a clothes-brush. I hope that doesn't make anyone feel she deserves what she then gets. Me, I was impressed by and sympathetic to both young women, and reflected that one function of the brunette's performance may be to suggest that her colleague must also to some extent be acting. After all, the latter does stay in her fictitious role and speak lines appropriate to it despite severe distraction.

And so to *College Classics 8*, the most recent of the series. Here's Mr B-P again, this time a headmaster with no name, in colloquy with Mr Hill, a school governor and potential apoplectic who has just had an egg hurled at him in the schoolyard. Send on the girls: two blondes and a brunette, respectively — Rifkind, Hurd and Clarke. (Let me hear no accusations of bias, however. *Punishment Platoon*, a video which falls outside the scope of this essay, concerns two young female army privates called Blair and Prescott. It's otherwise most notable for thrice using the exact same amused reaction shot of one girl watching her friend being spanked, as though the editor might be a failed student of Kuleshov.) When a season of chastisement films is screened at the NFT, perhaps these should open it, to encourage a political reading of the genre.

Hurd is an American at a British school, and disapproves vociferously of the spanking of her classmates. By contrast, Rifkind gets so bored with

watching Hurd receive the same treatment that she doodles on the blackboard. Brunette Clarke seems to be having the most fun; there's even a close-up of her smiling at the camera while being spanked. Was she directed to play it like this, or is her personality irrepressible? Neither she nor Hurd can quite contain their amusement at the spectacle of Rifkind being strapped. When it's Hurd's turn she resists and wriggles a good deal, but by now we may assume the audience is expected to perceive her acting to some extent *as* acting. Clarke suffers the fiercest strapping and yet, entirely to her credit, she can't hide a smile as she walks off camera at the end of the take. It seems poor Rifkind has to make up for her friend's frivolousness, but though she looks decidedly unhappy at the end of her own caning she has hardly adjusted her dress before she's asking "Can't I watch her caned, sir?" It seems a bit ungenerous to send her off pouting before the American schoolgirl has to play the last scene. Still, overall the film is as variously representative an example of the genre as you're likely to see. Where you would see it I don't know — perhaps in a booth in a shop beside the main canal through the red light district in Amsterdam. You'll find a roll of kitchen towel provided for some reason in each booth.

"HARD-HITTING CLASSROOM SCENES as two very naughty teenagers are caught misbehaving and summoned before a cane-wielding Headmaster. Discipline is definitely the order of the day during a major punishment session over the teacher's desk — and chair — AND LAP!" So claims the blurb on the box of *Schoolgirl Spanking*, one of dozens of Liquid Gold cassettes to be found in HMV and elsewhere. Can the '18' rating on the box be spurious, or is it the blurb? The latter, of course. It and the title bear so little relation to the contents of the cassette that cynics might think somebody was banking that the customer would be too embarrassed to invoke the Trades Description Act. Don't bother. On the basis of this cassette I'd advise any interested reader to steer well clear of Liquid Gold, a name which surely can't be an intentional synonym for piss.

Education Anglaise may not live up to any expectations I've raised in this article, partly because the censor has removed some of the scenes illustrated on the box. Though the French boarding school for young ladies in which it's set is based on "the British method of education" and its staff "pride ourselves on being severe", not too much of this is demonstrated. Some of it is carried out by a schoolmistress who proves to be an antisemitic transvestite — well, we

may assume that audiences are seldom expected to identify with the administrator of discipline. The girls go in for a good deal of bathing and lining up, plus a little fighting and pilfering for which they are, in this cut at any rate, very mildly chastised. Some of this takes place offscreen while the camera concentrates on the faces of other girls listening. Soon the transvestite tires of such straightforward activity and, having groped one girl while teaching her deportment, moves on to having girls spank each other while dressed in nun's outfits he keeps in his office. By now one takes the film to be a comedy, though no more comic than much of the genre. Its other major deviation (from the rules of the English genre, that is) sees Sophie leaving the school as a dominatrix.

Personally, I think the British have the edge, and it's about time our film industry came up with a big-budget production. Might Roman Polanski direct? Lord knows the censors have passed so many spankings in mainstream films, his included, that early issues of *Janus* devoted dozens of pages to listing them. It was Hammer and their competitors who revived the British cinema when, as so often, it needed something new and startling, and who's to say the chastisement movie doesn't have as much potential first to shock — not to mention giving the tabloid journalists yet another excuse for dusting off their wrath — and then to be clasped to the national bosom? All it needs is for the BBFC to show some leniency towards this, I would argue, harmless genre. I never thought I'd see *Black Sunday* or *Ai No Corrida* uncut in this country, and I propose the schoolgirl spanking movie next for reconsideration by the censor. Then perhaps a detailed history can be written, not just this bunch of interested reminiscences. ∎

(Above) **Education Anglaise** — *schoolgirls, as we know, need discipline...*

(Below) *And here's the best way to administer it...*

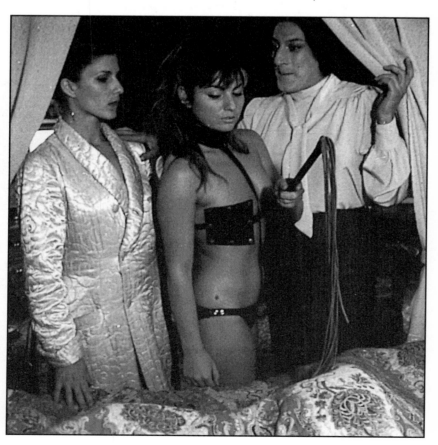

THE STATE OF THE ART FILM

BY ANNE BILLSON

There used to be a semi-jocular feature in the American magazine *Film Comment* in which famous directors were invited to list the films they regarded as 'guilty pleasures'. Mostly, they just cited a list of obvious critical no-nos. Martin Scorsese, for example, owned up to liking the kitschy Howard Hawks epic *Land of the Pharaohs*. This was hardly what you'd call a controversial choice: how can anyone *not* have a soft spot for a film in which Joan Collins gets buried alive?

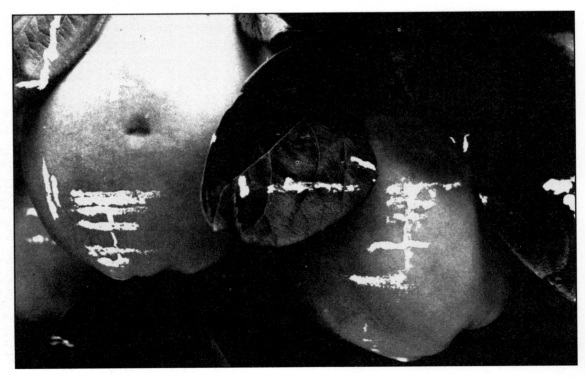

Some quince.

But it was John Waters' contribution to this same column which really twanged my chord. Waters — Pope of Trash — shamefacedly fessed up to a secret passion for the films of Robert Bresson and Pier Paolo Pasolini and the movies of Marguerite Duras. Now that's what I call really *guilty*.

Me, I grew up on precisely the sort of trash of which Waters was appointed pope. So did everyone whose teenage years coincided with some part of the seventies. Trashy commercial films were heaps more fun than arty crap like *Numéro Deux* and *Riddles of the Sphinx*. So when, in the eighties and nineties, would-be post-modernist publications such as *The Sunday Times* and *The Modern Review* began trumpeting pop culture as though it were some amazing new art form, I and other members of my generation scratched our heads in befuddlement. We'd always *known* movies with exploding heads or stomach-bursting aliens or disco-trashing Arnies were more artistically satisfying than pseudy foreign stuff in which nothing happened. Wasn't it obvious?

But exploding heads are two a penny nowadays; you don't even have to go to horror films to see them. And over the past few years, I have found myself watching helplessly as my taste in films has been infiltrated by a tendency so alien and pernicious that sometimes I wonder whether the body-snatchers got to me while I was asleep. I have found myself drawn towards the art film. Any old art film. The more boring and pretentious the art film, the better.

Here's what I think: *anyone* nowadays can watch scenes of murder and torture and mutilation in *Reservoir Dogs* or *Natural Born Killers* without feeling queasy or faint, but it takes a *Real Man* to endure all 137 minutes of *The Quince Tree Sun* — in which a Spanish artist sits in his back yard and paints a quince tree — without passing out.

It's not as though art movies are easy to find. Half the cinemas that used to show them have closed down, your local Blockbuster dealer thinks Antonioni plays for Inter Milan, distributors are increasingly reluctant to take risks on foreign fare and the few arty screens that *are* available tend to be clogged up with British or American independents. But the die-hard fan can still track down the occasional piece of bilge so pretentious and brain-deadening that it can't fail to leave you thankful to have emerged alive.

So what *is* an art movie? And how do you know when you've got one? Here, then, is the Billson Top Ten Criteria for Spotting an Art Film at Fifty Paces...

1 It must have subtitles. The term 'American art movie' is an oxymoron. (The term 'British art movie', for that matter, is a sick joke. I mean, how can you *tell*?). Directors such as Lynch or Hartley or Jarmusch have made strenuous attempts to ape the pseudo-intellectual conventions of the Euro-movie, but their films are too geared towards a self-consciously hip audience to count as the real thing.

It should perhaps be noted that subtitles are not *in themselves* an indication that what you are watching is an art movie. *Violent Cop*, for example, may be in Japanese, but it's more like a sukiyaki *Dirty Harry*; the Italian bodyguards-vs-the-Mafia thriller *La Scorta* is just too thrilling; while *La Reine Margot*, even though it's set during an obscure (at least to British audiences) period of French history, is simply two and a half hours of terrific-looking French and Italian film stars taking their kit off, getting covered in blood and dying horribly.

Besides, the subtitles give you something to read during the boring bits. Which brings us to...

2 A bit of a lack in the action department. This rules out the work of Jean-Pierre Melville, who hardly ever fails to insert at least a couple of scenes in which men in raincoats shoot the crap out of each other. Undiluted cerebellum-dulling art films, such as *Jeanne la Pucelle*, *Abraham Valley* and *Agantuk* (Satyajit Ray's last film — thank God), are full of scenes in which characters stand or (more often) sit around wittering about nothing in particular, often with long, meaningless pauses between witters.

3 Pretentiousness is a must. In *Abraham Valley*, a Swiss-Portuguese-French contemporary reworking of *Madame Bovary* by Portugal's most distinguished writer-director, Manoel de Oliveira, one of the characters declares, "There is a jeans bourgeoisie with bursts of righteousness against speculation." Then someone else says, "Like a belly, verandahs are a sign of authority." I'm sorry, I don't buy that, but *isn't it fun*? You don't get dialogue like that in the latest Kevin Costner pic.

Abraham Valley lasts more than three hours and is guaranteed to give you Repetitive Brain Injury. I watched it to the last bitter drop, primarily because I wanted to see the annoying heroine, immediate cause of my suffering, die a slow and horrible death. At long last, she trips over a loose board on the jetty, falls into the lake and drowns. Believe me, this wasn't nearly slow and horrible enough.

4 Gloom. When did you last encounter an art film with jokes in it? That's right, art films are about suffering, and we're not just talking about yours. In the Cambodian film *Rice People*, the parents say, "We were born to these rice fields, it's the only life we know." Then, in the subsequent 129 minutes, father steps on a thorn and dies, crabs eat the rice, mother goes mad, sparrows eat the rice and the seven daughters — Sokha, Sokhoeun, Sokhun, Sophun, Sophoeun, Sophat and little Sopheap — toil up to their waists in water. Not a lot of laughs there, unless

A sequence cut from **Zombie Flesh Eaters***... (Actually a life-affirming sniffing scene from* **Abraham Valley***, but who cares anyway?)*

(Above) Sandrine Bonnaire stands around being miserable in **Jeanne la Pucelle**.

(Below) Celine and Julie on Nitrous Oxide – a wacky art house 'hit'...

you count the scene in which a cobra gets clubbed to death, a long way beyond the reach of the American Humane Society.

But don't think for a minute that doom and gloom are the preserve of the Third World. In the César award-winning *Les Roseaux Sauvages* (and not for nothing is 'César' also the name of a brand of dog food), some intense French adolescents ask questions such as "Did you ever try to kill yourself?" and take each other on dates to Ingmar Bergman films. "I hate being young," says the token *fille*, "it's a huge burden." Ah, but not as much of a burden as being in a film by Andre Téchiné, a director who excels in what his publicity blurb calls 'psychological pointillism'.

5 Needless length. Jacques Rivette holds the record here; his *Out 1: Spectre* weighs in at 255 minutes — and *nearly all of them improvised* — but that's nothing next to the legendary, little-seen twelve-hour version of the same film. Even this director's one big audience-pleasing hit, *Celine and Julie Go Boating*, was 192 minutes long. More recently, he has given us 244 minutes of Michel Piccoli painting Emmanuelle Beárt in *La Belle Noiseuse*, and *Jeanne la Pucelle*, a 238-minute version of the Joan of Arc story, which had to be divided into two parts before anyone would agree to watch it. That's 238 minutes of Sandrine Bonnaire standing around and looking po-faced, a spectacle enlivened only when the English roll up and call her a trollop.

Honourable mentions in the bum-numbing stakes are also due to the dreary adaptation of Zola's *Germinal* (158 minutes) — and it takes a peculiar sort of talent to make one of the raunchiest writers of the nineteenth century dreary; Wim Wenders' excruciating *Faraway, So Close* (144 minutes), in which a lot of grown actors prance around wearing angels' wings and telling us to love one another; and a Franco-Argentinian effort called *The Voyage* (150 minutes), in which a young *hombre* rides his bicycle all the way from Tierra del Fuego, at the bottom of South America, to Panama, at the top. But the biscuit-taker in this department has to be Hans-Jurgen Syberberg's *Hitler, a Film from Germany*, which will gobble up a whopping great 437 minutes of your life. I lasted only the first 96 minutes, which were a riot of strobe-lighting effects, *Spitting Image*-style Goebbels puppets, little girls in Heidi outfits and men in swastika armbands ripping the heads off dolls. One day, I promise, I'll go back for

the remaining 341 minutes. Like when I'm dead.

6 Characters who look alike. In *Barnabo of the Mountains* (125 minutes), all the men, including Barnabo, have beards and it's virtually impossible to tell who's who. Neither can you work out who's been shot by whom, especially since each shooting is cunningly staged off screen.

One might also cite Alain Resnais' *Smoking/No Smoking* (293 minutes), in which Sabine Azema and Pierre Arditi play all nine characters from a series of plays by Alan Ayckbourn. Once you get over the novelty of two chic French *comédiens* playing people with names like Irene Pridworthy and Toby Teasdale, wearing frilly aprons and Barbour jackets, talking about the weather and brewing pots of tea, the prospect of never having more than two characters on screen at any one time begins to wear thin.

It wears even thinner when you realise that the story, which is not exactly rip-roaring to begin with, periodically grinds to a halt with the words "ou bien...", before *starting all over again*, but with minor changes. This is apparently meant to pack some message about a multiplicity of possible existences, though if you ask me, *Star Trek: The Next Generation* pulled it off more niftily in the forty-minute episode in which Worf got trapped in a kink of the space-time continuum and found himself married to Counsellor Troi.

7 Pure smut. The true art film can get away with stuff you'd never be allowed to see at your local multiplex. Thus, in *Annabelle Partagée*, those viewers who have not been rendered comatose by Annabelle's terminally boring love life can glimpse an erect penis, perhaps the first erect penis since ooh, I don't know, *Dr Jekyll et les Femmes* (which was a *monster* penis accompanied by lots of S & M and a famously ranting performance from Patrick Magee).

In *Germinal*, the women work topless in the mines ("I love my pit," says Gérard Depardieu, and who can blame him). And I bet you thought skinny-dipping was a speciality of the American slasher movie, didn't you? Well, you're wrong. Characters in art films are forever whipping off their togs and plunging into some sylvan pond or other; Daniel Auteuil in the Mogadon-substitute more generally referred to as *Ma Saison Preferée* springs to mind, but there must be hundreds more.

8 Water, lots of it. See comment about skinny-dipping above. See also *Solaris* (165 minutes), in which it rains indoors; *The Element of Crime*, set in a flooded Europe; and *The Voyage* and *La Frontera*, in which most of South America appears to be under water. Need I go on? You get the picture, and it's wet, wet, wet. Probably something to do with film-makers wanting to get back to the womb.

9 Irritating characters. An essential element in the straight-up, true-blue, bona fide art film. You don't want to have too much sympathy for these people, or they may start to engage your emotions and spoil the fun. And so, *Jeanne la Pucelle* whimpers so pathetically when she gets a teeny-tiny arrow in her armpit (what does she expect if she stands slap-bang in front of the archers?) that you want to slap the silly bint. *Barnabo of the Mountains* is such a bloody awful mountain ranger, and puts his colleagues' lives in danger so repeatedly by hiding behind rocks when he should be

out there bagging poachers, that you wonder why he doesn't just go off and become a zoo-keeper or something.

Possibly the most irritating characters in the history of cinema are to be found in the films of Eric Rohmer. In *A Winter's Tale*, a typical example, the protagonist gets married and moves from Paris to Nevers, and then almost immediately changes her mind and decides to leave her husband and move back to Paris again, which, as you can imagine, makes for excitement a-go-go. I don't normally approve of wife-beating, but for her I'll make an exception. I don't think I can improve on the words of the critic who once memorably summed up this director's entire *oeuvre* as 'skinny girls whinging'.

10 Style. It is not generally acknowledged that many of the best art films have more to offer in terms of design than philosophical thought. If you ever doubted that the early, funny films of Jean-Luc Godard were virtual primers of top-to-toe fashion, then look no further than *A Bout de Souffle*, in which someone reprimands Jean-Paul Belmondo for wearing silk socks with his tweed jacket.

The name of Krzysztof Kieślowski was known only to a handful of heavy-duty film buffs until he stopped making dour parables set on Polish housing estates and started making audience-pleasing arthouse hits starring good-looking Euro-cuties in tasteful designer wear and pleasing surroundings. *The Double Life of Véronique*, for example, set me off on a fruitless quest to find the *exact same tone of orangey-brown* as the walls of Irène Jacob's flat, even though I knew the colour was probably only a figment of film stock — my living-room still bears tell-tale daubs of Papaya, Cappuccino, Peach and Spice Island.

Trois Couleurs Bleu had me planning to move to Paris, dress like Juliette Binoche, and sit around being droopy and artistic in a series of sparsely furnished rooms in the Rue Mouffetard. This is the art film as lifestyle blueprint; *Rice People* didn't have a lot going for it there, but something like *Un Coeur en Hiver* takes it to the limit — classy soundtrack (Ravel), good-looking French actors with frozen emotions, colour-coded knitwear, understated little apartments and lots and lots of brasseries.

I need hardly remind you that many of the best art films are not in the least bit tedious. And yet... there is exquisite pleasure to be had from being bored. The boredom engendered by *The Quince Tree Sun*, for example, is an elevated type of boredom, of a different order from that commonly brought on by exposure to too much Meg Ryan or Pauly Shore. Admittedly, the lack of action in an art film can make the mind wander off, but at least it wanders onto a higher plane, there to dally with deep-dish concepts such as life, death, and the nature of, er, nature.

But what brought this on? Why do I now find myself bubbling over with glee at the wince-making portrait of a moribund relationship in *Le Mépris*, or *actively planning* a trip to Tower Video so I can stock up on all those early Antonionis in which people stand around and moan at each other, whereas I would once have run screaming from such low-concept, angst-ridden torments?

Perhaps it's no coincidence that 1994/1995 was the year of Tim Burton's *Ed Wood*. A sweet film, everyone was agreed — a film which celebrated friendship, and

differentness, and artistic endeavour of all kinds, and a bit of an eye-opener for me. *Ed Wood*, you see, made me feel kind of *guilty*. There we were back in the seventies — snotty-nosed, dope-smoking, middle-class students — crowding into late shows to sneer at things like *Glen or Glenda*. It never occurred to us that a laff-riot like that might have been put together (laboriously — it was never easy for Ed to raise the money) by a thinking, feeling, generous-hearted person with more genuine vision in his little finger than in all of today's working-stiff directors laid end to end. So what if that vision was laughable? At least he *had* one.

So trash has had its day, as far as I'm concerned. And I can't be the only viewer to have finally lost patience with celebrities like Jonathan Ross, as they recycle some crappy old movie for the umpteenth time (seen it, been there, done that) and imagine we want to listen to them babbling on about it, and not even as amusingly as we used to babble on about it ourselves. This is not just cheap programming — it's *lazy*. And I can't be the only reader to grit my teeth as some upstart video reviewer gets his facts wrong about Jean-Claude Van Damme, or some twelve-year-old columnist with a famous surname completely botches her statistics on *Batman Forever*. I mean, how slack can you get?

What has this got to do with my new-found passion for art films? Maybe it's just because they require a bit (oh all right — a *lot*) of effort, and I'm fed up with having my culture spoon-fed and being told what's in and what's out and what I should be thinking about everything, especially by journalists who are half my age. Or maybe it's a desperate attempt to keep one step ahead of the crowd by cuddling up to things that I know no one else is stupid enough to want to go and see. (Just you wait — in six months' time, the culture section of *The Sunday Times* will be running puff pieces about the exciting new phenomenon of the *art film*.)

Maybe some arty-farty director's pseudo-intellectual pretensions are a good deal funnier than *The Naked Gun* or *Hot Shots* or any of the other reference-heavy spoofs that pass for film comedy these days. Maybe it's masochism. Maybe it's the onset of middle age. Or, let's face it, maybe I'm just a pretentious git. ∎

(Above) The author practises freezing her emotions for a French Art Movie audition... (In reality it's what's'ername from **Un Coeur en Hiver***, but we don't care about such trivialities.)*

(Below) **A Winter's Tale** *– possibly the most nauseating, morally reprehensible still* **Shock** *has ever run...*

The Last Taboo! There's a phrase to be seen on the cover of many a paperback, and it usually turns out to refer to cannibalism. I wonder. There seems to be a general feeling that, in extreme circumstances, eating people may be excusable. Suppose, though, the survivors of that notorious Andean air crash, rather than eating their dead fellows, had — well, you know...

In the endless list of strange sexual activities, all of which are enjoyed by

A COFFIN NAMED DESIRE

NECROPHILIA IN THE MOVIES

BY COLIN DAVIS

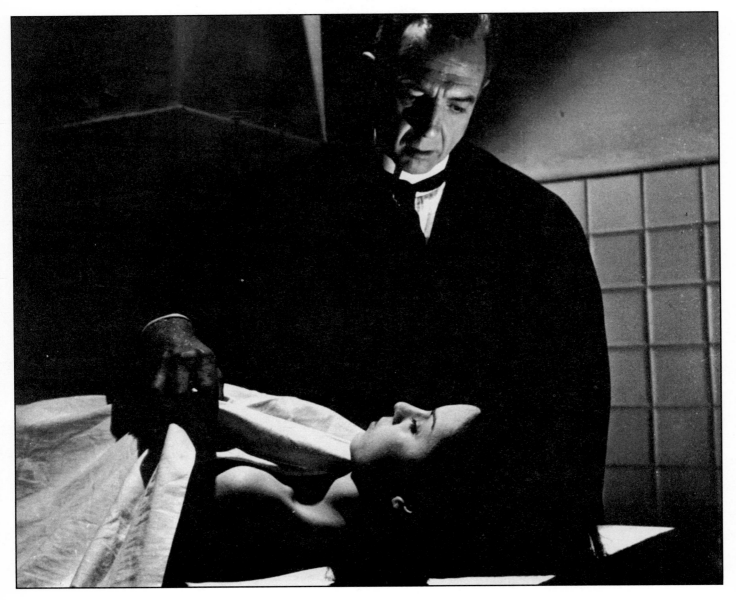

someone, somewhere, necrophilia must rank pretty highly on the taboo scale. Furthermore, it may be the most extreme perversion to have been portrayed in generally available films.

Public outrage over crime and depravity has always been accompanied by prurient fascination. The media are ever eager to spice up a mundane crime with suggestions of perversity. Herodotus, writing over 2,000 years ago about Egyptian funeral customs, claimed that beautiful women were never handed over to the embalmers while still fresh, lest the corpse be molested. I fear the obvious symptoms of death and dissolution would not discourage the protagonists of some of the films we are about to consider.

Moving on to the nineteenth century, Thomas Rowlandson's satirical drawing *The Resurrectionists* portrays the body snatcher, a lecherous grin on his face, clutching a female corpse in a fashion implying a more than mercenary interest in the booty. The documentation of necrophilia fills many pages of such classics of abnormal (to put it mildly!) psychology as Krafft-Ebing's *Psychopathia Sexualis*, Stekel's *Sadism and Masochism* and Hirschfeld's *Sexual Anomalies and Perversions*. Two of the more notorious 'textbook' cases are those of Sergeant Bertrand — 'a man of delicate physical condition and peculiar character' (we'll encounter a few of those...) — and 'Ardisson' — 'He was caught after he had taken home the body of a child three and one half years of age... On this he gratified his sexual desires even whilst the putrid body was falling to pieces. The stench filling the house betrayed him. Laughingly he admitted everything — A. (Ardisson) was small of stature, had a protruding jaw, and was feeble.' Well, that explains everything...

Like sadism, necrophilia is a term much bandied about and often loosely applied. Not every cruel act is sadistic, and not everyone — in film or reality — who fools around with dead bodies is a necrophile. Our criteria will be rigorously implemented: no time wasters need apply. To qualify, it is not enough to carry a head around in a bag — the candidate must demonstrate overt sexual intentions toward said object. Losers collecting body parts in the attic, grieving widowers giving their embalmed spouses a place of honour in the family mansion — morbid and unhealthy they may be, but necrophiliac, for our purposes, not necessarily so.

The protagonists of the few 'classic' necrophilia films have sex with dead people, and they do so *because they are dead*. Borderline cases have no objection to live partners but, if for some reason only a corpse is available, well — shrug — that will do. Then there are those who don't even realise the dead one *is* dead. Of course, we must always remember, when we seek to explain the behaviour of characters in a film, that their actions spring not from childhood trauma or whatever, but from the screenwriter's imagination, and their purpose is to make an effect. If a movie does attempt explanations, they need to be at least superficially convincing and, as we shall see, a case history can seem as unreal as a 'fictional' gross-out.

Let's begin, dipping a careful toe in the moral cesspool, by looking at some non-qualifiers or near misses. A small beginning: Michael Dunn in *Frankenstein's Castle of Freaks*. Remarkably for a dwarf actor, Dunn's CV did include a few decent roles, but this surely was not one of them. Genz is your standard evil henchman, incompetently assisting Count Frankenstein, played by Rossano Brazzi a long way

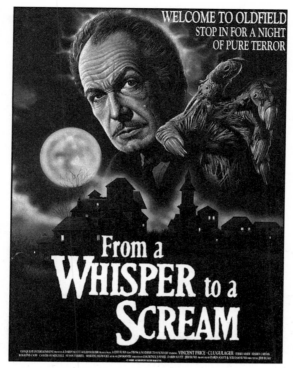

from *South Pacific*. We see Genz kneading the breasts of a freshly disinterred girl, evidently leaving a mark, for he is upbraided by Frankenstein: "You necrophile!" This being one of the few intelligible remarks to emerge from Brazzi's presumably self-dubbed English. Later, though, the little chap jumps enthusiastically on a live captive girl, showing his earlier behaviour to be opportunistic rather than true-blue perversion.

If a perverse movie is to be made, who better to direct it than the extraordinary Brazilian José Mojica Marins? *The Strange World of Coffin Joe* is a trilogy introduced by Marins, playing his usual screen alter ego Zé do Caixao. In the second episode, a hunchback (Jorge Michel) hopelessly adores a beautiful girl from

(Previous page) Robert Flemyng takes a rocket to the morgue in **The Terror of Dr Hichcock.**

(Below) Brazilian weirdo José Mojica Marins hams it up in a still that's essentially irrelevant to this article.

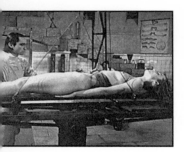

afar, while treasuring a pair of her shoes. On her wedding day she is murdered by another woman, and the hunchback is later able to consummate his love, afterwards leaving the shoes in her coffin.

Flesh for Frankenstein contains one of the most memorable (and frequently misquoted) lines in modern horror — "To know death, Otto, you have to fuck life in the gall bladder" — ranted by Udo Kier in a, shall we say, bravura performance... While the scene falls short of necrophilia *per se*, there's little doubt what Kier's sweaty horizontal hi-jinx on a female Frankenstein monster, arm buried up to the elbow in a gaping cavity, actually represents...

The first episode of another omnibus movie, *From a Whisper to a Scream*, introduced by a frail Vincent Price, tells a similar story. Stanley (Clu Gulager) is an archetypal middle-aged wimp, yearning for stately Grace (Megan McFarland), who ignores him, while his social life is restricted to caring for his complaining invalid sister, whose attachment to him his unhealthily intense. Grace eventually lets him take her out to dinner, but when he tries to kiss her on the way home she puts him down very smartly, whereupon the over-excited Stanley strangles her, dumps her on the lonely road and escapes unsuspected.

Night-time, and here's Stanley at the funeral parlour, pouring champagne to toast Grace as she lies in her casket. "We can't let a little thing like this interrupt our romance," he murmurs, unbuttoning his collar as the scene fades discreetly.

An ominous caption reads 'Nine months later', and we see Stanley back in his routine, perhaps slightly more contented now he has a night of passion to remember. However, his patience with his sister finally snaps and he kills her, afterwards settling back with a sigh of relief, apparently free at last. But what is that

furtive scrabbling, that small half-glimpsed intruder? Yes, it's Stanley and Grace's demonic offspring (the film was in fact entitled *The Offspring* in the US), fresh from the cemetery, gurgling "Daddy" as it pounces on the hapless Stanley.

This is one of the few fantasy films we are considering (*what, are the others all factual then? Ed.*). Oriental cinema swarms with solidly corporeal ghosts, likely to rot suddenly in a lover's embrace, but they are not properly speaking corpses, and the unfortunate victim is seldom aware of their true nature. A possible borderline case (though not Oriental...) is the cable movie *The Dead Can't Lie*, in which private eye Tommy Lee Jones falls for Virginia Madsen, having been hired by her husband, whom she is harassing, to keep her away from him. Trouble is, she's dead. She switches her attentions to the detective, who cannot shake off his infatuation even when her appearances become more and more unpleasant, as when he opens the fridge to have her tumble out cold and very corpselike. She mocks him, saying it will get worse. He doesn't actually have sex with her, and in the end comes to his senses, but his feelings must be considered something close to necrophilia. The film itself is good, particularly for a TV movie.

Mad killers are much more likely to be inadequate nobodies than charismatic incarnations of evil, and this presents a problem for film-makers. Even if you can't afford Anthony Hopkins and a good screenplay, some tacky fun can be had with cheap gore and the rantings of an amiable ham in the Cameron Mitchell mould, but it is a lot harder to make a watchable movie about a pathetic misfit, as is demonstrated by *Crazed*. Much of *Crazed*'s running time is devoted to establishing the plight of Graham (Laslo Papas): rejected by his adoptive parents, can't deal with

(Above) Udo Keir about to discover the only sensible use for the gall bladder.

(Right) Otto finds the missing script for **Flesh for Frankenstein**.

women, dead end job... We spend nearly as long getting to know Karen, a diabetic would-be writer who leaves her protective boyfriend to make it alone, staying in the very boarding house where Graham lives. Discovering her drowned after a seizure in the bath, he hides her in the attic, slaughtering all who interrupt his idyll. This provides twenty minutes of violence to wake up the viewer before Graham is carted off to the institution. Although he fits the corpse with a wedding dress, there is no indication of sexual activity, so the verdict must be 'not proven.' This film should not be confused with the British *Craze*, a poor black magic effort wasting Jack Palance among others, or with the retitled version of *Poor Albert and Little Annie*.

Living Doll presents us with another of life's failures. This one's named Howard (Mark Jax), and he is a medical student, paying his way with vacation work at a New York hospital morgue. Both his job and his studies are suffering because his mind is on Christine (Katie Orgill), the girl in the lobby flower shop. All nerds must have a best friend who is a devil with women and regards the nerd with tolerant contempt, right? Working with Howard is fellow student Jess (Gary Martin) — note the careful choice of their names. (*Actually, I don't — what on earth are you on about, Davis...? Ed.*)

Howard's sleazy bed-sitter is papered with secretly snapped photos of Christine, and every morning he is pathetically grateful for a word of greeting as he passes the flower shop. But as Jess says, "She doesn't know you exist." She has a boyfriend, Steve, an obnoxious stud who treats her casually, even roughly. Arriving at the morgue one morning, Howard is told to prepare a fresh corpse for the pathologist, and to his horror it is Christine, killed in a car crash. "You ever done this before?" inquires the pathologist briskly. "Simple as skinning a rabbit." Howard is of little help, watching as his beloved is opened up with scalpel and saw. The actual cuts are off-camera, but we eventually get a good look at Miss Orgill (a former Page Three girl), with her magnificent new autopsy scars, which must have provided a nice job for the make-up man.

Howard manages to filch Christine's wallet and, leafing through it at home that night, he reads — or perhaps imagines he reads — a card stating that she suffered from catalepsy, and subsequently dreams that she is calling for his help. The following day he rushes to the morgue only to find her gone, and we see him next at the cemetery, lurking in the background as Christine is buried. Needless to say he returns after dark with a spade, and the body is soon laid tenderly on his bed. "We're safe here," he murmurs. "It's not much, but it's ours."

From this point Howard retreats into his fantasy world, bounded physically by his dingy room. The corpse rapidly decomposes, but to him — and to us when we look from his viewpoint — it remains the same Christine, turning her head and smiling when he speaks to her. Kitting her out in bridal dress he takes a wedding picture, declaring, "I think it's time we formalised our relationship." Alas, formalin would be more appropriate — Howard never attempts any sexual act with his rotting bride beyond a chaste caress or a peck on the cheek.

Continually hassled by his landlady, Howard takes advantage of a transfer to night shift to move Christine to a drawer in the morgue. But she begins to make awkward demands: "I want Steve! I want him here beside me... I want you to do it." An unfaithful

corpse? Interpreting her motive as revenge, Howard reluctantly carries out the killing. When he returns, bloodstained, he kisses Christine for the first time, perhaps emboldened by his deed, and the spell breaks: he sees what we see, that he is kissing a rotting corpse. He flees in disgust, but later returns to rant at Christine, "You filthy bitch." She has left her slab and is dancing with Steve, inviting Howard to join them in death. After some futile shots at the apparition he slumps in a corner, gun to his head. "What a day!" he murmurs, smiling wearily. Bang.

Howard is an excellent example of a madman who, though devoted to a dead person, is not a necrophile. The moment he takes in the fact of Christine's true condition he recoils from her. Ironically, he would have fared better if he had been a straightforward necrophile, since he is ideally situated to get her properly embalmed. He could have used some tips from the real Count Karl Tanzler von Cosel, who performed running repairs on his dead fiancée so as to continue their sexual relationship for several years.

Living Doll, the credits announce, is a Spectacular Film Production. Well, not quite, although it took two people, Peter Litten and George Dugdale, to direct it. It was shot 'on location in London and New York' — one suspects the New York exteriors were filmed with the aid of a cheap excursion ticket. Howard is a little more sympathetic than some of our heroes, and Mark Jax gives a decent performance, but is still irritating sometimes — bemused and preoccupied, rather than insane and grandly obsessed. Acting is generally competent, with Orgill required only to look pretty and lie around naked, which she does very well. Another actress, Nicola Turner, plays dead Christine in her more advanced state of putrescence. The landlady is played by 'special guest star' Eartha Kitt, of all people; she has little to do, having presumably been hired for 'marquee value', though it seems doubtful that her fans would watch this kind of film... Heard over the closing credits, the titular song is sung by Martin, but of course it will always be associated with our own Sir Cliff Richard. It does give you a warm glow to think of the paragon of wholesomeness being connected, however tenuously, with a film like this...

In *Henry, Portrait of a Serial Killer*, the brief episode of corpse-molesting is casual and unpremeditated, a mere diversion amidst the carnage. Henry himself (a truly

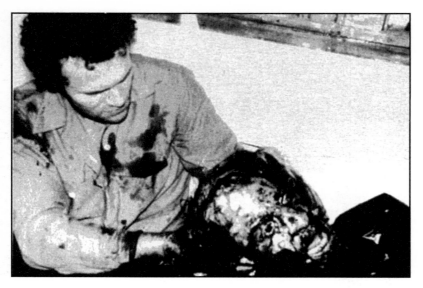

(Above) Michael Rooker prepares 'Ferman a là mode' for the BBFC Whist Drive and Tea Dance...

frightening performance by Michael Rooker) regards his victims, once they are dead, as so much garbage to be disposed of. He seems uninterested in sex — perhaps incapable of it — and although driven to kill takes little pleasure in it, or indeed anything else. It is his repulsive acolyte Otis (Tom Towles) who has fun, nervous at first but soon laughing as he pumps bullets into his first victim. "Feel better?" inquires Henry with a thin smile, and Otis certainly does.

In the film's most notorious scene, Henry and Otis watch a video of their slaying of an entire family. Grinning at the camera, Otis enthusiastically gropes a screaming woman, then snaps her neck like a chicken's and proceeds to maul her with even more enjoyment. He pauses to wave her limp hand at the viewer before returning to further activities which we have to guess at. Otis is not specifically a necrophile so much as a polymorphous pervert (as someone described Albert Fish). Anything is worth trying as far as he is concerned, and in the intervals between the murder sprees with Henry he makes a pass at a young man and tries to rape his own sister. An unsettling consequence is that we find ourselves siding with Henry, who seems by comparison almost noble in his austere ruthlessness. He protects Otis' pathetic sister and even seems to have some affection for her, but in the end she must die too.

Crazy Love, was inspired by the work of the late Charles Bukowski, and is another (Belgian) trilogy, presenting three episodes in the sad life of Harry Voss. In the first he is an adolescent making a clumsy foray into sex, and in the second a teenager doomed to celibacy by the world's worst case of acne — a horribly convincing make-up job. The last episode is the only one drawn directly from Bukowski, being based on his story 'The Copulating Mermaids of Venice, California'. The adult Harry (Josse de Pauw) is an alcoholic deadbeat in the best Bukowski tradition. He and a friend steal a girl's corpse on its way from hospital to mortuary and, after making love to the body, agree that it was the best woman they've ever had; we suspect Harry, at any rate, hasn't had many. The dead girl is played by the actress who represented romantic love in the first story. For Harry, the act of necrophilia is romance.

A few steps away from textbook necrophilia are those eccentrics who simply refuse to acknowledge the very fact of their partner's death, usually making no

physical demands on the dear departed. Boris Karloff in *The Climax*, a 1944 *Phantom of the Opera* rip-off, and future US Congressperson Helen Gahagan in the 1935 version of *She*, are examples. In *Neither the Sea Nor the Sand*, Susan Hampshire is somewhat crazier. Her lover dies but keeps on walking about, apparently galvanised by the power of love, and although he does decompose she is so obsessed she doesn't notice. Scripted from his own novel by former TV newsreader Gordon Honeycombe, this odd attempt at macabre romance is generally thought to have fallen between all available stools. Imagine what the Italian *giallo* version would have been like...

A sort of subdivision comprises those who would like to make love to their latest conquest in the same bed with a dead previous partner. The, er, hero of tasteful Joe D'Amato's *Beyond the Darkness* prepares for the threesome by disembowelling and embalming his dead girlfriend — on screen, naturally. While preparing the body, our man pauses to munch on her internal organs, and he kills another girl by biting out her throat — only she's not really dead and revives inside the furnace... You get the idea. Anything and everything is thrown at us simply for shock value, not to present any coherent account of the man's insanity (*gee, I'd have never expected that of Joe D'Amato...Ed.*). He is a taxidermist, whom we see first preparing a baboon, and the surprise here is that D'Amato somehow neglected to include a perverse act with the animal. When the dead girl receives a passionate kiss, it is not because she is dead but because she is his great love. He pursues live women — though they tend not to stay live for long — and has a sexual relationship with Iris, the Sinister Housekeeper.

Earlier, the old master Mario Bava brought us *Lisa and the Devil* — a piece of dream-like illogic whose plot is impossible to follow, let alone summarise — in which a young man, scion of a strange old family, beds a drugged Elke Sommer beside the decayed remains of his previous lover. A fully paid-up necrophile would have preferred the corpse to Elke —

now that would be *really* perverse... In literature, a brilliant treatment of the refusal to relinquish a dead love can be found in William Faulkner's early short story 'A Rose for Emily', and there have been numerous examples in real life.

Heads. Just start counting the pictures in which severed heads are carried about, spoken to, hidden in beds and generally treated as one of the family. Usually the head is a trophy or a conveniently portable stand-in for the original owner, rather than a sexual object, but a notable exception can be found in Joel M. Reed's infamous *Blood Sucking Freaks*, when Ralphus the dwarf has sex with a severed head. Once again we have a random selection of gross acts rather than any real interest in human behaviour. The details of this particular perversion worry me — how does one deal with teeth? Please don't write and tell me.

On a higher cultural plane, opera fans will be familiar with the following scene in Richard Strauss' *Salome* (1905), based on Oscar Wilde's play. The heroine, having failed to seduce the prophet Jokanaan during his life, and having sworn that she would eventually kiss his mouth, fulfils her promise with his head, which was brought to her as reward for her dance of the seven veils before her stepfather. High culture has generally been a rich source of naughtiness; this opera could have been staged in Britain when no film of such activities would have got past the censors. All right, I'm cheating, it's not a movie, but there are several video versions, in two of which Maria Ewing and Catherine Malfitano respectively prove that not all opera stars are fat ladies by ending the dance totally nude. Eat your heart out, Madonna.

Where were we? Ah yes, body parts. There are those who like to conduct a sort of jigsaw puzzle campaign, collecting bits of young women with a view to assembling a perfect specimen. This no doubt happens in real life — what doesn't — but I can't offhand remember reading of a case. Both *The House That Screamed* and *Pieces* deal with such hobbyists. Since they don't manage to finish their projects, we cannot be certain of their intentions toward the completed bodies.

One of the best and most entertaining portrayals of a psycho remains Roberts Blossom's performance as Ezra Cobb in *Deranged*. As everybody knows, this is based on the case of Ed Gein, the Wisconsin Ghoul, and the film follows his story fairly closely, but with an important difference of emphasis. When Ezra dresses up in the flayed skin of a corpse and sits round a table with a bunch of mummified bodies, he seems to be doing it for company, and he does not keep a special collection of dried female pudenda as Gein did. The sexual motivation of Gein's behaviour is clear, but Ezra has been put off sex by the ranting of his mother. No doubt his activities could be diagnosed as sublimated sex, and since his last victim is an attractive young girl, he could be moving toward straightforward necrophilia. Depicting the bare legs of a strung-up corpse, the movie's poster (with the somewhat misleading subtitle '...The Confessions of a Necrophile') reads 'Pretty Sally Mae died a very unnatural death!... but the worst hasn't happened to her yet!' This recalls British serial killer and pedantic dullard Dennis Nilsen's puzzlement at the fact that people seemed less outraged at the killings than at what had been done to the bodies afterwards.

Nilsen himself was the subject of a film, the little seen *Cold Light of Day*, written and directed by Fhiona Louise. There is a disclaimer that this is not an exact

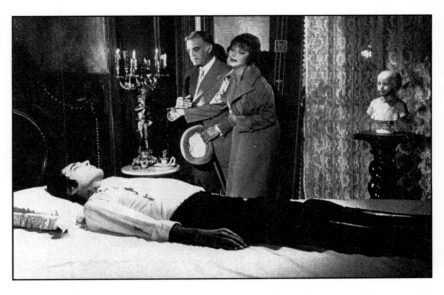

Not a necrophilia scene, but the nearest we could get from **Lisa and the Devil***...*

account, and the character is renamed Jordan March, but the Nilsen story is followed pretty closely.

It's something of a rarity for British cinema: a cheaply made independent production of the kind the United States churns out by the thousand. After accompanying all those psychos across the underbelly of American life, with its sleazy bars and endless cheap motel rooms, it is, for a British viewer, strange to follow this murderer through the shabby homegrown hell of London lodging houses and public lavatories.

March (Bob Flag, a veteran musician, performer and all-round entertainer), a minor civil servant living alone in a seedy flat, seems to have no friends, though he is kind and helpful to a frail elderly fellow lodger. He picks up a young drifter and invites him to stay at the flat, passing him off as his nephew to the other tenants. A low-key sexual relationship with the diffident March soon bores the young man, who treats him with open contempt while cruising public lavatories in search of more stimulating encounters. When he decides to leave, he is strangled by March, who curls up sobbing with the corpse, which he keeps in his bed for several days before hiding it under the floorboards. The body is eventually dismembered and flushed down the toilet.

Another transient, an even less engaging individual, is killed almost at once, and from then on March seeks out young men specifically to murder them. He has discovered a great truth: hateful though the act of murder is, a corpse is, for a few days anyway, a companion, who makes no demands and gives him no trouble. But the plumbing proves unequal to his demands, and soon enough there is a blockage. A young plumber, called in by one of the other tenants, remarks trenchantly, "I may not have been in the business long, but I know what shit smells like." The body parts come to light, and the law knocks on March's door.

The film begins with the arrest, and the action takes place in a series of flashbacks as March is interrogated by a bullying police officer, who rants at his prisoner, continually telling him how disgusting he is. This is rather pointless, since March is perfectly willing to admit to the murders, though reluctant to go into further details.

"Did you fuck their bodies?" shouts the inspector.

"No, they were too beautiful for mere crude sex."

In a later flashback, however, we see a half-clothed

March strenuously performing some uncertain act with one of his victims. A connection is suggested between his problems and the boyhood viewing of his much-beloved grandfather's corpse. In this flashback, a briefly glimpsed priest is played by jazz musician Lol Coxhill, looking a bit like Donald Pleasence. In the end March tells the inspector that his interest was in death itself. If he killed himself he would know death only once, but in killing others he can repeat the experience endlessly. The real life Nilsen was rather fond of this kind of facile intellectual construct.

Bob Flag, who bears a strong resemblance to Nilsen, gives a fair performance in a sketchily written part, and the various young men are good enough; the majesty of the law is served less well in this respect. The sex scenes are treated with great discretion, and the dismemberments are quite mild, no doubt due to budgetary restrictions. The whole affair is low key and certainly cannot be accused of glamorising its subject. A sort of earnest home movie, then, best viewed with some prior knowledge of the Nilsen case. (*Even better not viewed at all in my humble opinion. Ed.*)

Jordan March, if not sympathetic, is pathetic, and this is even more true of our next hero, whose story is also said to be based on fact. Swiss horror films are something of a rarity: the only one that springs to mind is *The Devil's Plaything*, a seventies vampire effort chiefly notable for the participation of porn actress Maria Forsa. Perhaps the makers of *Bloodlust* planned not a horror film but a serious psychological study: its original title (*Mosquito der Schänder*) does not suggest exploitation, and the lurid retitling of respectable foreign movies is a time-honoured custom both here and in America. In fact, *Bloodlust* is a clinically accurate title, but any serious intentions do not long outlast the opening proclamation: 'This film recreates events that happened not very long ago.'

Our hero, seen behind the credits on the absurd little motor scooter that seems an extension of his personality, is an inadequate, quiet young man — literally quiet, for childhood abuse left him a deaf-mute. In a typically heavy-handed flashback, doctors' faces peer down at us and voices intone, "Deaf and dumb for life... incurable... beaten by his own father." Another flashback shows the beating, and very unconvincing it is.

The young man — he is given no name — is neat

and well-groomed, and holds down an unspecified office job, but his private life exhibits strange obsessions. His room is filled with dolls, and on the black-painted walls are funeral notices clipped from newspapers. Although he is too shy to show it, he seems interested in a pretty young neighbour, a girl who is dreamily romantic to the point of hilarity. Told by an older woman, "I think he loves you," she replies, "In love? I'm in love with the clouds. One of these days I'm going to dance over the rooftops and caress the whole world." "You're a silly little dreamer," replies the woman, showing remarkable restraint. Possibly the English dubbing has rendered this exchange sillier than it was, but I suspect not...

The man goes off with a hefty prostitute, but seems to want nothing more than a cuddle and she throws him out. Back home he roughs up one of his dolls — it has black hair like the whore — then impulsively pours ketchup on his hand and licks it off. His quirks are taking a dangerous turn. At the office, crass colleagues mock him, causing him to spill red ink on his hands, and to underline this symbolism we have another flashback, showing him being bullied at school with a similar inky result.

His obsessions becoming more focused, he breaks into a mortuary where, after a moment's nausea at the sight of a real corpse, he makes a small incision in the dead woman's neck and licks the blood. He scratches 'MQ' on the wall, and the next day at the office repeatedly scrawls 'MOSQUITO' on his blotter — in red ink, naturally. On his next mortuary visit he gouges the eyes from a blonde corpse, played by the least convincing dummy you ever saw. The eyes go on display in a jar at home, but luckily for us he is content with one set, so at least this doesn't turn into another eyeball film, a sub-genre whose probable nadir, *The Headless Eyes*, found its way onto the *SX* list of 'The Fifty Most Boring Movies.'

Next time he cuts off a corpse's head — using nothing but a razor! — but doesn't take it with him. The newspapers are full of the Mosquito's exploits, and the folks at the office tut over what the world is coming to: "They should bring back the death penalty." "At least he hasn't killed anybody..."

A mortuary attendant lies in wait and seizes the young man, but he batters his captor and escapes, leaving him dead or unconscious — we never know. Undaunted, he moves to his next phase, buying a glass pipette to suck the blood of his victims: his identity as the Mosquito is now complete. But another emotional blow is in store for him; the fey young girl makes good her promise to dance on the rooftops and duly falls to her death.

In search of distraction the Mosquito visits a brothel, staffed with caricature beefy tarts in fetishistic underwear; if this picture is any guide, the Swiss like 'em sturdy. He requests a lesbian show, but keeps getting flashbacks of his innocent 'girlfriend' and flees in disgust. At the cemetery, he exhumes his love, tears his wrist, smears her lips with his blood then kisses it away. He leaves the corpse propped up like a scarecrow on a seat, but we hear nothing more about it, even though the woman neighbour clearly saw him lingering after the burial.

Back in his mortuary routine, he uses the pipette for the first time, and seems to have settled into a pattern that satisfies him, though you wonder if he ever got an unexpected mouthful of embalming fluid. He follows a courting couple into the woods and, infuriated by the contrast between their frank lustful

Cold Light of Day.
(*The original caption has been censored.*)

behaviour and his imagined idyll with the dead girl, stabs the couple to death and drinks their blood, the man's as avidly as the woman's. This time he drops a personal document at the scene, and is arrested at the office. The end credits appear over shots of that girl dancing in the woods.

This ought to have been a grim and pathetic story, but any initial good intentions have been subverted by the style. The lesbian scene is filmed as soft porn, far beyond what is necessary to establish a contrast with the man's romantic daydreams. On the only occasion when he interferes with the dress of a corpse, a real girl is used, so we can admire her breasts. At least she manages not to breathe. The endless daydream sequences may well portray the Mosquito's stunted imagination, but more likely that of their creators. The fey young girl is frankly ludicrous, and students of the great Molesworth will be reminded of Fotherington-Thomas with his cry of "Hello clouds, hello sky!" Music, by David Llywelyn, is used throughout to underpin the mood, but more often it undermines it. A romantic choral theme associated with the girl backs the man's dreams, turning sour and edgy as his sinister impulses take over. The idea is fine, but the romantic theme itself is slushy nonsense, albeit suitable to director Marijan Vajda's style.

Apart from its tacky approach, the screenplay (by Nagnoi Supasi — surely an anagram) has many loose ends. Worst of all, no attempt is made to explain the psychopath's problems; the flashbacks account only for his physical state. This man may be pitiful, but he is complex, with his doll rituals, his obsession with blood and his adopting the title Mosquito. After all, if the film really was based on a true story, professional literature must have been available.

Lastly, Werner Pochath's performance as the Mosquito is lightweight, failing to generate the sympathy we are obviously meant to feel. Only for a moment is he frightening, when after the double murder he smiles to himself, all contact with reality gone. Although he is not a necrophile in the most obvious sense, blood sucking is considered to be one expression of arrested sexual impulse. A detailed depiction of this condition can be found in Theodore Sturgeon's 1961 novel *Some of Your Blood*.

The Terror of Dr Hichcock takes us into the realm of straightforward, classic necrophilia. Riccardo Freda has been called the godfather of Italian Gothic, since the first of his contributions to the genre, *I Vampiri*, predates the work of Mario Bava, who was photographer on the latter and even directed part of it. Freda worked in the busy world of Italian commercial cinema, many of his films being historical spectacles, like *Theodora, Slave Empress* (or, as printed in *Halliwell's Filmgoer's Companion*, *Slave Express*, one of my favourite typos), and varying greatly in quality.

With *The Terror of Dr Hichcock*, Freda continued the practice he had established with *Caltiki* of Anglicising everyone's names — he became Robert Hampton — leading *Cahiers du Cinema* to assume that the picture was English. The two lead actors, of course, were English. Barbara Steele, launched in Bava's *Black Sunday* as the reluctant queen of European horror, is not the central figure here. The professor, to accord him his proper status, is played by Robert Flemyng, who already had a long career (including stage experience) behind him. He was later seen in *The Blood Beast Terror*, trying to keep a straight face while coping with a daughter who is really a giant vampire moth.

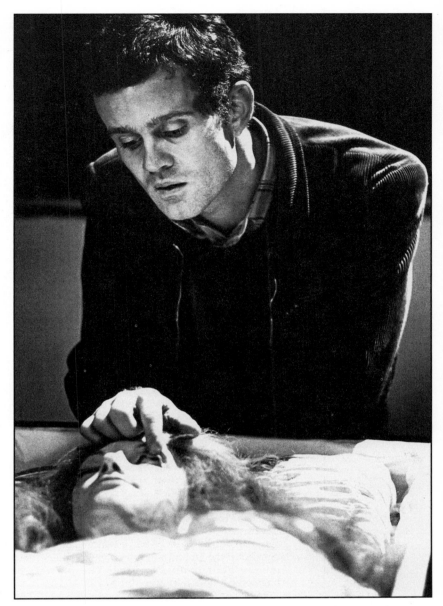

Hideous little pipsqueak Werner Pochath pokes around in **Bloodlust**.

The rest of the cast of Freda's film, apart from Harriet White's Sinister Housekeeper — this one's called Martha — are mere cyphers.

An opening night shot of Big Ben is captioned 'London 1885.' As the bell strikes nine (the clock shows 9:30!), we see a grave-digger toiling by lamplight, a fresh coffin by the graveside, and a dark figure creeping through the bushes. The grave-digger is felled, the coffin prised open and gloved hands tremblingly caress the face of the girl within. The intruder's cape swings forward, blacking out the screen...

A sign says 'University College Hospital', and we hear Big Ben again, striking eleven as Hichcock enters the operating theatre. His patient is the grave-digger, who is saved with the aid of Hichcock's invention, an anaesthetic that slows bodily functions to a corpselike state. Significantly he remarks, "We must hurry... I don't know how long my anaesthetic will last, it's very variable."

Our suspicions about the identity of the necrophile are soon confirmed. Arriving home, Hichcock cannot wait to get rid of guests and repair with his beautiful

Martha, My Dear... The batty old housekeeper from **The Terror of Dr Hichcock.**

young wife to the special locked room, whose purpose is symbolised by a nude statue. The sombre hangings, the candles and the bier indicate the particular nature of his desires. Margarethe is laid out, the special anaesthetic is administered and he embraces her still form... 'His secret was a coffin named desire!' proclaimed the posters, 'The candle of his lust burnt brightest in the shadow of the grave!' Margarethe submits willingly to her husband's little foibles, though you would think she must be missing the fun...

The game soon goes awry, and Margarethe dies before the horrified Hichcock's eyes. Devastated, he moves out, leaving his mansion in charge of Martha, who was a party to his domestic arrangements and now apparently runs the place on her own! Twelve years later he returns, looking no older, though still a trifle mature for young new wife, Cynthia (Steele). Martha, who has at least gone grey, greets them coldly. While they are talking, a scream is heard. That, says Martha calmly, is her mad sister, but she's off to the asylum tomorrow. "I see," says Hichcock, with commendable British phlegm. Husband and wife go off to their rooms — there is never a hint of a physical relationship — and Cynthia's Gothic tribulations begin. Windows blow open, a white-clad figure is glimpsed in the grounds, footsteps approach her room and the door handle is tried. The portrait of Margarethe broods over everything.

Every day Hichcock is busy at the hospital, and Cynthia mopes at home, beginning to believe that Margarethe is haunting the place. Her husband seems distracted, and his meagre affection dissipates. When a young girl dies at the hospital his old lusts are rekindled, and he twice sneaks into the morgue, interrupted just as he touches the corpse.

One night Cynthia, exploring a secret passage, spies on Martha serving tea to a mysterious somebody. Later Hichcock himself glimpses a veiled woman playing the piano, and runs around calling his first wife's name. Giving way to his familiar impulses, he drugs Cynthia and carries her to the secret room, but before he can betray the memory of Margarethe with her successor, clawing hands grab him.

Now thoroughly unhinged, the doctor poisons Cynthia's bedtime milk — to make things easy for us the bottle is labelled 'poison' — but she tricks him, taking the milk to Hichcock's handsome young colleague. By the time he's had it analysed and grasped the danger, Cynthia, back at the mansion, is suspended upside down with the mad Hichcock babbling happily to the mysterious veiled woman, who is of course Margarethe, buried alive but rescued by the faithful Martha. He will use his new wife's blood to restore the first one's youth, he raves. We can't see Margarethe's face properly, but it seems she has not lasted well, though it's only been twelve years. I suppose premature burial ages one...

The ending is rather perfunctory: the young doctor arrives in the nick of time, pushes Hichcock off a balcony and Margarethe into the inevitable fire, carrying Cynthia to safety as the mansion burns.

Musically, Italy is above all the land of opera, with which the Gothic cinema has much in common. Characters are simply drawn and broadly played, the emotional charge being carried by the music in the opera, by the visual imagery in the Gothic film. Of course, music can contribute greatly to the cinema, but Roman Vlad's score for Freda, though in the right style, is undistinguished.

Although Barbara Steele has said that Freda was easier to work with than Bava, he shows no gift for directing actors. He creates a dream world, or rather a nightmare, prowling unhurriedly about his sombre settings, using coloured lighting to heighten mood, though not as exuberantly as Bava was does. When a sceptical producer demanded "Where's the monster?" about *House of Usher*, Roger Corman, thinking quickly, replied, "The house is the monster." You could say of *Hichcock* that the atmosphere is the co-star. The storyline is straightforward, especially when compared to later work by Bava and Argento.

Flemyng is good, staring wildly as his reason totters or licking his lips with furtive tongue as some female cadaver stirs his interest. The part might also have suited Michael Gough. As I suggested, this is not really a Barbara Steele picture; her part is passive, merely that of a damsel in distress. For my taste her unique personality is better suited to more ambiguous, or even villainous roles. That said, her unusual looks make a change from the very-modern bimbos who grace so many period movies, and there are striking moments, such as when she gazes wide-eyed through a storm-lashed window, her face illuminated by the lightning: with Steele, 'wide-eyed' takes on a new meaning. Later, she wakes from a drugged sleep to find herself in a coffin, her terrified face seen through the glass panel as she screams soundlessly.

In America the film lost, in the words of *The Psychotronic Encyclopedia of Film*, 'twelve minutes of sexual deviation.' As a result, *Castle of Frankenstein's* original review mentioned only 'hints of necrophilia,' while David Hogan, in *Dark Romance*, synopsised it without even mentioning the perversion.

A decade after Freda's Gothic melodrama came a picture whose setting and style could scarcely be more different. When *Love Me Deadly* begins, a service is drawing to a close in a funeral chapel; at the back an elegant blonde sits alone. As she watches the other mourners file up to view the deceased, she seems detached, almost bored, toying with her necklace and smiling a little behind her veil. When everyone else has gone, she approaches the coffin, eager now, draws back her veil and kisses the dead man passionately on the lips. She is not in fact alone: the undertaker watches her intently from behind a curtain. Then behind the credits we see a flashback, bathed in warm amber light, of a little girl playing happily with her father. On the soundtrack, unfortunately, is a sentimental song: 'Love me deadly, kiss me deadly... This secret love I have is mine alone.'

Lindsay (Mary Wilcox) is not a mourner, far from it.

She scans the papers for funeral notices and gatecrashes the services, hanging back until she can claim a kiss from the corpse. This seems to satisfy her and she appears poised and in control, but her happiness is fragile. When an over-eager friend tries for more than a kiss, she reacts violently, scratching his face; after he is gone, she miserably hugs a teddy bear, cueing a flashback of Daddy presenting the toy to her.

Worse problems develop. Lindsay is accosted by the undertaker, who recalls her visit to his premises: "I couldn't help noticing your, ah, affection for the deceased. The word is necrophilia." He must, we think, be about to blackmail her — but no, there is something worse. There is, he tells her, a group of like-minded individuals... She makes her escape, but soon receives a letter: 'We who share your passions and needs will meet tomorrow evening... Our subject is particularly attractive.'

Impulsively, Lindsay rings Wade, he whose advances she had rejected, asking him to take her to dinner, but she can't overcome her inhibitions and won't ask him in afterwards. She has torn up the letter, but now cannot resist going to the funeral home. However, when confronted with a room full of naked people and a corpse on a slab, she flees in horror.

After the brief platonic relationship with Wade, she begins to date Alex (Lyle Waggoner), who reminds her of her father. We know this is so because as she looks at him Dad's images fades in over his... Despite the inevitable problems, she is happy with Alex, but after one of their abortive attempts at love-making she receives a phone call from the undertaker and talk of "a more personal arrangement" sends her off to the funeral home again. This time, however, she is seen by Wade, who follows her and sneaks into the building. Just as Lindsay is about to climb aboard a cadaver, she hears screams and runs into the next room in time to see Wade murdered by the undertaker's assistant. She escapes in hysterics but, incredibly, doesn't sever relations with the group.

She marries Alex, but is unable to consummate the union. Surprisingly — this being America — he does not hustle her off to the analyst, but neither does he show much sensitivity. Matters are not improved when he discovers her at the cemetery, in a girlish dress, dancing round Daddy's grave and talking to him. She slips back into her old funeral visit routine, but this innocent pursuit is no longer sufficient and another letter finds her back at the necrophile club. But Alex sees the letter and follows, with the inevitable result. He bursts in to find a crowd of naked celebrants and Lindsay astride a corpse. He is killed before her eyes.

A sedated Lindsay wakes up at home, and the undertaker tells her he has 'prepared' Alex and brought him home. Now she must rest. After he leaves the room, there is an extended flashback purporting to explain all: little Lindsay comes across a loaded gun in Daddy's den and accidentally shoots him. At night, she comes downstairs to see her father, laid out in his coffin, and snuggles up to him affectionately.

Adult Lindsay totters sleepily into the next room to see Alex/Daddy, only to find the undertaker indulging his own desires, mutilating the corpse with a knife. She smashes his skull with an ornament, climbs into bed and snuggles up to her dead husband. To the accompaniment of that song, the camera pulls back and back, Lindsay's image dwindling on a black screen, isolated in her mental darkness.

Love Me Deadly is an oddity, and curiously likeable.

The killings are gory, and there is a queasy moment when Lindsay, on one of her early funeral expeditions, caresses the face of a man who, unknown to her, was maimed in a road accident. The rebuilt nose crumbles under her fingers. Yet this is not exactly an exploitation film, the general approach being that of a TV soap, as emphasised by the characters' dress and lifestyle, not to mention the presence of Lyle Waggoner.

Mary Wilcox is rather good as Lindsay, as indeed she is in a small comic role in the undervalued *The Big Bus*. As Fred McSweeney the undertaker, Timothy Scott is quietly creepy rather than frightening.

Lindsay's obsession is the film's central concern, yet all those flashbacks, leading up to the final revelation about her childhood trauma, in the end fail to provide an adequate explanation. She would plausibly have grown up fearing that if she really loved someone, they would die, and since for an adult loving fully would mean sex, she would be unable to respond to the men in her life. However, her violent reactions suggest repugnance rather than a concern for a partner's life, even though her sexual drive is strong enough to make her consort with homicidal Fred and his friends: writer-director Jacques La Certe might have managed her case history a little better, without resorting to tedious lectures of course.

The best-known modern necrophile is a woman, Karen Greenlee. In an interview in *Headpress* magazine she named *Love Me Deadly* as a favourite movie, remarking how good-looking the corpses are. Well, that's an original critical angle...

With the Belgian entry *Lucker* we move, as it were, under the counter, where ratings or certificates have no place. So-called video nasties provide much entertainment for some lost souls, so they tell me, but you'd have to be really strange to find *Lucker* entertaining, though it is quite an experience.

We are in a hospital bed, with faces peering down at us. A male nurse has brought a female colleague to see the new inmate, John Lucker, and tells her something of his case history: "Some years ago he killed eight girls and raped their decomposing bodies." She protests that Lucker should not be in a private clinic,

TERRIFYING...BIZARRE...

"Love Me Deadly"

Colour
Time 95 minutes

but is reassured: he is thoroughly sedated. As they are leaving, she cries out in alarm that Lucker opened his eyes. Naturally the man laughs it off and, needless to say, Lucker climbs out of bed as soon as they are gone, groggy but functioning. He is an unappetising figure, overweight but powerful, with plump sensual features.

Padding off in his hospital smock, Lucker kills a doctor with a screwdriver through the eye, steals his clothes, and goes out to a waiting car driven by the victim's girlfriend, whom he strangles. Driving to a quiet spot, he rapes the corpse: in long shot we see the car shaking rhythmically, a shot which, on its own, would fit a bawdy comedy. Having slept untroubled in the car, Lucker continues on foot, striding with increasing urgency through a deserted urban landscape. Almost as a diversion, he gorily knifes a girl in an alley, and eventually he arrives at a block of flats where a girl named Cathy Jordan lives. She was the only one of his victims to survive after he stabbed and raped her — which means he had sex (horrid thought) with a live person. No doubt he intends to get it right this time.

He cannot get into the flats, but follows one of the residents, a prostitute named Vicky, to a nearby bar where she duly picks him up. On the way to her flat she prattles on to the unresponsive Lucker, telling him he'll get his money's worth. Sadly, this is true. Only one of the other flats is occupied, she tells him, so he can make as much noise as he likes. Soon enough she is handcuffed to the bed, still voluble, now with mixed indignation and fear. Lucker cuts her throat and she dies, thrashing about to the accompaniment of a radio interview with a psychiatrist. "His sexual and sensorial obsession led him to commit sadistic crimes through which he hopes to assert himself."

Lucker covers the body and waits. And waits. Captions and an off-screen voice tell of the days — six of them. He pulls back the sheet to reveal the body, horribly discoloured and glistening with slime. He cuts away the clothing and peels it from the corpse, which he fondles ecstatically. Stroking the dead woman's groin, he avidly licks the fluids from his hand, then strips and flings himself on the body, his flabby buttocks pumping away at the fade-out of what must be one of the grossest scenes on film.

Temporarily satiated, Lucker dismembers the corpse and conveys it in plastic sacks to the utility room. A young man, passing him on the stairs, offers to help, remarking on the weight of the bags but curiously not noticing the smell. When he accidentally drops a bag, spilling fragments, Lucker kills him and stashes him in a cupboard. Meanwhile, two of Vicky's girlfriends come to visit, only to find a hideously stained bed. One girl, running for help, meets Lucker on the stairs and is killed, then the other is dragged to the utility room and suspended from an overhead pipe. After watching her hysterics calmly for a while, he rubs Vicky's severed head in her face before going in search of his real prey.

Cathy Jordan is busy in her bedroom, but before long she too is in the utility room, tied to a chair, adding her hysteria to the other captive's. Seemingly unnerved by all the screaming, Lucker goes berserk, pummelling the suspended girl like a punchbag, then messily knifing her. Cathy has managed to free her hands, and when he comes for her she contrives, rather implausibly, to get the knife from his pocket and stabs him. Badly wounded, he pursues her along dark deserted passages, with Cathy trying endless doors, all locked. Finally she manages to push him down a lift shaft.

In contrast to *Bloodlust*, *Lucker*'s opening credits declare, 'This motion picture is purely fiction.' One can only breathe a sigh of relief. Johan Vandewoestijne, who directed and co-wrote with the director of photography, John Kupferschmidt, obviously intended the picture to be both disturbing and disgusting, and it most certainly is.

Hardly ever off screen, John Lucker is the whole film. We never really know him, let alone understand him, but in Nick Van Suyt's convincing, if necessarily one-note performance, he is real enough. He does not change or develop during the action, his psychosis being already fully established. His three female victims are dispatched with extreme sadistic violence and in unblinking close-up; these scenes, perhaps more than the necrophilia, would make British release impossible. Three men are killed, but two merely to get them out of the way. The other, Vicky's drug dealer, is bizarrely choked with a salt cellar, and this grim symbolism is the film's closest thing to a joke, the only sign of any impulse in Lucker beside his overriding mania. We never see him eat, though he smokes and drinks to pass the time, and his resistance to sedatives, though probably indicating nothing more than medical incompetence, hints at Jason-like invincibility.

Vicky's corpse, constructed by production designer Flip Beys, is revoltingly realistic, and the actresses convey fear and hysteria harrowingly well. The grim story has appropriate settings: the clinic, glimpsed at the beginning, is the only building with any character, all else being urban bleakness. The only jarring note is a feeble song, 'John Lucker's Back in Town', behind the closing credits, sung by someone calling himself William Powell. The Thin Man must be turning in his grave!

Nekromantik and its sequel are probably better known to genre enthusiasts, and more discussed, than any other films in our survey, yet are unknown to the general public, difficult to access, and apart from club showings, unlikely to be legally available in any form in Britain unless there is a major change in attitudes.

The story, which proceeds unbroken through the two films, is simple. A young couple collect human body parts, eventually obtaining a decomposed corpse which they use in their sexual activities. The girl leaves, taking the body, and the young man kills himself. Another girl digs him up and uses his corpse in its turn. She forms a relationship with a living man, but is not satisfied and hits on a spectacular and gory compromise.

These are underground movies, with some sporadic claim to being art films. *Nekromantik* begins with a quotation, 'What lives that does not live from the death of someone else?' and a warning, 'Some of this film may be seen as offensive,' neatly indicating both aspects of the enterprise. The quotation is of dubious relevance, but the warning is justified. The pre-credits sequence gets straight down to business with a woman having a roadside pee — close-up of urine splashing noisily on the turf. She rejoins her husband in the car and they crash — close-up of extravagantly mutilated corpses. Then the credits roll, backed by dark-hued, tragic-romantic music. Rob (Daktari Lorenz) has the ideal job, working for Joe's Cleaning-Up Operation, a group responsible for, literally, picking up the pieces after accidents or crimes. He collects souvenirs, and after the brisk disposal of the car-crash victims he has some more trophies for the jars displayed in the shabby apartment he shares with Betty (Beatrice M.).

The next death, which provides Rob with his big opportunity, is a ludicrous accident. A blond macho type sits in his garden, drinking beer and toying with his gun, enjoying what sounds like Third Reich march music on the radio. He probably owns a pit bull. Firing at a bird, he shoots an apple-picking neighbour. Betraying only mild irritation, he loads the corpse on a wheelbarrow and dumps it in a ditch, whence it is later retrieved by Joe's operatives and stolen by Rob, leading to the film's centrepiece.

Rob and Betty unwrap their prize to scraping, nervy music, but the following sex scenes are backed by romantic piano. Visually, too, the scenes are softened by arty effects: slow motion, strobing and multiple images. Although the corpse is an almost skeletal mummy, it implausibly retains one eye, which Rob at one point sucks into his mouth during the threesome. Betty furnishes the cadaver with a wooden phallus, on which she commendably fits a condom. You can't be too careful. A later scene features a predictable juxtaposition: Rob and Betty eat meat, swimming in dark juices, while the corpse, hung on the wall, drips its own fluids into the bowls on the floor. Can the other tenants not smell anything?

After he loses his job and Betty deserts him, taking their playmate, Rob becomes even more deranged. Picking up a prostitute, he takes her to a graveyard — where else? — but proves impotent. Incautiously she laughs at him, he strangles her, and then he can perform, after which he falls asleep, to be wakened by a startled gardener, whom he slays with a spade, severing the head just above the mouth, a novel effect.

Finally Rob commits suicide, a blackly comic affair with him ripping his belly with a knife while ejaculating copiously from an enormous and obviously fake penis. The film ends with its best joke: a lingering shot of Rob's grave, into which a spade is suddenly driven by a high-heeled shoe. (*A real laff riot, that one...Ed.*)

Nekromantik has plenty of the flaws of underground cinema: uncertain pacing, artiness, sometimes unconvincing effects, though the corpse, which cost £80 to construct, is realistic. The characters, though pitiable, are hardly sympathetic, but that may have been the intention. The picture does succeed in depicting people with skewed minds, living in a sort of

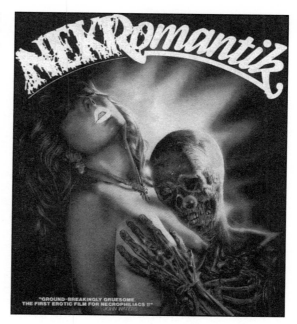

grimy, claustrophobic annex of life.

Nekromantik 2, unusually for a sequel, begins at the exact moment the first film ended. Another quotation, 'I want to master life and death' — a pretty vague sentiment — and we're back at the cemetery where the digger turns out to be, not Betty as we might have expected, but Monika (Monika M.), a young lady who has read about Rob's suicide and decided he is the corpse for her. However, necrophilia is not as easy as she thought, and when she first takes him to bed, she flees to the bathroom to vomit. But she perseveres. This body is newer than *Nekromantik*'s, more human-looking and so more disturbing. Monika lays it out neatly, with flowers at the head of the bed. They wilt instantly.

Life becomes more complicated when Monika meets Mark (Mark Reeder), a young Englishman. She decides, sensible girl, that a live Englishman is better than a dead German, and reluctantly cuts Rob up for disposal. But she cannot bring herself to jettison her old love completely, so keeps the head and genitals. The rest is dumped back in his open grave (which nobody seems

*(Below) Titan censored the stills with big rubber cocks and corpse-fucking, so here's another boring shot from **Nekromantik**. Yawn.*

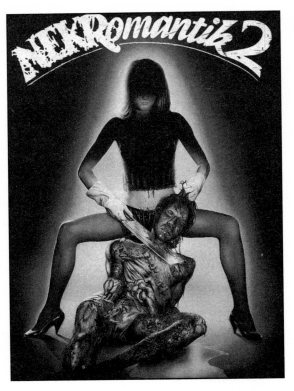

As the Universal horror series of the thirties and forties ran out of steam, the icons of the genre were reduced to the status of straight men for Abbott and Costello. There is nothing that could be called a tradition of necrophilia movies, just a number of unconnected curiosities, but it is interesting that the last film we have to consider is a comedy.

Mortuary Academy proclaims in its title the market it is aiming for. William Kelman's screenplay does plumb memorably low levels of taste, but the movie just isn't very funny — less so than *Abbott and Costello Meet Frankenstein...*

Stars Paul Bartel and Mary Woronov work hard, he managing to be suavely creepy and she her usual rather intimidating self. Dr Paul Truscott and Mary Purcell run Grimm's Mortuary Academy ("You snuff 'em, we stuff 'em," the receptionist cheerfully greets callers), and his necrophiliac credentials are immediately established, with Mary stretched motionless on a slab, his verbal foreplay making it clear what game they're playing. Called away, he promises to take up later where they left off. "Do I have to take another ice bath?" she asks plaintively.

This touching relationship is undermined by the arrival of a pretty cheerleader who choked to death on popcorn on the seventeenth birthday. The doctor is soon sneaking into the morgue with a bunch of flowers, whispering sweet nothings to his inert love (Cheryl Starbuck, on a strange, if restful, acting assignment), but nothing more. He doesn't believe in going too far on the first date.

Later he takes the body for a moonlight tryst on the beach, rolling in the surf in a grotesque parody of *From Here to Eternity*. While he swigs wine, she floats away, to be found by a bunch of partying yuppies who welcome female company. Only in the morning, with the arrival of an indignant Truscott seeking his 'fiancée,' do they realise they've been gang-banging a corpse. As he drags her off, Truscott murmurs reassuringly, "We'll overlook what happened... I know you could never feel anything for them."

Miss Purcell overhears the doctor booking one-way honeymoon tickets to Virgin Islands — requesting refrigeration facilities — and plots revenge. She and the students fit a vacuum cleaner into the corpse, hide in the morgue, and when the doctor is engaged with his chilly girlfriend they switch on, persuading him to sign over the Academy. "Shall I turn it up from wood floors and lino to shag and deep pile?"

Truscott stalks off unrepentant, and the last we see of him, the happy pair are reclining in deck chairs on the cruise liner, with Truscott swatting flies clustered on his bride's veil. The captain, a cameo by veteran Cesar Romero, insists on shaking Mrs Truscott's hand, which comes off messily in his grasp. "She's dead!" he howls, but the doctor calmly answers, "Well, let's face it, Captain, nobody's perfect." Perhaps we ought not to be too superior. An equivalent British film might have been just as bad — imagine *Carry On Up the Shroud...*

The nominal main plot concerns two tedious orphans, Max and Sam (Perry Lang and Chris Atkins), who, to inherit their uncle's fortune, must graduate from the academy he founded. The other students include a psycho, a Jew, a cool black guy, and so on through the stereotypes. The *Police Academy* series at least features some likeable characters (*Whaaaaat? Ed.*); this lot is merely boring. Life at Grimm's Academy ("You kill 'em, we chill 'em") follows the hackneyed traditions of such comic institutions. Naturally there

to have noticed in the meantime), and later we see Betty arrive, too late to renew her relationship. So she does still love him — isn't that sweet?

Monika is not fulfilled by her affair with Mark, though he is perfectly happy. He does come across the genitals in the fridge, but being English is too polite to mention it. Distraught after a tiff, Monika accidentally knocks over one of those plastic anatomical models, which she has been using as an ornament. As she reassembles it, she has an idea...

There is a reconciliation at Monika's flat, but she is still unable to reach orgasm. From beneath the bed she takes her trusty cleaver and, without missing a stroke, as it were, cuts off the prostrate Mark's head. Tie a ligature to sustain his erection, pop Rob's rotting head on his shoulders, and at last Monika can attain fulfilment.

This time, director Jörg Buttgereit had apparently gone too far. *Nekromantik 2* ended up on Germany's banned list, accused of 'glorification of violence.' Screenings in other European countries met with endless problems: the full story can be found in David Kerekes' book *Sex Murder Art — The Films of Jörg Buttgereit*, together with lots of other information and some pretty pictures.

Nekromantik 2 lacks its predecessor's oppressive gloom, and the artistic pretensions are also more obtrusive. At the cinema where Monika meets Mark, we are treated to a lengthy black and white parody of a French art movie. Whatever its merits, and they are few, the episode is irrelevant and breaks the mood. Buttgereit has said he did not intend "shock for shock's sake." Hmm... The final scene, though so over-the-top as to mock the accusations of glorifying violence, does present a deed more extreme than any of Rob's; he never really planned to kill anybody. What may have upset the authorities more is that Monika doesn't commit suicide. In the end, though, the film does convey a moral: if you find severed body parts in your girlfriend's fridge, chaps, head for the hills.

are endless opportunities for corpses and assorted body parts to be treated disrespectfully. There is some stuff about a rock band (managed by Wolfman Jack, another cameo) who are killed in a car crash, then fixed up by a clever student so they can play a last gig to raise money for the bankrupt academy. At the concert the electrical cadavers burst into flames, but the audience is delighted and all ends happily. Shy Max wins a pretty student, while his cocky brother ends up with Mary — serves him right. A funnier, and nastier, mechanised corpse episode is to be found in Tom Sharpe's novel *The Throwback*.

It is interesting that *Mortuary Academy* is freely available on video in Britain; I can imagine some people finding it more offensive than the grisly horrors of *Lucker*. Presumably the extreme bad taste of the former escapes banning because the 'influence' charge is so patently absurd in the case of a film about necrophilia: nobody expects the audience to rush out and head for the nearest cemetery, stopping off at the garden centre to buy a spade.

How should we sum up? As I said, these films form no tradition. They are too few, and too little connected, for any talk of schools or influences, and the closest thing to a series is the *Nekromantik* two-parter. For visceral impact, *Lucker* is in a class of its own, a coldly efficient account of a week in the life of a monster. *Nekromantik* deals more with misfits than with monsters, and its rough edges and uncertainty of style let it down, but there are poignant moments, and there have been many worse underground movies. *The Terror of Dr Hichcock* is not a masterpiece, but it is perhaps the best effort of an uneven director, and surprisingly frank for its time. And there is Barbara Steele. *Love Me Deadly* is a curious hybrid, somehow surmounting most of its undeniable faults. As for *Mortuary Academy*, the less said the better. Considering the nature of the subject, the absence of big budgets, big stars and really famous directors, necrophilia in the movies has furnished plenty of interest, some shocks and more craftsmanship than might have been expected... ∎

Thanks to Brigitte Bruneau for coming to the aid of my inadequate schoolboy French in translating passages from **Lucker.**

ADDENDUM:

As of this edition we haven't been able to 'dig up' copies of the following:

El Asesino de Munecas. 1974. According to Phil Hardy's Aurum Film Encyclopedia: *Horror* this one's "a classic Hispanic tale of surgical horror..." concerning a young man who kills courting couples and subjects them to "outlandish surgical practices." Director Miguel Madrid apparently "chronicles the boy's necrophilia in revolting detail." That's one to look forward to then...

Bacchanate. 1970. Uta Erickson has an incest trauma with her dead brother — "I guess that explains why the naked gal was writhing about on her brother's grave and jerking off a corpse." (*Shock Cinema*)

Darkest Soul. 1994. "Two losers, both fired from a series of menial jobs, become grave diggers and start stealing bodies for money. Tommy, who wears all black, gets a new girlfriend but still pays for hookers and apparently becomes an (offscreen) necrophiliac." (*Psychotronic*)

Inner Sanctum 2. 1994. A Fred Olen Ray movie which features "a sex with a rotting corpse scene". Can't wait. (*Psychotronic*)

Schramm. 1995. Mr Kerekes tells us "in the great disjointed manner of the movie, there is a series of intercut flashbacks to where the serial killer, Lothar Schramm, is cutting the underwear off one of his dead female victims (not identified), caressing her and spreading her legs. Necrophilia is strongly implied, but there is no concrete, physical evidence of intercourse(!). (The sequence is intercut with Schramm nailing his dick to a table.)" Okay...

The Torture of Japan. 1985. A three part anthology — "in its first segment, a grieving widow fishes her bloated husband's corpse out of the river and indulges her necrophiliac desires upon his cold and clammy rotten flesh..." — one of the many Japanese filth epics 'reviewed' in Todd Tjersland's *Sex, Shocks & Sadism* — a magazine so appalling (in every conceivable sense) that even the editor had problems consuming it...

2002: The Rape of Eden. 1992. Plague has killed off most of the human race... "When a bounty hunter accidentally kills a virgin, he has sex with the corpse while it's 'still warm'." (Mr Kerekes again...)

The Wicked Caresses of Satan. 197?. Features "...a wild necrophilia scene in which a handyman pays a lover's call to the bedroom of the Duke's busty housemaid — murdered yet newly revitalised..." (*Video Watchdog*)

The **Bloodlust** *nerd bores another victim stiff...*

AN ENCOUNTER WITH TRACI LORDS

BY DAMON WISE

Meeting Traci Lords was a strange experience. Surprisingly enough, she seemed skinny, angular and almost birdlike in the flesh, a few pounds burned off in the transition from struggling starlet to hard-working actress. Amazingly, too, she didn't seem to carry a presence, betraying none of the 'va-va-voom' John Waters has teased from her in two consecutive

movies, projecting instead a slightly cultivated normality that seemed odd simply because it was so... normal.

Like many Americans, she appeared, at first, to be impervious to irony, stopping the conversation with little questions or for clarifications that seemed so deadly earnest it was almost funny. In fact, I didn't think we'd got along too well, and listening back to the tape I was surprised how frank and dry she'd actually been. Tired and jet-lagged, she'd not long arrived in London, with a management circus in tow that I'd presumed would babysit her during the interview. But Lords didn't stonewall a single question — and neither did she portray any overt flicker of annoyance. Which made it all the stranger, really: no limits were ever set, but Traci's formidable, full-on gaze (and certain moments of almost imperceptible brusqueness in her voice) warned away from certain areas while my stammering attempts to bring the p-word nonchalantly into the conversation sounded really rather desperate on playback.

And, quite frankly, Traci Lords has had quite enough of the p-word — which was perhaps the most unsettling aspect of our encounter. Because for all her rehabilitation (on the big screen, on TV, on the airwaves), her brief but legendary porn career has left an indelible, psychic imprint that — while not being a psychiatrist — I'd wager has plenty to do with her unwitting remoteness. I think I genuinely believed she'd put it behind her, the way Americans generally do, and that she'd be ready with the obligatory 'hilarious', deadpan reminiscence, or some equally print-worthy moral sermon. In retrospect, one's teenage years are perhaps better spent indulging in sex and drugs, either separately or, if the two must mix, without the presence of a film crew. In truth, I think she's plain mortified — and who wouldn't be?

As it stood, Traci was ambivalent about her past, refusing to tidy it up with a forced laugh or take the Susan Atkins route to born-again repentance. To be honest, I felt kind of grubby that I was even trying to talk about it at all, and I couldn't help thinking of an interview with the Dark Brothers, in which Gregory Dark had outlined his reasons for retiring from the whole porn genre. "It's not that I have any problems with sex films," he reflected, "it's that I have a problem with the industry itself. Not only the perception of the industry but also the people within the industry. They're people I don't want to do business with, if I can help it." Or as Traci once put it: "The people behind it have no conscience and they don't care. They don't care about anything. They don't care about what they do to the women, the men, anybody. All they care about is making a fast buck, and if you dropped dead tomorrow, so what? You're just a piece of flesh, that's it. If you went and got an ID from a Cracker Jack box, that'd be fine. And I think I'm being kind."

Traci Lords' crossover, it strikes me now, shouldn't be taken lightly; after all, no other ex-porn actress has ever really pursued mainstream success with the same degree of tenacity. Her last 'adult movie', *Traci I Love You*, was filmed in Paris, a few months after she turned eighteen, and in a state of total confusion she sold the rights to raise money for a modelling portfolio. When she cleaned up her act a little, she tried to buy it back, but each time they raised the price. It's the only one of her seventy-odd X-rated titles still legally available and she seems resigned to the fact that it's out there, even

if she doesn't like it. This level of defiance is reflected in the way she handled her first wave of notoriety — any man who approached saying he recognised her was greeted with the words: "And how would *you* know?" Cynics suggest she is trading on her past, but Lords hasn't disrobed since her appearance in *Not of This Earth* back in 1988 and her current image bears little resemblance to the clichéd, gormless porn pin-up — standard-issue stripes of blusher and Seka-style, sub-New Romantic loin cloths — she threatened to become before the FBI came calling. And let's face it, Ron Jeremy and Brandy Alexandre are never likely to give the Academy any sleepless nights.

Traci's forays into the film world haven't always been successful, in fact many never even saw the light of day in the UK. She's perhaps most obviously linked with John Waters, who used her to such great effect in *Cry-Baby* and *Serial Mom*, but without his shrewd, sympathetic direction, Lords is likely to come a cropper. One such disappointment is an offbeat crime thriller, *Ice*, directed by Lords' husband Brook Yeaton, son of Waters' casting manager and confidante Pat Moran. Lords plays a safe-breaking, coffee-house singer and delivers what I first assumed to be the funniest line I'd ever heard spoken in a movie. A white cop is talking to Traci about the blues. "Do you play?" she asks. I thought she'd said, "Are you black?" It was the

Traci, back in the, um, halcyon days of **New Wave Hookers**...

Traci guests on **Baywatch...**

Roseanne, on which a post-credit sequence mocked Traci's porn past in a ridiculous, slapstick manner. (She was also the only remotely acceptable element in the otherwise atrocious Stephen King TV turkey adaptation of *The Tommyknockers*.) Her recording career has also proven surprisingly strong — having encountered techno in London's clubland during a modelling stint in the early nineties, Traci turned her back on some laughable soft-rock/limp-pop opportunities and found time to craft her début video in the image of an Eon 007 production, replete with a three-nippled Scaramanga, gold paint and a dramatic death scene for John Waters.

Traci considers herself big in her homeland and pockets of Europe, but although London is no longer alien to her, she still considers it something of a challenge. "What's really difficult about London is that I'm not known here for what I *want* to be known for," she admitted. "I'm known more for being infamous than I am for being anything else. And that's really hard to deal with when you want to be judged on your music. It can be frustrating."

The conversation that follows took place shortly before the release of her début album...

DW: Why did you choose techno?

TL: I knew that I wanted to do dance music, but I wanted something with a harder edge — although I didn't really know what that meant yet. And then I sort of discovered techno [in London]. I forgot about it when I got back to the States, cos it wasn't really happening there, but about three months later I found it again at a big rave in LA. It was massive, like, 4,000 kids. I was, like, 'Wow, what the fuck is *this*?' And I knew that that's what I wanted to do, but I didn't know how to go about doing it, cos I was approaching different record companies and looking for a deal, but everything that had come up was really the wrong deal, and the last thing I wanted was to get stuck in a record contract with the wrong deal.

People really wanted to package me as the next pop diva. Like, bubblegum pop music — and that's *not* what I wanted to do. It was like, 'okay, you can be the new Samantha Fox...' I said no thanks. Nothing against Samantha Fox, I just didn't wanna go that way. I knew I *didn't* wanna go that way.

DW: Back in 1989 you told *Film Threat* you were listening to Jane's Addiction, The Cure and Depeche Mode. I'd anticipated a more industrial, Ministry-type sound.

TL: I love Nine Inch Nails, they're one of my very favourite bands, and I love Courtney Love. I love her record, (*Hole's*) 'Live Through This', I think it's probably one of the best records I've heard in ages. I think my music has a bit of that in it. The fact was, growing up, I was listening to a lot of rock, and I love rock, but I've always been, since I was really little, really into all different kinds of music. I mean, I would listen to AC/DC and Black Sabbath when I was going to high school, and then I would listen to Elvis Presley, and I loved Blondie.

DW: Was music a soundtrack to your rebellion?

TL: Definitely. Music has always been a way to escape. Always. Like being pissed off at your parents or ditching school and blasting your stereo, locking the door and not letting anyone in. Running out the back door and spending every last dime you have on records, going to concerts, T-shirts... I loved music. I mean, I *was* Debbie Harry. But I didn't think about

highest point of an unremittingly dull film; unsurprisingly, she didn't seem too eager to talk about it. (In fact, Traci's voice developed a curious frostiness on this subject — perhaps tellingly, the two have apparently now separated.)

Conversely, Traci was more satisfied with her role in Brett Leonard's *Virtuosity*, a vaguely enjoyable (if predictable) cyber thriller from the man who gave us the distinctly unenjoyable (and predictable) *The Lawnmower Man*. The club scenes she appears in were meant to climax with Traci being given a pair of morphed wings as she performs 'Fallen Angel', a track from her début album, *1,000 Fires*. Instead, she just has a glorified walk-on; presumably the wings are on the cutting-room floor somewhere. But *Virtuosity* was a $30,000,000 movie from a major studio (Paramount), and recently Traci came even nearer to the mainstream with a close call on Martin Scorsese's *Casino*, losing a gift of a part as Robert De Niro's mistress to Sharon Stone. As Waters says, it's not like she lost "to someone on *Baywatch*".

Lords seems to have had most luck on the small screen, where she's been easily assimilated by sharp network executives (film-maker Richard Kern has suggested, quite plausibly, that Traci is sometimes drafted in "so guys'll watch it and women'll have someone to hate"). Most tellingly, she was also inducted into America's most subversive sitcom,

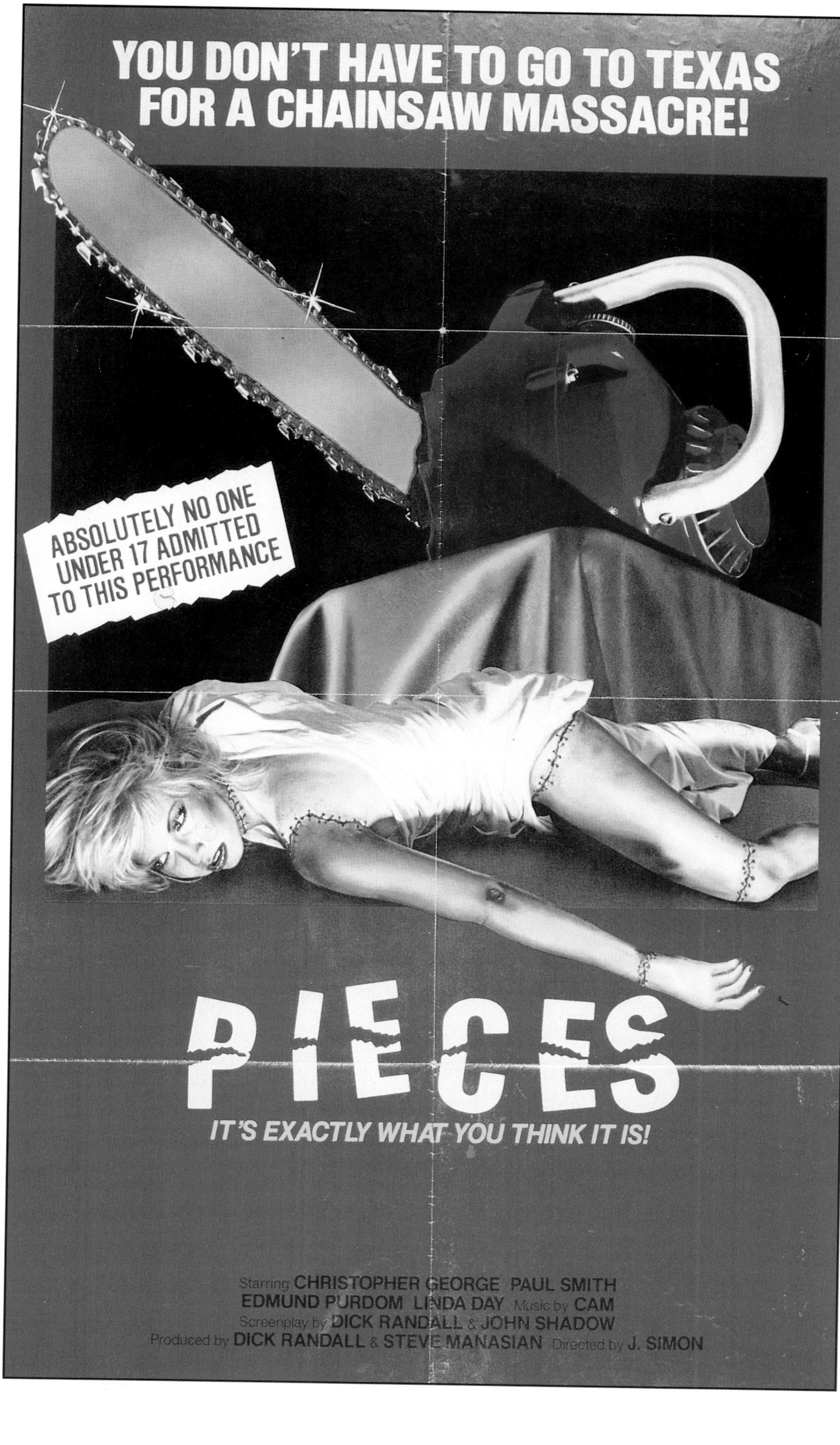

YOU DON'T HAVE TO GO TO TEXAS
FOR A CHAINSAW MASSACRE!

ABSOLUTELY NO ONE
UNDER 17 ADMITTED
TO THIS PERFORMANCE

PIECES

IT'S EXACTLY WHAT YOU THINK IT IS!

Starring CHRISTOPHER GEORGE   PAUL SMITH
EDMUND PURDOM   LINDA DAY   Music by CAM
Screenplay by DICK RANDALL & JOHN SHADOW
Produced by DICK RANDALL & STEVE MANASIAN   Directed by J. SIMON

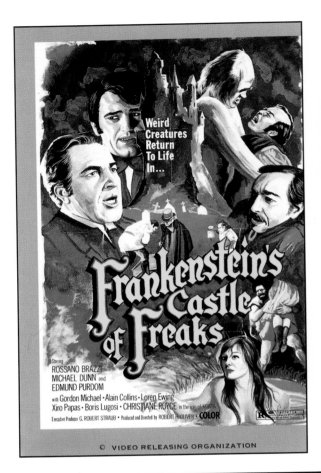

DWAIN ESPER PRESENTS

FREAKS

LOUELLA PARSONS SAYS—
FOR PURE SENSATIONALISM "FREAKS" TOPS ANY PICTURE
YET PRODUCED. IT'S MORE FANTASTIC AND GROTESQUE
THAN ANY SHOCKER EVER WRITTEN.

EXCLUSIVE FOREIGN DISTRIBUTION CONTROLLED BY
EXCELSIOR PICT. CORP.
NEW YORK 19, U.S.A.

DWAIN ESPER
PRESENTS

THE STORY OF THE LOVE LIFE OF THE SIDESHOW

DO SIAMESE TWINS
MAKE LOVE?

CAN A FULL GROWN WOMAN
TRULY LOVE A MIDGET?

WHAT SEX IS THE
HALF MAN HALF WOMAN?

FREAKS

LOUELLA PARSONS SAYS—
FOR PURE SENSATIONALISM "FREAKS" TOPS ANY PICTURE
YET PRODUCED. IT'S MORE FANTASTIC AND GROTESQUE
THAN ANY SHOCKER EVER WRITTEN.

EXCLUSIVE FOREIGN DISTRIBUTION CONTROLLED BY
EXCELSIOR PICT. CORP.
NEW YORK 19, U.S.A.

BARBARA STEELE

5 TOMBE PER UN MEDIUM

WALTER BRANDT · MARILYN MITCHELL

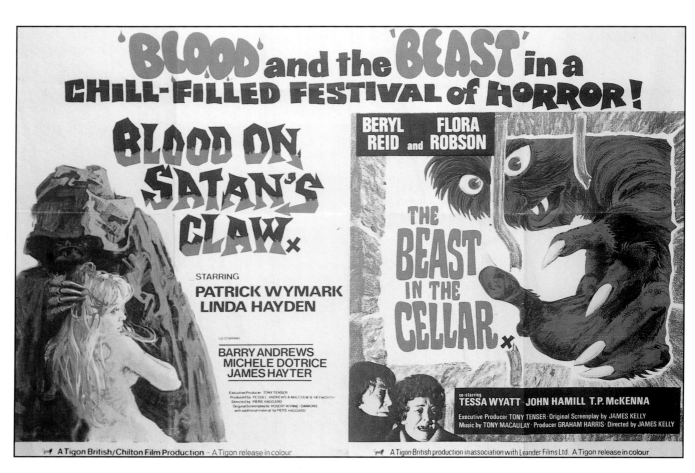

'BLOOD' and the 'BEAST' in a CHILL-FILLED FESTIVAL of HORROR!

BLOOD ON SATAN'S CLAW x

STARRING
PATRICK WYMARK
LINDA HAYDEN

CO STARRING
BARRY ANDREWS
MICHELE DOTRICE
JAMES HAYTER

Executive Producer TONY TENSER
Produced by PETER L. ANDREWS & MALCOLM B. HEYWORTH
Directed by PIERS HAGGARD
Original Screenplay by ROBERT WYNNE-SIMMONS
with additional material by PIERS HAGGARD

A Tigon British/Chilton Film Production – A Tigon release in colour

BERYL REID and FLORA ROBSON

THE BEAST IN THE CELLAR x

co-starring
TESSA WYATT · JOHN HAMILL · T.P. McKENNA
Executive Producer TONY TENSER · Original Screenplay by JAMES KELLY
Music by TONY MACAULAY · Producer GRAHAM HARRIS · Directed by JAMES KELLY

A Tigon British production in association with Leander Films Ltd. A Tigon release in colour

growing up and making a career or a life around it.

DW: Do you think things would have been different if you'd stayed in Ohio?

TL: Oh yeah.

DW: Or would you have rebelled in a different way?

TL: I probably would have found some way to terrorise the world, yes. I can't see myself ever, like, having been grown up and been a housewife and having some kids. I mean, it *could* happen, I suppose, but...

DW: You turned your back on one sleazy, drug-riddled world — but then you went into the music business! Are you concerned about that? Do you keep that at arm's length?

TL: No, I... What do you mean?

DW: We hear stories of the porn industry being sleazy and drug-fuelled, but the music industry is just a more upmarket version.

TL: So is Hollywood.

DW: Did you learn any lessons...?

TL: Are you talking about *temptation*?

DW: No, just that you've turned your back on one set of values...

TL: I don't know that I've turned my back on it, I've just sort of grown from there, moved on. It's no big secret that I was a bit of a mess when I was younger. I guess that would be an understatement, really. Fifteen, sixteen, seventeen were really hard for me. I did a lot of drugs, I made movies, I posed nude and really just didn't give a fuck. I was extremely destructive. Didn't think I would live to be twenty-one, and I did. It's just a matter, I think, of hitting my own personal rock bottom and saying, 'What the fuck am I doing?' And I did that sooner rather than later.

And now, with music and with film, as much as I *hate* parts of my past, and I *hate* things that I've been through, in a way, as far as writing and stuff goes. Cos I can go way deep. I've had some things in my life that have really messed with my head, and in music and acting I have a lot to pull from because of that.

DW: So you don't subscribe to the notion that drugs can enhance creativity?

TL: No, I wouldn't say I'd agree with that. You can't just say that as an overall statement. I've been very creative when I've been stoned off my ass, yeah. And the truth is, in the past, I've had fun doing drugs. I'm not like, 'Oh, don't do drugs,' I just know that, now, I hate death drugs.

DW: Have you ever lost any friends through that?

TL: Through drugs? No.

DW: How pivotal was your role in *Not of This Earth*? It's generally credited as coming at a time in your career when you were given a break when you needed one. Is that how it was?

TL: Yeah, that's the way it started. I was eighteen and it was the first and only time I really did nudity in a film as an adult. I've never done it since. It was for Roger Corman and it was a B-movie — I don't think anyone would disagree with *that* — and I'm really glad that I did it, because it gave me a different kind of attention, for something new. That was when I was getting hit hard with, 'porn, porn, porn...' That's all I could really *expect* to get hit with at that time, cos I had *done* nothing else.

DW: What kind of work were you being offered before *Cry-Baby*?

TL: Well... I thought it would be very easy to be stuck into sort of a B-movie category, and I resisted that. I didn't do that.

DW: What kind of movie?

TL: Well, just like I said. B-movies. Cheap, low-budget films. Just exploitative, really, and that's not where I wanted to go. So I went to TV. I started doing *Married... With Children*, *Wiseguy*, *MacGuyver*, movies of the week, and just taking 'the good film role' that came along every once in a while.

DW: Whose idea was the porn spoof in *Roseanne*? I was surprised to see you doing that.

TL: That was actually her idea, and she brought it to me. Because it was a way of answering people without answering. And it was done as a joke, because I think the whole thing *is*, basically, a joke. It's been *so* long now, and people still seem so fascinated by it. But the fact of the matter is that I did *Melrose Place* and *Roseanne*, so I was on two of the very best, top-rating shows in the States. My single reached number two in the *Billboard* dance charts, I've done six movies and ten other TV shows... I've got all these credits and I've gotten all this, y'know, *critical* acclaim, really, and still people tend to latch onto porn this, porn that. It's a bit tired, really, I think.

DW: Most men's magazines over here won't sign a release form unless the model has proof that she's over eighteen — and a lot of that came directly from the scandal you were involved in. In retrospect...

TL: Do I think that's positive? Well, if that's the case, and that's what happened from it, then maybe it's good. Because I do think that when you're fourteen, fifteen years old, that's not really a decision you're ready to make at all. When you're fourteen or fifteen you probably *think* you're ready to make it, but I don't think you can see the long-term effects of a decision that big.

DW: Is it a relief to know those films are no longer available?

TL: Mmm. Definitely.

DW: You seem to have emerged from porn with a very strong sense of your identity. Was that always the case?

TL: No. I would say I tried very much to hide that at first. I changed my name and I was really trying to hide it, reinvent myself. I changed my name when I was doing fashion and print work and going to acting school. The problem I had was that people knew anyway, and it was this double-edged sword of 'Oh, you're trying to lie about it, you're trying to hide this.'

I finally got so fed up with defending myself, I just said, 'Okay, you're right — I *am* Traci Lords. Fuck you!'

And I dealt with it more like that. 'This is my work, this is what I do, hire me or don't hire me.' Well, they started to hire me after a while. Because I was completely relentless. It's been very, very difficult.

DW: Is Nora a convenient name to hide behind?

TL: No, it's impossible. It didn't work! That's what I'm saying!

DW: But do you feel more like Traci or Nora?

TL: Well, Traci Lords is just a name, but I've been Traci Lords for a long time. I haven't been Nora since I was a child. Really, a name is just another title. Especially as an actor, I mean, God, you're a different person every day. It's not even really an issue.

DW: I've noticed, in terms of basic fact-checking, that not a great deal that's written about you actually seems to be true.

TL: They get things a bit jumbled, hahaha! It's always amazed me. I love the press, I really do, I see why it's necessary, but I always find it really astonishing, and kind of crazy, how... they screw up everything! I know that a lot of magazines make a big show of fact-checking, but the way they go about fact-checking is really amusing. If they read something more than twice, they consider that fact-checking.

DW: How did you find working with John Waters? I understand that one piece of advice he gave you was to take what people think of you and use it against them.

TL: I think he's fearless that way. John Waters definitely doesn't look at the world from a... He's slightly off to one side. I think he tends to see the truth in a lot of things, which is very cool. And most people are afraid of the truth."

DW: Did it feel strange having Patty Hearst as your mother in _Cry-Baby_? How did you get on?

TL: I don't really know her very well, to tell you the truth. I met her on a couple of occasions. She's always been very sweet to me, being somebody else that's been through some weird things in her life, to say the least.

DW: How about Iggy Pop?

TL: He was really mellow, actually. He was very funny. He was probably the most together, low-key person on that cast.

DW: Did you suggest yourself for the role in _Serial Mom_?

TL: No, he did. I think John has a tremendous amount of control in his films. He chooses the people he wants to work with and goes after them very aggressively. I auditioned for _Cry-Baby_, I got in, I did a really good job and he was pleased with it. And then when _Serial Mom_ came up there was a small part, and he said, 'Will you do this for me? It's only a couple of lines.' I would do _one line_ for John Waters, because I think he's brilliant.

DW: Even if that one line is, "Ooh, Franklin Mint"?

TL: Yeah. Which is not an easy line to deliver. Where do I find my motivation for _that_?

DW: None of the pre-publicity mentioned that you were even in the film.

TL: Mmm. Because it wasn't something where I wanted billing or felt I deserved billing. It was just a funny role and it was a good time to do it. It was a favour.

DW: Do you think John Waters is jealous of the fact that you were busted by the FBI?

TL: I don't know! It's a good line, though. I'll have to ask him.

DW: What happened with the part in _Casino_?

TL: I never got it. There were several actresses up for that, and I really went the distance. I had a really good shot at that, but they ended up hiring Sharon Stone. And who can blame them? She's definitely box-office.

DW: How far did you get?

TL: Close. Real close.

DW: That must give you some kind of satisfaction.

TL: Yeah. To be in that running. If you're gonna lose a role, you might as well lose it to Sharon Stone.

DW: Did you always want to be famous?

TL: Never wanted to be famous. That's probably the hardest part about it, because I think you lose a lot of your freedom. It's a double-edged sword that way. Sometimes it can be fun, but more times than not it's just a pain in the ass.

DW: Do you live in Hollywood?

TL: Yeah.

DW: How do you find that?

TL: Hmm. _Interesting._

DW: In one interview, you're quoted as saying you're considered to be the 'biggest prick-tease' in the music industry, because you carry all this baggage from your past. Do you have that problem when you go for film roles?

TL: Not so much, no. I mean, I've had it in my past, but over the last two years... I think I have a lot of respect, actually, with casting directors. They know my work and I'm known for doing good work. Thankfully. And so, it's not so much that as in my private life...

DW: Will you be working with your husband again? I saw the film, _Ice_, that he directed with you...

TL: I have no plans right now for that.

DW: How was that. Did it feel strange?

TL: No, not all. It felt completely natural. It was a really good experience.

DW: I thought it was very strange that, in one scene, you were making love in the shower with your underwear on.

TL: It was the way it was written, and it was the only way I would have done it, to be quite honest with you. I haven't done any nudity since I turned eighteen. I've always said I would if I thought it was appropriate, and it never has been. I never wanted to go the cheap exploitation route — I always felt like I already did that. I've done the sex, drugs and rock'n'roll. I can't see any reason to repeat it, really.

DW: How do you see the future? Do you ever see a point at which you may have to choose between singing and acting?

TL: I think that that's like... That would really *suck*. And I think it's actually really *ridiculous* the way they put you into certain categories. I mean, labels are for cans and jars, they're not for people. In Old Hollywood, if you look at it, you had Greta Garbo, you had Marilyn Monroe, you had Veronica Lake... What did they do in their films? They were singers, they were dancers and they were actors. They were all of the above — they were *performers*, that's what they did.

So, I can't see why you can't, as a performer, perform in any way that works, really. I mean, maybe the problem is that people have tried to do it before, and they've done it really badly! So maybe that's why people don't think it's possible. Whether or not it's possible, I guess, remains to be seen.

DW: Are you a Method actress, or do you prefer to switch off when you get home?

TL: I've studied, like, all different things, and Method acting was the very first I studied at the Strasberg theatre, and it was the first thing I learned, actually. I still find it really helpful, but I studied comedy and... you couldn't be a Method actress and do slapstick comedy, it just doesn't work. I can't see Roseanne doing that.

DW: What do you feel you've achieved over the last ten years? Do you feel validated?

TL: I don't know, because I think that if you say validated that means you're looking for everybody's approval and acceptance, and I can't really say I'm looking for that. I mean, it's nice when people like your work, but I don't know how important that is. And I only say that because if you go into a project thinking, 'Oh God, I better do it like *this*, because this is what's acceptable, and this is what could bring me acceptance and acclaim and praise', I think you would censor yourself a lot and really go by the rules of what has worked in the past. That would be really safe and it would really put you in a box. You wouldn't be able to explore much.

Doing my album, I certainly didn't do that. Because the safe route would have been to do, like, a little pop record with a producer who had done successful pop records before.

DW: Why did you call the album *1,000 Fires*?

TL: Well, there's a track on the album called 'Fly', and part of the lyric is "1,000 fires burning in the rain". I just think that's an awesome visual image. Fire's something that's fascinated me for as long as I can remember. Because I think it's the most powerful thing on Earth, really. It can suck you in and kill you; if you get too close it can burn you up and you're gonna die. Or, if you get close enough, it can protect you. Save you, really. It's a total contradiction. And that's what I think I am. It seemed appropriate.

DW: What was the reason behind making the video for 'Control' a pastiche of Bond movies?

TL: It was funny, but while I was doing press and stuff in the United States, people tended to think the lyrics had a lot to do with sex. I could see how they thought that, but it wasn't what we wrote it about, it was more about addiction and obsession — possession — and I guess that could be sexual, but it was from a lot of different perspectives.

Anyway, in doing the video, I wanted to make sure it was something totally the other way. It's about control — and who is the ultimate character that was always in control? Bond! 007! So it became about a female James Bond.

DW: Was that one of your reasons for doing *Ice*? It's a very untypical role, particularly for a woman. You seem to indulge in a lot of...

TL: ...boyish traits? Uh-huh. I guess I just have a macho side to me!

DW: Does it worry you, being blonde? Because you're immediately measured up against that pantheon of blonde female singers...

TL: I've never really thought about it. I mean, I've been just about every colour — purple, green, blonde, black...

DW: What's your natural hair colour?

TL: Dirty blonde. In *Details*, there's a shot where my hair's really dark. I did dark hair for *Vogue*.

DW: What sort of modelling did you do?

TL: Fashion, swimwear, print, commercials...

DW: Did you enjoy that?

TL: No, I hated it.

DW: Do you ever see a time when you'll give it up?

TL: Modelling? Oh, I haven't modelled in ages. I *pose* now, for interviews and stuff. But I *hate* it... ∎

ATTACK ON REASON

THREE PROPAGANDA FILMS EXAMINED

BY JACK STEVENSON

Kenneth Anger likened the film medium to a "crystal ball... that could create visions... manipulate time and space and transcend realism." War has historically provided the ultimate rationale and impetus for state-sanctioned manipulation of motion picture footage in the service of a host of patriotic, nationalist and racist causes which, despite their often radically opposed goals, produces a cinema of amazing similarity as it hits upon the same universal human nerve endings. The most extreme products of wartime editing rooms are brutal character assassinations, overflowing with fear, hatred and mistrust. Such films focus on a specific 'enemy' and proceed to provide lavish historical documentation on why this individual/race/country/culture is alien and dangerous to us, producing 'evidence' within a heavy mist

of paranoia and emotion that retards refutation via rationality or reasoning. The 'active ingredient' in such a concoction is an almost viral dose of pure paranoia, while the historical documentation provides a *sense* of 'proof' if not the commodity itself. The unapologetic, unambiguous directness of these films, their partisan belligerence, imbues them with a pungency and power that their logic and research hardly merits. Their arguments could never be sustained on paper, but on screen they thrive. They do indeed seem more akin to the magic of the crystal balls that Anger speaks of than 'film' as we conceive of it today — either as entertainment or educator...

The most notorious use of manipulated footage during the Second World War period — and perhaps ever — was *Der Ewige Jude* (*The Eternal Jew*), a clumsily lobbed though noxiously poisonous forty-five minute cocktail of unparalleled racism and cultural assassination aimed at the Jew. Scripted by Dr Eberhard Taubert and supervised by Dr Fritz Hippler, it is still considered dangerous despite its dated techniques, vulgarity and the crudity of its thrust. "You must use caution with this film, and my warning has nothing to do with censorship," warned Claude Lanzmann, producer-director of the Holocaust

Nazi propaganda film **Der Ewige Jude** *— 'a noxiously poisonous cocktail'.*

documentary *Shoah*, in 1991, going on to call it "extremely dangerous". Its showing in Europe and America is *still* suppressed outright or allowed only in carefully controlled circumstances.

The film opens in 1939, with shots of crowd scenes and street life in the Nazi-controlled Warsaw ghetto. The German narration, delivered documentary newsreel style, describes the Jews as a lice-infected people who thrive on usury and who, through deception, have infiltrated the highest echelons of government and financial institutions with the goal of world domination.

It presents unattributed statistics, as well as quotes from the Bible, the Talmud and various newspapers, while delivering a staccato of grossly out of context found footage to hammer home its message. The "Jewish take-over" of Europe is illustrated by arrow map graphics, while Jewish "infestation" is visualised by close-ups of swarming rats. The decadence of an exhausted American culture is symbolised in turn by footage of wild dancing and a Negro jazz band.

An extended excerpt from the 1934 feature film *House of Rothschild* is shown to illustrate Jewish greed and deception, as a family dodges the tax collector at feast time. None of that film's comic intent is discernible here.

Towards the conclusion, the viewer is treated to more grotesque footage: the slaughter of a cow in accordance with kosher ritual, intended to show the brutality and monstrosity of the Jewish nature. (Any type of cattle slaughter is just as brutal.) The scenes of slaughter are followed by a closing montage of high-stepping, smiling Aryan soldiers and flower-bearing women bringing "order" to a "poisoned" world.

The Allies themselves would employ similar editing techniques in propaganda tailored for both the domestic audience and the post-war occupational forces. The vile depiction of Jews by Nazi film-makers is surely equalled in its offensiveness by the depiction of the 'Jap' by American propagandists.

Your Job in Germany was a fifteen minute 'anti-fraternisation' film shipped to US occupation troops in a just-conquered Germany on 13 April 1945. It was scripted by Theodore Geisel, who would become famous after the war as a writer/illustrator of

children's books under the pseudonym of Dr Seuss, and by Anthony Veiller, who in 1952 would produce and co-script *Red Planet Mars*, the anti-communist Christian science fiction film. Directed by Anatole Litvak, *Your Job in Germany* was a product of the Frank Capra film unit that already had to its credit a large catalogue of war and propaganda documentaries. Capra himself directed Sergeant John Beal's narration.

Your Job in Germany is an up-tempo hodge-podge of diverse footage orchestrated into an effective whole by dramatic, emotive narration. The film seeks to blatantly prejudice the GI against his new host: the "dangerous and untrustworthy" German people, who are credited with starting two World Wars, accompanied by footage from old feature films about Bismark and Kaiser Wilhelm. This is, of course, rather an over-simplification of history — in fact, *Your Job in Germany* is a masterpiece of over-simplification, dire warnings and wholesale character assassination. Rightly called one of the most bitter and angry films of the war period, it placed the blame squarely upon the German *people* as opposed to their Nazi leadership — as did most Allied propaganda up to this point.

The GI is warned to remain ever "aloof, watchful and suspicious" of Germans, as crowded street scenes (some of which could be from anywhere) are presented to evoke the spectre of "the mob" and the hidden danger of the hatefully-intentioned individual lurking anonymously therein. "Your enemy is still there, watching you, and hating you..." More crowd and street scenes. "They're out of uniform now, just part of the crowd. You won't know them, but they'll know *you*. Just one mistake can cost you your life. Trust none of them!"

In its original version, *Your Job in Germany* opens with some of the first graphic, corpse-laden images of concentration camps, which at this early stage were still in the process of being liberated. (This footage was deleted on the film's first re-release in 1982.) Further grotesque footage flashes on screen throughout: a crushed child pulled from the debris of a collapsed building like a flattened doll; glimpses of dead and badly wounded soldiers; cities in flame; Nazi slave labourers; children hung by the neck, swaying in the wind.

The film hinges on a series of dramatic crescendos and on skilful use of counterpoint that juxtaposes these horrors with beautiful Bavarian countryside, children at play, folk dancing and crowded, friendly beer halls. The message to the GI is "don't judge these people by what you will see in three dimensions, judge them by that fourth dimension you cannot see — their history, their soul." The film signifies this by peeling away the layers of calm and beauty to expose the bare wood of their past. The lesson is one that

might be addressed to any army of occupation: don't be lulled into a false sense of security. But unlike the Asiatic Japanese, who would always remain 'other', most Americans and Germans shared a similar racial heritage and friendships — or romances — and had no great barriers to overcome. Hence the film's theme could not be hammered home forcefully enough.

The most poignant and obvious use of counterpoint appears in the closing montage of dancing, gay German peasants in folk costumes intercut with exploding shells as the narrator acidly relates, "We are determined that the vicious German cycle of war, phoney peace, war, phoney peace, war, phoney peace shall once and for all time come to an end!"

Much of the footage used was drawn from captured Nazi archives, under license LM-185 relating to seized enemy materials. Dramatic footage shot by Leni Riefenstahl of a Nazi youth rally, focusing on blond boys marching and beating drums, is used here not to convey the glory of symmetry, discipline and purpose that Riefenstahl intended, but to evoke the evil spectre of masses of brainwashed youth. "Guard particularly against this group" — close-up pan shots of stern-looking young blond boys — "these are the *most* dangerous: German youth." The scene works completely in this new and totally opposite context, demonstrating how dependent images are upon music, narration and contextual underpinning.

Despite the occasional absurd moment generated by use of very old feature film footage that predates the war by a comfortable margin and meshes strangely with the angry narration, the film *still* packs a potent emotional punch. Not so much because of the information it relates but because of the way it relates it. In our modern age of sophisticated media messaging techniques and the subliminal soft-sell, *Your Job In Germany* packs a wallop of pure fiery propaganda that hits like a missile.

Our Job in Japan was an eighteen minute companion piece to *Your Job in Germany*, made a year later in March 1946 for showing to US troops occupying defeated Japan. It was the last film made by Frank Capra's film unit, the 834th Signal Service Photographic Detachment (though none of the films contain any personal screen credits). Capra himself, however, was now out of the Service and back in Hollywood. Ted Geisel supervised *Our Job in Japan* and co-wrote it with Carl Foreman, the talented and soon-to-be-blacklisted scriptwriter of future classics like *High Noon* and (uncredited, though he received a post-humous Oscar) *The Bridge on the River Kwai*.

Almost identical to *Your Job in Germany* in pacing, structure and its free-wielding use of found footage, *Our Job in Japan* differs by placing the blame more upon the leadership than the people. The film blames the Warlords for reawakening a bloodthirsty fanaticism endemic in ancient Japanese culture, and then turning the native Japanese aptitude for modern technology to military ends to give the monster its claws.

The Japanese were "led into waging a war so disgusting, so revolting, so obscene, that it turned the stomach of the entire civilised world," hisses the narrator, as pictures of dead children are superimposed over Japanese rally scenes. (Such a statement could be made about any war.)

Japan is depicted as "an old, backward, superstitious country" — cut to old images of a Japanese farmer peddling paddle-wheel irrigation — "just beginning to learn the new stuff" — cut to shot of a street car driver

— "except that (*suddenly we see a glinting sword*) this group had plans... the Warlords."

The Warlords intervene and force through their own agenda by taking over and repopularising Shinto, "just one of many religions, a tired religion, an old religion just lingering along with its dim, hazy, almost forgotten Gods..." They "hop up" Japanese thinking with Shinto by using it to rekindle latent supremacist urges, to "bring back ancient hatreds, bring back ancient nightmares" — cut to feature film footage of torch-carrying samurai knights — "up from Japan's murky, barbarous, bygone past, *bring back the mumbo-jumbo!*" Cut to footage of traditional Japanese folk and religious rituals scored with shrill chanting voices and horn music, strange to American ears. These images evoke the idea of a strange people, a wholly alien culture steeped in absurd and ridiculous — but somehow darkly menacing — rituals and superstitions.

It's a common theme of American wartime propagandists: here is an ancient culture that is not only strange, incomprehensible and in all ways foreign to us, but is somehow threatening to our new American culture — to all things American. It's a conspiracy of cultures to undermine us and suck the world back into the black hole of this "mumbo-jumbo". The recurrent theme of *Our Job in Japan* is that we must force the Japanese to stop making war and "start making sense." If the Germans were just plain bad, in the parlance that any GI could understand, then the Japs were just plain "nuts".

Unattributed feature film footage is presented throughout *Our Job in Japan*, such as repeated shots of a charging, shouting Japanese soldier, which is used as a bridge into modern war scenes. Footage of the same wounded American GI that appears in *Your Job in Germany* is also glimpsed, while some of the battle sequences could easily be of European origin.

Towards the end, while narration lectures GIs to lead by example and show that "our idea is better than the Japanese idea", footage appears of white soldiers in a cafeteria line. "Most Americans do believe in a fair break for everybody, regardless of religion, creed or colour," the narration continues, with a quick cut to two smiling black GIs apparently waiting in the same line. In fact, the US Armed Forces remained segregated until 1949. The scene is a lie. Segregation had caused great unrest in America during the war years. In Europe, black American GIs were not even allowed to enter cafeterias serving German POWs.

Like *Your Job in Germany*, *Our Job in Japan* was aimed at the gut, not the intellect, and veers between crudely wrought cultural assassination and effective drama. In between the lines these two films say more about America than Germany and Japan... ■

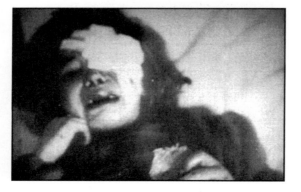

(Above and below) More from **Your Job in Germany**.

ARE YOU NOW OR HAVE YOU EVER BEEN...?

BY KIM NEWMAN

Strange Invaders opens with nostalgic recall of America's 1950s, 'when the only things we had to worry about were the Communists and rock 'n' roll.' Michael Laughlin's retro-chic science fiction film captures rather well this naïveté, synthesising popular images of the immediate post-War era as at once cosy and uneasy. The Mouseketeer-level nuclear preparedness films excerpted in *The Atomic Cafe* have a similar pitch, acknowledging the Cold War's dreadful possibilities but neutering them with cartoon turtles and absurd civil defence measures.

One of the most-repeated but least-examined assumptions about fifties genre films is that, somehow, whether the actual subjects are giant locusts or organised crime, they are 'really' about Communism. It is a given that everything from *Conquest of Cochise* through *The Phenix City Story* to *I Married a Monster From Outer Space* either allegorises the red threat as external invader or, more rarely, evokes a formless paranoia that relates equally to fears of Commie subversion and to fears of the quixotic anti-Communist purges of Senator Joseph McCarthy and others.

A myth that needs addressing is the name given the period. In *The American Inquisition 1945-1960* (1973), Cedric Belfrage notes that 'the domestic arm of the Cold War was a calculated campaign to wash America's brain. The distortion of the reality of that campaign begins with the label now firmly and hygienically attached to it: "The McCarthy Era", referring to the late meteoric senator from Wisconsin. If any single American deserves his name on the label, implying fatherhood and rearing of the monster, it would be J. Edgar Hoover.'

At the risk of belabouring Belfrage's point, picture this: McCarthy first claimed to "have in my hand" a list of card-carrying Communists in the State Department in 1950, fell out of favour with the collapse of the Army-McCarthy hearings in 1954 and died drunk in 1957. Naming the era after him limits it to the years between 1950 and 1954 when, admittedly, the witch hunts were at their most ferocious, farcical and widespread. J. Edgar Hoover began a career of professional red-baiting with the Palmer Raids of 1919, was appointed director of what would become the Federal Bureau of Investigation in 1924 and was still on the job at the time of his death *forty-eight years* later in 1972. For Hoover, anti-Communism was an obsession pursued at the expense of fighting the Nazis during World War Two and resisting the rise to power of all-American organised crime throughout his period of office.

In Hollywood, McCarthyism began in 1947, three years before anyone had heard of McCarthy, with the House Un-American Activities Committee hearings into alleged Communist influence in the movie industry. Here, Chairman J. Parnell Thomas put the squeeze on the 'unfriendly' witnesses who became known as the Hollywood Ten. They would have been the Hollywood Eleven, but Bertolt Brecht pretended not to understand English well enough to answer questions in his first session with HUAC, then got out of the country one step ahead of a Contempt of Congress rap. After years of appeals, Ten-ites Lester Cole and Ring Lardner Jr were sent to Danbury Prison only to find among their fellow inmates Congressman Thomas, convicted in the interim of dipping a hand into the federal till.

The Hollywood Communists suffered for slipping 'subversive' dialogue into scripts: the line "share and share alike, that's democracy" (from *Tender Comrade*) tipped off Ginger Rogers' mother that writer Dalton Trumbo was a red, though the film as a whole is drenched with sickening patriotism. The film *Fellow Traveller* theorises that Hollywood reds were deliberately sacrificed by their Soviet masters because the kerfuffle about McCarthyism took the sting out of criticism of Moscow purges in which dissidents ended up dead rather than unemployed. Actually, this paranoid thinking accepts whole-heartedly the central tenet of McCarthyist thought: that American Communists were agents of a foreign power, working against the interests of the United States by smuggling out atom secrets or stirring up violent unrest.

The American Communist Party of the period was, in fact, a 'nut' group, packed with cranks and procedural hair-splitters, incapable of organising the proverbial piss-up in a brewery let alone a fifth column in the amazingly unlikely event of a Soviet invasion (as we now know, Russia's list of countries to invade mainly consisted of places attached to its immediate borders). The ACP's memorably inane slogan was 'Communism is twentieth century Americanism.' Most 'fellow-travellers' hauled before HUAC were middle-of-the-road leftists who had once, during the New Deal or in the allied spirit of World War Two, expressed something akin to approval either of Communism or the USSR (indistinguishable in the collective mind of the American people in the fifties).

It is hard to detect traces of anything that might genuinely (Ginger Rogers' mother aside) be called red propaganda in any of the films, good or bad, made by the Hollywood Ten. The Ten were Cole (writer of *The Invisible Man Returns*, which has a miner's strike sub-plot), Lardner (who later wrote *MASH*), Trumbo (*A Guy Named Joe*, *Spartacus*), Edward Dmytryk (director of *The Devil Commands*, *Captive Wild Woman*, *Tender Comrade* and *Murder, My Sweet*), John Howard Lawson (writer of *Blockade* and — uncredited — *Terror in a Texas Town*), Herbert Biberman (director of *Meet Nero Wolfe* and *Salt of the Earth*, one of four people blacklisted for that particular film, and writer of *King of Chinatown*), Adrian Scott (producer of *Murder, My Sweet* and *Crossfire*), Alvah Bessie (writer of *Objective, Burma!*), Albert Maltz (writer of *This Gun for Hire*, *The Man in Half Moon Street* and *The Possession of Joel Delaney*) and Samuel Ornitz.

Other 'unfriendly' witnesses — former or current radicals eventually blacklisted in the industry — included actors Gale Sondergaard (*The Spider Woman Strikes Back*, and wife of Herbert Biberman), J. Edward Bromberg (the vampire hunter of *Son of Dracula*), Kim Hunter (*The Seventh Victim*, *Planet of the Apes* and *Tender Comrade*) and Lionel Stander (*Once Upon a Time*

(Above) "Dad, you hide under the toilet lid from the nuclear blast and I'll rid the world of Commies." More Cold War madness from **The Atomic Cafe.**

(Previous page) Not even a dirty filthy fifth columnist Commie pinko faggot would dare to lie on the Bible! The righteously demented **My Son John.**

(Below left) What lurks beneath the skin in **Strange Invaders**?

EVEN IN THE GRADE SCHOOLS...

REMEMBER! YOU ARE SUPPOSED TO OBEY THE STATE, NOT YOUR PARENTS.

the State Supre

(Above) A principle not far removed from today's 'nanny state' ideals...

(Below) I love a man in uniform — Hume Cronyn (left) as **Brute Force's** *'swishly sadistic fascist'.*

THE GREATEST PRISON-BREAK FILM OF ALL TIME!
BURT LANCASTER
HUME CRONYN · CHARLES BICKFORD · YVONNE DE CARLO · ANN BLYTH
"**BRUTE FORCE**" 'A'
A MARK HELLINGER PRODUCTION · DIRECTED BY JULES ("RIFIFI") DASSIN

in the West, The Eroticist); writers Guy Endore (author of *The Werewolf of Paris*, and scripts for *Mad Love* and *The Devil Doll*), Dashiell Hammett (who went stubbornly to jail), Carl Foreman (*Bowery Blitzkrieg*, *Spooks Run Wild*) and Michael Wilson (*The Bridge on the River Kwai*, *Planet of the Apes* and *Salt of the Earth*); and directors Joseph Losey (*M*, *The Prowler*), Abraham Polonsky (*Force of Evil*), Michael Gordon (*Boston Blackie Goes Hollywood*, *Pillow Talk*) and Cy Endfield (*Hell Drivers*, *Mysterious Island*, *Zulu*, *De Sade*). Most of these people had, at one time or another, been 'card-carrying' Communists, which is to say members of the American Communist Party. It is a signal of just how completely washed-up Bela Lugosi was in the fifties that nobody bothered to blacklist him on political grounds: he had held office in the Communist government of Hungary in the early twenties. He prepared a statement of current anti-Communism for HUAC in 1950 (arguably perjuring himself), but they weren't terribly interested.

Under Thomas, HUAC obsessively alleged that red writers insidiously worked the party line into MGM musicals or Fox thrillers, polluting the minds of innocent American audiences. The only actual films they could produce in evidence were odd and embarrassing pro-Stalinist wartime efforts (*Mission to Moscow*, *The North Star*, *Song of Russia*) that try to do for the USSR what *Mrs Miniver* does for Britain. Under questioning, Jack Warner and other moguls justifiably complained they had been forced to make these films, mostly box office bombs, not by subversive screen-writers but at the request of the US government. The supposed point of the HUAC attacks on the film industry was to keep red propaganda off screens, just as the intent of similar attacks on universities was to keep it out of classrooms.

Investigations failed to turn up *any* concrete incidences of subversion in movies beyond Lionel Stander whistling 'The Red Flag' while waiting for a lift. Subtly, the thrust of the crusade changed. As in investigations into the civil services, universities and everything down to dentistry and the US Mail, the purpose of the hearings in Hollywood was to render unemployed and unemployable anyone who was or had been a Communist or was sympathetic to leftist ideas.

Though sifting through filmographies does not unearth specific Communist influences in American film of the late 1940s, it is actually understandable that J. Parnell Thomas and others of his stripe would go to the cinema and feel something was wrong. Wartime films are aggressively upbeat and trivial — which goes for *House of Frankenstein* as well as *Reveille With Beverly* — and almost lobotomised in their patriotic frenzy. At the upper end of the quality scale, we have an irrepressibly dancing James Cagney as George M. Cohan in *Yankee Doodle Dandy*, but more frightening are flag-draped collections of frozen smiles and hollow gestures like such all-star musical-comedy-revue-atrocities, let's-all-salute-the-flag efforts as *Thank Your Lucky Stars* and *Hollywood Canteen*. HUAC presumably wanted Hollywood to keep making these films after the War was over. Instead, they got dreams and dead ends: returning servicemen flocked not to musicals and comedies but to social problem pictures (*The Best Years of Our Lives*) and thrillers (*The Blue Dahlia*) reflecting their own experiences. The late forties was rich in desperate *film noirs* and psychological malaise.

Crossfire, from the Ten-ite team of Dmytryk and Scott, was seen as an important picture by both its makers and its audiences because it addressed a 'social problem': villain Robert Ryan commits an impulse murder, for which hero Robert Mitchum almost takes the blame, because he is anti-Semitic. The strange thing is that the film remains watchable (unlike HUAC squealer Elia Kazan's similarly anti-anti-Semitic *Gentleman's Agreement*) because it isn't very interested in its supposed message (which was grafted onto the project; in Richard Brooks' novel, *The Brick Foxhole*, the Ryan character kills a homosexual). *Crossfire* now looks like a great film not because of Robert Young's speech about bigotry being a bad thing, but because, along with other great *noirs*, it depicts a nightmare American city awash with lonely, alienated, war-maddened, terminally nervous characters. Ryan and Mitchum are indeed interchangeable, GIs without a war lost in a city they can't recognise, and they are no better off than Gloria Grahame's pathetic drab or the hash-slinger (Paul Kelly) who is hopelessly in love with her.

Crossfire could claim to be a Communist movie, in that it was made by a coalition of liberals and

Communists, but the same desperation informs late forties films made by directors of all political persuasions. Frank Capra, a right-wing Republican, was despairing enough to make the Potterville segments of *It's a Wonderful Life*, with Grahame again as a streetwalker, as horrific as any analysis of American malaise from the far left. Now, *noir* is analysed in terms of masterpieces (*Double Indemnity*, *Mildred Pierce*, *Out of the Past*), but its power lies in the aggregate impression that must have come, in an era when everyone went to the cinema all the time, from a weekly diet of, to list just the Ds, *Detour*, *Deadline at Dawn*, *The Dark Corner*, *Dead Reckoning*, *Desperate*, *Dark Passage*, *The Dark Past*, *Dark City*, *The Damned Don't Cry*, *D.O.A.* The titles almost tell the story: dark, desperate, dead, damned...

To single out at random any picture from the late forties is to be confronted with an America which has won its war but found the victory hollow. After *House of Dracula*, Hollywood wasn't making traditional horror movies, but when the childish Universal monster rallies and Abbott and Costello pictures abdicated the job of the horror film, other types of film stepped in and set out to be seriously disturbing. The prison movie *Brute Force*, from to-be-blacklisted Jules Dassin, is not the product of a society happy with itself, choosing to allegorise America as a jail run by a swishly sadistic fascist (Hume Cronyn), with inmates who tear each other to pieces or die in regular, doomed escape attempts. 'Nobody crashes out,' the film concludes, contradicting the romanticism of *High Sierra*: even in death, there is no freedom.

The irony is that HUAC, hoping to clean up the post-war screen and restore a land fit for Deanna Durbin, actually contributed to the perpetuation of the fear and loathing. In the War, Hollywood responded to the patriotic call by making anti-Nazi films; now, accused of Un-American Activities, the studios tried to cover themselves by cranking out anti-Communist programmers. Many a fifties red-baiting picture feels like a remake of a forties Nazi-bashing movie: *Walk East on Beacon*, in which the FBI smashes

a Commie spy ring, is exactly patterned on the template of *The House on 92nd Street*, in which the FBI smashes a Nazi spy ring. William Cameron Menzies's *The Whip Hand* was initially *The Man I Found*, about a heroic journalist (Elliott Reid) discovering Adolf Hitler alive and evil in a small town on the Canadian border. It was partially reshot and completely re-edited by RKO to make Commies rather than Nazis the bad guys, though one major thug character remains a stereotypical blond Aryan stormtrooper and the Dr Moreau-ish villain (Otto Waldis) is one of many movie ex-Nazis who shift allegiance to the reds after World War Two. Movie ex-Nazis who shift allegiance to the *West* after World War Two are rare outside of the Werner von Braun biopic *I Aim at the Stars*, to which wags appended the sub-title *But I Hit London*. *The Whip Hand* boasts a wonderfully overwrought finish in which Reid tries to talk Waldis out of unleashing the plague in America with "have you forgotten that the Nobel Prize committee once considered you the scientist who had done the most to benefit mankind?" only to have the mad scientist sneer "I *am* benefiting mankind, by ridding the world of all the people that stand in the way of Communism!"

The half-heartedness of the anti-red McGuffins of these films can be measured from French release prints of Sam Fuller's *Pickup on South Street*, in which Communist villains are transformed by dubbing into gangsters and the object of the eponymous pickup is not microfilm but a cache of drugs. Incidentally, *Pickup* is the best film in the batch, thanks to the squirmy characterisation of pickpocket hero Richard Widmark and the independent Fuller's refusal to whitewash the American values Widmark stands for, which amount to cold beer and the right to commit petty crimes. 'There are a lot of scumbags in America,' Fuller says, 'and it's their country too.' Authority is represented by a cop who says of Widmark, "there's one cannon (pickpocket) I'd like to see get the chair."

Howard Hughes, who initially supported the Hollywood Ten out of anti-government bloody-mindedness but transformed into an anti-Communist

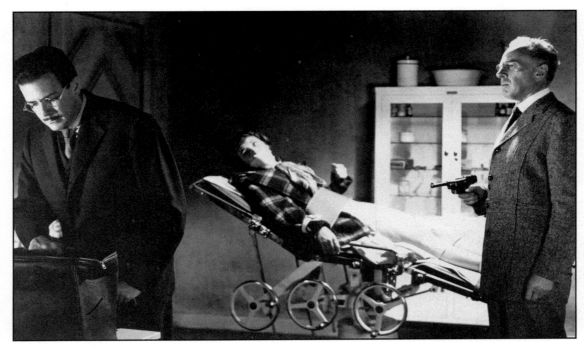

"Inject the babe with Commie juice and you're a free man" — **The Whip Hand** *metamorphosed from anti-Nazi to anti-Commie in a jiffy...*

ideologue, came up with a test for prospective employees. In order to gauge a director's political sentiments, he would assign them a terrible script called *I Married a Communist* and examine their reasons for turning it down. The first to see it was Joseph Losey, who naturally passed up the opportunity to absolve himself of the taint. Finally, with the pressure on for every studio to turn out an anti-Communist picture, Hughes's RKO pressured Robert Stevenson (*Mary Poppins*) into shooting the film, better known now by its re-release title *The Woman on Pier 13*. Old friend Robert Ryan is a self-made shipyard executive who has risen from the ranks of the stevedores; he is blackmailed by old associate Thomas Gomez, who remembers him as a red hard man in the thirties, and ordered to stir up trouble on the docks. The politics are hilarious — with the famous Party Membership Card passed on like the rune in *Night of the Demon* — but as a standard *noir*, the film is serviceably doom-haunted.

I Married a Communist was swiftly followed by *I Was a Communist for the F.B.I.*, a biopic of an ex-red-turned-informer that became embarrassing when its real-life inspiration Matt Cvetic was repeatedly shown up as a liar. This spun off a similarly-themed TV series about infiltrator Herbert Philbrick (Richard Carlson), *I Led Three Lives* (1953-6). No Hollywood film cared to think too deeply about why anyone would actually make a political decision to join the Communist Party. Therefore, these films show Communists as typical *noir* freakos, degenerates, bizarros and sadists. Anti-Nazi films, with slightly more justification, had done the same: Signe Hasso plays a lesbian transvestite fascist in *The House on 92nd Street*. *I Married a Communist* offers typical comrades like Janis Carter as a high society nymphomaniac, Gomez as a sweaty sleazeball and William Talman as a cheap hood who runs a shooting parlour. There is a token attempt to show why Ryan ("embittered, violent by nature") joined in the thirties, but John Agar swallows the party line because Carter sleeps with him (the situation recurs in *The Red Menace*). The Communist Party of

these films is a cross between a fifth column and Dr Mabuse's crime empire, dividing its time between stirring up unmotivated industrial unrest and rubbing out informers. In *The Red Menace*, a poet expelled from the Party for 'politically objectionable' work ("we contend that Marx had no basis in Hegel") is driven to suicide; in *Big Jim McLain*, John Wayne's contribution to the crusade, reds summoned before an investigating committee are drugged by their superiors so they are unable to testify. Again, at the risk of labouring a point, there are *no* recorded real-life cases of American Communists murdering comrades who broke with the party, not even those who in turn informed at length on former friends.

Most of the anti-red paranoia movies were tawdry trash on the level of *Shack Out on 101*, a drama of infiltration set in a greasy spoon diner, or *Invasion, U.S.A.*, a nightmare in which Dan O'Herlihy hypnotises the patrons of a New York bar into imagining a Russian invasion, prompting a ploughshare manufacturer to rush out and convert his factory to sword-production. The major artefact of the breast-beating boom is Leo McCarey's astonishing *My Son John*, whose confused ideology is not much helped by having to use snippets of *Strangers on a Train* to fill out scenes because Robert Walker died during production. As a consequence, the climax — in which John (Walker) addresses his old school with an impassioned anti-Communist speech — consists of a dramatic spotlight falling on a lectern as a tape-recorder grinds out the speech. Walker had recorded the speech before he died: we are supposed to believe his character has taped it in case the Commie rats get him before he can deliver it. It's yet another film in which the Party murders one of its own to prevent him making a statement.

Again, Hollywood can only imagine Walker going Commie through neurosis. In a touch which can hardly have comforted die-hard anti-Communist/closet homosexuals J. Edgar Hoover, Roy Cohn and Cardinal Spellman, *My Son John* suggests its main character is pink because he is gay. Mincing with Bruno Anthony mannerisms and hugging his mother (Helen Hayes), Walker — who works in Washington, suggesting he is one of McCarthy's State Department 'card-carriers', the reds who lost China — drips camp acid wherever he goes. "Well, I'll see you all in the bomb shelter," he sniffs, later adding homosexual relish to his statement "I love humanity, mother. I love the downtrodden, the helpless minorities."

Strangely, the film is more incisive a dissection of the destructive influence of typical American parents than *Rebel Without a Cause*: without overplaying the Mr Magoo mannerisms, Dean Jagger's Dad is a

(Above right) "So just remember — no more red apples in Mom's Apple Pie." Un-American goings-on in **My Son John**.

(Below) Senator McCarthy holds a meeting to discuss removing the red from the Stars and Stripes... (**I Married a Communist/ The Woman on Pier 13**)

drunken, abusive, patriotic bigot who makes up dreadful songs about Uncle Sam and literally hits his son with a Bible; Hayes's smothering Mom is a sentimental Norma Bates, forever sobbing on the point of menopausal crack up ("modern science has pills for women of my age, John"). *My Son John* is a grotesque, rarely revived because of its embarrassing sentiments, but its hidden psychology offers more cutting and saddening an analysis of American failings than any left-wing picture of the period. In *Running Time: Films of the Cold War* (1982), Nora Sayre muses that 'contrary to the director's intentions, one could easily conclude that mothers cause Communism.'

On the whole, the explicit anti-Communist films of the late forties and early fifties were ignored by the public. Just as many fervent anti-Communists despised Joe McCarthy for, as they saw it, making a joke out of their cause, most knee-jerk anti-reds *still* couldn't take *Big Jim McLain* — which thanks HUAC in its closing credits and commends them for being 'undaunted by the vicious campaign against them' — seriously. *Pickup on South Street* got by on being a good picture, but Mark Robson's interesting if obnoxious *Trial* was a flop because the audience didn't care for a lecture. Like *I Was a Communist for the F.B.I*, *Trial* touches on the real life fund-and consciousness-raising that went on around such show trials as the Scottsboro Boys and the Sleepy Lagoon cases, alleging that reds deliberately botched the defences of minority innocents accused of rape or murder so they could keep the donations coming and finance a revolution. Arthur Kennedy, always reliably devious and cowardly, masterminds the plot.

The worst thing about the red scare movies is their enormous collective insincerity. Leo McCarey and John Wayne might have been McCarthyite tub-thumpers, but most of these films were made by studios running scared. They thought cranking out an anti-Commie picture would mean their writers, stars and directors would be left alone. Starring in *I Married a Communist*, Robert Ryan exorcised the 'taint' of *Crossfire*. Jack Warner had certainly felt a personal involvement in the studio's anti-Nazi films (Warners mounted *Confessions of a Nazi Spy*, after a Jewish employee was murdered in Germany by brownshirts), but cynically made *I Was a Communist for the F.B.I.* to get HUAC off his back. These films, unlike a great many genre items that allegorise the situation, are not about Communism or McCarthyism. The irony is that while science fiction pictures and westerns were evoking or discussing the issues, the films that were supposed to be *about* them were just spy or gangster movies in disguise.

Given how quickly things changed, it is hard to recall that the first wave of 1950s science fiction films were made with intellectual or political agendas. *Destination Moon*, from a novel by extreme right-winger Robert A. Heinlein, is explicit propaganda for rocketry but also favours big business over weak-willed government, proposing a moon race in which a coalition of private industry and the military best agents of an unidentified foreign power — which alert audiences would assume to be located East of Poland and West of China. Later, the point was underlined when Walt Disney, exactly the kind of private enterprise demagogue Heinlein idolised, used his *Man in Space* (1955) TV series and the Tomorrowland exhibit of his new theme park to convince President Eisenhower that America should mount a serious space programme.

Though Robert Wise's somewhat smug liberalism and that paternalist final speech about siccing the Gorts on us if we don't discontinue atomic testing now seem irritating, *The Day the Earth Stood Still* was a remarkably courageous, progressive film to be made at the height of McCarthyism. It seems likely that it

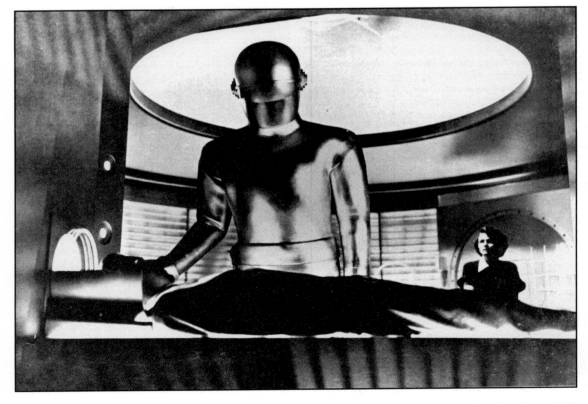

The Day the Earth Stood Still — *a comparative oasis of sanity in the rabid McCarthyist fifties.*

slipped through because no one took 'that crazy *Buck Rogers* stuff' seriously or was more concerned with the obvious religious allegory (Klaatu's Earthly cover name is 'Mr Carpenter') than any political relevance. Dr Barnhardt (Sam Jaffe), the saintly scientist who welcomes the alien, is obviously based on Albert Einstein, then held in deep suspicion because of much-publicised regrets that his theories had led to the atom bomb.

When a Presidential envoy tells the alien "I'm sure you recognise from our broadcasts the evil forces that have produced the tension in our world", Klaatu (Michael Rennie) snaps, "I'm not interested in the internal affairs of your planet." Such genuinely above-it-all sentiments are almost unique in fifties SF (they aren't repeated in *The Day the Earth Stood Still* rip-offs like *Stranger From Venus* and *The Cosmic Man*). If aliens were not allegorised red invaders, then they were divine (like Mr Carpenter) and on the side not only of the United States but of Tail-Gunner Joe and Cardinal Spellman. *Red Planet Mars*, an embarrassing but unusual use of science fiction in the C.S. Lewis rather than H.G. Wells tradition, is entirely wrapped up in supposedly heavyweight but actually *Reader's Digest* level philosophising. It shares its lack of interest in SF extrapolations of alien civilisations with *The Day the Earth Stood Still*. In *Keep Watching the Skies*, Bill Warren spends paragraphs criticising the scientific inaccuracies and inconsistencies of *The Day the Earth Stood Still*; for all the concern Wise and screenwriter Edmund H. North have about faster-than-light drives and robot-run societies, Klaatu could as well be an angel. In *Red Planet Mars*, God literally speaks from Mars.

Like the almost as cringe-inducing *The Next Voice You Hear*, in which God speaks from the radio, *Red Planet Mars* addresses middle-American know-nothing religiosity with a now-terrifying mix of smugness and sanctimony. These are the type of films Dean Jagger as John's Dad would have loved. Peter Graves establishes contact with Mars and receives messages about their super-technological civilisation which send the world into a panic (informed that Martians live 300 years, someone wonders how the economy can pay out pensions for 235 of them). However, the tenor of the messages changes (the early ones are part of a sneaky plot by Russian Communists and a Nazi mad scientist) and religious preachments from outer space prompt a religious revival behind the Iron Curtain which overthrows the Communist Party and reinstates a doddery Patriarch of the Orthodox Church as ruler of all the Russias. These scenes, ridiculous as they are in their low-budget mix of stock footage and false-bearded extras, feel even stranger after the real collapse of Soviet Communism.

Red Planet Mars is like an artefact from Ancient Egypt: it seems the product of a society utterly foreign to us, with incomprehensible beliefs, rituals and conventions. It patronises its assumed audience as if its makers felt it was important to pretend to be stupid in order to get across their message that religion is *good* and Communism is *bad*. *Red Planet Mars* seems functionally insane, but it is not the only film of its type. *The 27th Day* is another allegory, in which plot device aliens subject humanity to a test designed to reveal that Communists are scum: five representatives from different countries are abducted by a flying saucer years before it was fashionable and given Pandora's Box capsules capable of exterminating all people within 3,000 miles. The American and the German puzzle about moral quandaries, but the Russian is hauled up before his leader, who wants to use the capsules to wipe out the West and, when the ordinary Ivan resists, decides in a paranoid spasm to nuke the West before they can use their capsules on the Soviet Union. In an ending even more mind-boggling than that of *Red Planet Mars*, our side work out that the capsules can be used for good; when they are opened, 'every enemy of peace and freedom' in the world *drops dead*. In *Science Fiction in the Cinema*, John Baxter dryly notes that 'one assumes that it is only a coincidence that the President of the USA is not mentioned after this event.'

Aside from the hysteria of *Red Planet Mars* and *The 27th Day*, the anti-Communist credentials of most SF

films were sublimated. Slaps at the reds tend to be on a level of pettiness exemplified by giving the unsympathetic scientist of *The Thing From Another World* a hat and a beard that make him look Russki (though he has the deeply Anglo character name of Carrington). These are sign-of-the-times asides of no more significance than the use of buzz-words like 'radiation' then or 'nanotechnology' now. Nevertheless, there are constant reminders of the Cold War: *The Flying Saucer*, made before everyone equated UFOs with aliens, has Our Side and Them competing to get hold of the eponymous machine, which has been developed in secret by an enterprising scientist; a cliché sub-plot of *Lost Continent* has all-American hero Cesar Romero distrust unemotional Russian scientist Rostov (John Hoyt) until he delivers a speech about how Communism has ruined his homeland; in *The War of the Worlds* (1953), the Martians come from a *red* planet and the Russians are the only major power not seen to be resisting the invasion; and *The Deadly Mantis* opens with a tiresome documentary chunk about the Distant Early Warning system of Arctic bases, though in this case the alarm is triggered not by Russians with snow on their boots but by a giant prehistoric insect.

Many alien races or insect threats from fifties films echo the pop image of the Soviet Union as a hive mind, with a centralised evil brain sending unemotional, interchangeable drones out to do or die for the cause. *It Came From Outer Space*, *The War of the Worlds*, *Killers From Space*, *Them!*, *This Island Earth*, *The Beast With a Million Eyes*, *The Brain Eaters*, *I Married a Monster From Outer Space* and *Invisible Invaders* all have menaces on this pattern. In *Invaders From Mars* and *It Conquered the World*, the USSR is equated with bug-eyed brains and American Communists with mind-controlled slaves of the Central Intelligence who betray their own kind. Over and over again, these films harp on freedom and emotion as the keynotes of those American-Earthly values we are supposed to be defending. By contrast, British SF was still fighting World War Two: our invaders, most notably the Daleks or the bureaucratic body-snatchers of *Quatermass 2*, are explicitly fascists from outer space; even *Battle Beneath the Earth*, which has the fiendish Chinese tunnelling under America, makes a point of having its villain be a renegade warlord rather than a Maoist.

It Conquered the World offers Lee Van Cleef as a scientist who collaborates with It, sees through It's Utopian promises and, like a good HUAC informer, turns vehemently on his monstrous turnip master ("I welcomed you to Earth, and you made it a charnel house!"). The Cold War mindset of these films combines to give the unhelpful impression that Russians aren't human beings and that Communism is not a debatable political philosophy but an utterly alien and unknowable condition. While Exeter (Jeff Morrow) of *This Island Earth* and the alien husband (Tom Tryon) of *I Married a Monster From Outer Space* succumb slightly to American-Earthly culture, they will never fit in and, like Robert Ryan in *I Married a Communist* or Robert Walker in *My Son John*, must die for having once been alien. *Forbidden Planet* is a warning against becoming *too* intelligent: in the fifties, those most at risk from Commie contagion were 'egghead' intellectuals who tend to show up in SF films as trouble-makers like Carrington or, even more unpleasantly, the literally swollen-domed monsters of

Invasion of the Saucer Men. How often have you heard this: those aliens may be clever but it's our god-darned human *emotion* that makes us stronger.

The classic of the alien infiltration sub-genre is Don Siegel's *Invasion of the Body Snatchers*, scripted by Daniel Mainwaring from Jack Finney's novel *The Body Snatchers* (1955). Though few doubt its effectiveness as a paranoid horror film, there is a great deal of controversy as to what stance it actually takes on the fearful fifties. The Italian critic Ernesto G. Laura opines 'it is natural to see the pods as standing for the idea of Communism which gradually takes possession of a normal person, leaving him outwardly unchanged but transformed from within.' Peter Biskind elaborates: 'the pod society is the familiar mechanistic Utopia usually (and rightly) taken as a metaphor for Communism. This is a world in which "everyone is the same", a collectivist millennium to which all citizens contribute, as they do here, systematically distributing pods in a parody of political activism.' Siegel himself originally claimed the film as "a satire on right-wing complacency", but modified the view to "the fact that the world is peopled by pods was sufficient reason to make a picture like *Invasion of the Body Snatchers*, be it an attack on McCarthyism or an attack on Communism."

The body snatchers can be seen as embodiments of a deadening and devalued Americanism or of Communist infiltration: in both cases, they look like us but harbour alien, oppressive beliefs. As Biskind notes, the pods' unemotional hive-mind attitudes are typical of SF film's allegorised Communists; but, crucially, they are *Americans* and not even the shifty, sweaty fifth columnists of *I Married a Communist*. The body snatchers replicate exactly the folksy small-town values of the people they replace and the mounting hysteria of the still-human hero (played, with inevitable ideological connotations, by Kevin *McCarthy*) marks him out as a target for persecution by monstrous forces who have usurped the faces and voices of Andy Hardy's home town. Ideological confusion is the motor of a great many American films of the fifties. *High Noon*, written and produced by liberals (Fred Zinnemann, Carl Foreman) but starring an arch-conservative (Gary Cooper), and *Invasion of the*

Communist turnip from outer space...

EVERY MAN ITS PRISONER... EVERY WOMAN ITS SLAVE!

IT CONQUERED the WORLD CERT X

STARRING PETER GRAVES BEVERLY GARLAND LEE VAN CLEEF.

The ingeniously ambiguous **High Noon**.

Body Snatchers, written by the paranoid radical Mainwaring and directed by the romantic reactionary Siegel, can both be read equally well as pro- and anti-McCarthy statements. In *High Noon*, Cooper's Sheriff, the lone man of integrity who stands up to the outlaws, could as well be crying out against the blacklist or incarnating McCarthy's self-image, a lonely voice accusing Communists while liberal America (the townsfolk) turn their backs.

Apart from *Invasion U.S.A.*, nuclear war films of the period (*Rocketship XM*, *Five*, *The Day the World Ended*, *World Without End*, *The Space Children*, *Teenage Caveman*, *The World, the Flesh and the Devil*, *Last Woman on Earth*) are surprisingly apolitical, failing utterly to blame the Russians for starting fictional world wars. Atomic Armageddon is an evil for which all mankind, represented by nebulous groups like 'politicians' and 'scientists', is responsible. Often, children or other innocents provide a voice of saintly reason that sets the complex geo-political man-oeuvring of the Cold War on a level with playroom squabbles about who has the most toys. In *Terror From the Year 5,000*, a time-travelling mutant from the future addresses a contemporary heroine with "our history clearly records how the women of the twentieth century stood idly by while the atmosphere was contaminated and the children of the future doomed." With modest radicalism, these neglected quickies imply that the West is as responsible for the Cold War as the Soviet Bloc.

While most films that profess to be worried about Communism are manifestly insincere, there is a real bite to films that dare to be worried either about the horrible potential of the Cold War or the society-sapping dangers of McCarthyite witch-hunting. If the body snatchers are only arguably stand-ins for the witch-hunters, it is undeniable that westerns about lynch law are as obviously tackling other issues as Arthur Miller's examination of historical witch-hunts in *The Crucible*. Some film-makers, secure in the knowledge that westerns were even less thought of as serious than science fiction, were remarkably daring. In *Johnny Guitar*, Nicholas Ray casts Ward Bond (a vocal member of the red-baiting Motion Picture Alliance) as the brutal head of the mob that the rabid

Mercedes McCambridge sics on Sterling Hayden (who cracked up after being forced to name names and became an exile), a fellow-traveller with a near-Communist outlaw gang. One can imagine Ray's delight at hearing veteran screen heavy Bond mouth sentiments exactly similar to his off-screen views and exciting audience hisses.

Allan Dwan's underrated *Silver Lode*, one of a run of one-man-against-the-whole-town westerns (cf *A Man Alone*), has Dan Duryea as a sneering agitator named 'McCarty' — Dwan leaves in a take where an actor misreads a line and calls him 'McCarthy' — who makes an unjust accusation against the respected Sheriff (John Payne) and turns all his former friends against him. "Well, Sheriff," sneers McCarty as the lynch mob close in, "looks like law and order is back in control." There are a few westerns — Charles Marquis Warren's rabid *Arrowhead* is the most flamboyantly obnoxious — that equate Red Indians with other reds and adopt an ultra-McCarthyist policy of extermination, but most high-profile oaters of the 1950s suggest an almost subversive analysis of capitalism. Big business, the bogey of the radical left, is responsible for far more trouble in fifties westerns than anything remotely collective: corrupt cattle barons figure in *The Furies*, *Man in the Saddle*, *Shane*, *Rio Bravo* and dozens more. When creating the TV western series *Branded* (1965-6), Larry Cohen explained that his high concept was 'a blacklisted cowboy'; though Chuck Connors is unjustly accused of cowardice rather than political activity, the underlying theme of the show is the accusation that its hero is 'soft on' red Indians.

It was not until the sixties that the need to disguise the issues with ray guns or chaps passed and films could come closer to the truth. John Frankenheimer's *The Manchurian Candidate*, scripted by George Axelrod from Richard Condon's 1959 novel, doesn't need to dress up its McCarthy figure in western duds or pretend he is an alien invader. Senator John Iselin (James Gregory) is a spot-on parody of McCarthy, outrageously seen in fancy dress as a tipsy Abe Lincoln, limbo-dancing 'How Low Can You Go' at a party. Comparison with *Point of Order*, Emile De Antonio's skilful editing-together of TV footage from the hearings, shows that Gregory perfectly matches McCarthy's blowhard bluster and die-hard ignorance.

The Manchurian Candidate is based on the premise, much expressed at the height of his campaign, that if McCarthy "were a paid Soviet agent, he could not do more harm to this country than he is already doing now." A profoundly acid movie, which fades out on Frank Sinatra mumbling "hell... hell", *The Manchurian Candidate* one-ups the witch-hunters by depicting a Communist conspiracy even more extensive than the one imagined by HUAC. Here, the Chinese and the Soviets, represented by such engaging villains as Khigh Dhiegh, Henry Silva and Reggie Nalder, back the anti-red campaign of Senator Iselin, which is master-minded by his truly frightening wife (Angela Lansbury). She uses her brainwashed son Raymond (Laurence Harvey) as an assassin to manoeuvre her husband towards the Presidency, whereupon she will assume "powers that will make martial law look like anarchy."

Though it operates in a political arena, *The Manchurian Candidate* is as much a family drama as *My Son John*, as Lansbury's monstrously committed momma, who is the logical development of Helen Hayes's menopausal ditherer, shapes and tortures her own son into the ideal Communist agent, all the while concealing her fascist aims from her red masters. When Iselin complains that his wife won't tell him how many Communists there are in the government and he is always being tripped up for giving a different number to the press, she tells him to pick a number he can easily remember: he looks at the bottle of Heinz ketchup in his hand and, in a witty cut, is denouncing '57 card-carrying Communists'. Lansbury, with tight hairdo, is a revelation, taking vicious little sucks on a cigarette as she coos over her zombie son. An attack on the worst impulses hiding behind American values which is also patriotically fervent in its belief in the worth of those who lay down their lives for an ideal, *The Manchurian Candidate* predictably aroused the ire of the John Birch Society and the American Communist Party. Its makers must have been delighted.

From this, it was a logical step to *Dr Strangelove: or How I Learned to Stop Worrying and Love the Bomb*, in which the Cold War is seen as an enormous collective expression of the sexual insecurities of middle-aged men in power. Sterling Hayden, still eaten by guilt, is General Jack D. Ripper, who starts World War Three to compensate for his impotence, launching bombers which are as phallic as his cigar. Professional anti-Communism is represented by Buck Turgidson (George C. Scott), the increasingly manic general who giggles over casualty figures in megadeaths, and Dr Strangelove (Peter Sellers), a cyborg ex-Nazi with an uncontrollably heiling erectile arm. Even the more sober *Fail Safe* suggests that nuclear war could only start through an *American* technical error and depicts the anti-red adviser who suggests the President take advantage of the mistake to wipe out the Soviet Union is an arrant maniac with a bizarre name (Walter Matthau as Dr Groeteschele). By the sixties, the Cold War was either spoofed or seen cynically, removing it from any political differentiation into the Fu Manchu-like fantasies of *Dr No*, the plague-on-both-your-

houses despair of *The Spy Who Came in From the Cold* and the combination of the two in *The President's Analyst*.

McCarthy was such a clown — irresistibly reminiscent of the bullying chiseller played by Broderick Crawford in *Born Yesterday* — that he was being made tentative fun of even while he was a powerful force (both Walt Kelly's *Pogo* and *Mad Magazine* ran skits). As soon as he was gone, McCarthy became fair game for impersonations like James Gregory's Senator Iselin and set a precedent for the increasing depiction of senators and other authority figures as out-and-out villains (cf Charles Laughton in *Advise and Consent,* Cliff Robertson in *The Best Man,* Robert Vaughn in *Bullitt*). But McCarthyism was not just a craze espoused only by obvious bastards and dunderheads, it was a broad-appeal political position adopted by mainstream American figures from John and Robert Kennedy to Richard Nixon. While McCarthy died embittered, these men rose to the Presidency and set the political timbre of the 1960s and seventies.

The blacklists ebbed somewhat in the late fifties and early sixties, but trace elements remain to this day. Lionel Stander ended up on *Hart to Hart* and Abraham Polonsky emerged from exile with the script for *Madigan,* but Joseph Losey never made a film in America again — it has been suggested that the Stateside butchering and throwing-away of *The Damned* by Columbia was politically rather than commercially motivated — and some key figures couldn't come out of the cold because they were dead. Nevertheless, and despite the intense personal involvement many film-makers had in the issue, it took as long for Hollywood to get around to making films *about* the period as it did for the studios to back pictures about Vietnam. *The Way We Were,* a love story set against thirty years of American history, was recut before release to play up the romance and down the politics, excising much of the material about the fifties and the Hollywood Ten. Even in the somewhat

(Left) **The Manchurian Candidate** — *you've got to suspect brainwashing when Laurence Harvey's fellow troopers all say what a nice guy he is...*

couple patterned on Julius and Ethel Rosenberg; Nicolas Roeg's *Insignificance*, from Terry Johnson's play, is a collision of real-life characters, with Tony Curtis as a mean-spirited Senator obviously standing in for Tail-Gunner Joe; *J. Edgar Hoover* reprises the Cohen film in a TV movie minor key, with Treat Williams as Hoover and Charles Hallahan as McCarthy; even Richard Attenborough's *Chaplin* hauls out Hoover (Kevin Dunn) to persecute its hero and drive him into political exile.

Meanwhile, television (also hit hard by the blacklist) turned out a few effective biopics: William Devane is blacklisted radio commentator John Henry Faulk and George C. Scott his crusading lawyer Louis Nizer in *Fear on Trial*, a rare instance of dramatising a genuine rather than a representational case; Peter Boyle is a blustering McCarthy in *Tail Gunner Joe*, carrying the attitudes and tactics of *Joe* onto the floor of the house; and James Woods is perfectly verminous as Roy Cohn, McCarthy's lawyer, in *Citizen Cohn*, with Joe Don Baker as McCarthy and an apt cameo from Frederic Forrest as Dashiell Hammett, which is framed by Cohn's reminiscences from a hospital bed as he dies of AIDS (also a theme of the play *Angels in America*). The oddest TV effort is Paul Schrader's *Witch Hunt*, which happens to have the same premise as my own story, 'The McCarthy Witch Hunt' (1994), and is set in an alternate world where a McCarthyite Senator (Eric Bogosian) is persecuting actual witches, burning them at rallies.

similar showbiz-politics of *For the Boys*, George Segal's blacklisting is relegated to a sub-plot, though the film features a potent scene when the calmly drunk victim turns on the friends who won't support him.

As a part of the panorama of twentieth century crookedness, McCarthyism continues to feature in many biopics or through-the-decades stories: there's a tiny sub-plot in *Marathon Man* about the blacklisting of Dustin Hoffman's academic father and the thesis he is writing to assuage his guilt; Larry Cohen's *The Private Files of J. Edgar Hoover*, though more concerned with other crimes, shows Hoover (Broderick Crawford) leaking information to McCarthy (George D. Wallace); Sidney Lumet's *Daniel*, from E.L. Doctorow's novel *The Book of Daniel*, is about the legacy of both radicalism and anti-Communism on the children of an executed

The first film *about* the purges is Martin Ritt's *The Front*, which proudly lists in its end credits its own creative personnel who were blacklisted. Taking an unusual angle, the film is about a struggling, apolitical schmuck (Woody Allen) who agrees to lend his name

(Above) Zero Mostel sets 'em up in **The Front**.

(Right) Norma Jean discovers the theory of relativity in **Insignificance***: Now we know who had her killed...*

Ron Silver fails to notice the Commie disguised as a sack of onions behind him in **Fellow Traveller**.

to TV scripts written by blacklisted writers. The film is rich in detail about the day-to-day lives of the victims of McCarthyism: a nice moment has the swell-headed Allen returning a script to its author because it isn't good enough to carry his name. Zero Mostel (who claimed on a televised hearing that his gutless employers were 'Eighteenth Century Fox' and thanked the inquisitors for getting him on TV for the first time since his blacklisting) is moving as a comedian who once went on a Communist march because he wanted to get laid and is now driven to suicide. This is a minor equivocation: emphasising people who were 'unjustly' persecuted (and many were, through mistyped names or lying informants) implies that real Communists or fellow-travellers were *justly* blacklisted. A few, like Mostel, put on a show of defiance when hauled up before HUAC, but most took the Fifth Amendment or caved in and named names. *The Front* opts for a rousing finale as Allen, radicalised by his experiences and suspect because of pink sentiments in the scripts credited to him, finally snaps back at the Committee grilling him, "I question your right to ask me these questions, and furthermore you can all go fuck yourselves."

Walter Bernstein, the blacklist survivor writer of *The Front*, returned to the theme with Peter Yates's conventional fifties-set thriller *The House on Carroll Street*, with Jeff Daniels as an FBI agent and Kelly McGillis as a blacklisted journalist. The McGuffin is the contrast between the Evil Government's persecution of suspected American leftists with its open-arms welcome for convicted Nazi war criminals, who are being brought into the country because they can help the West jockey for power in Eastern Europe. Entirely competent, *Carroll Street* is distinguished solely by Mandy Patinkin's wickedly witty, subtly menacing turn as an inquisitorial master villain obviously modelled on Roy Cohn. Philip Saville's British *Fellow Traveller* is another conspiracy item, but

more intriguing in its recreation of the period, straddling the slow drift to suicide of a John Garfield-like star (Hart Bochner) who remains in poolside internal exile in Hollywood, and the struggles of a writer (Ron Silver) exiled to a rainy London where he grinds out scripts for a *Robin Hood* TV series. The suppression of Silver's politics in this toil is wonderfully expressed by his back-pedalling on an initial suggestion that Robin should be 'a man of the people' to see the outlaw hero as 'a Battle of Britain pilot type'. Daniel J. Travanti features as a triple-agent Hollywood psychiatrist (a real-life figure whose odd role in the blacklist is examined in Victor S. Navasky's *Naming Names*) in the *Manchurian Candidate* business of backing McCarthyism for Moscow.

Unfortunately, the first major Hollywood studio movie about McCarthyism is Irwin Winkler's *Guilty By Suspicion*, which is riddled with showbiz bullshit, deeply mendacious juggling of actual history and just-plain irritating earnestness. The central figure is hotshot director David Merrill (Robert De Niro), another 'innocent' who once attended a few CP meetings for vaguely humanitarian reasons, but was thrown out for arguing, and whose name is given in testimony by a career-saving rat of a screenwriter who is seen squirming under committee pressure in the opening scene.

Overnight, Merrill goes from A-list to blacklist, being dropped by Fox studio boss Darryl Zanuck (*Guilty By Suspicion* is a Warners film) from a big budget international picture, hounded by the FBI even when he takes a job repairing camera equipment in a New York slum and, in the final indignity, being replaced as the pseudonymous director of a poverty row western (which looks more like a 1942 movie than a 1952 one). As Merrill stands firm in refusing to name names, all around him crack up: blacklisted movie star Patricia Wettig (whose gaunt gorgeousness would not have got her a screen test in the chubby-chasing 1950s) commits suicide when her cringing husband

names her; and jovial writer George Wendt (we see him doing rewrites on *Gentlemen Prefer Blondes*, two years before it went into production) is as obviously destined to sell out just as Merrill, a man of movie hero-ish unbending integrity, is not.

Though *Guilty By Suspicion* is about naming names, it is remarkably reluctant to do so itself: Zanuck (played uncannily by Ben Piazza) is the only real-life character who appears, though Lionel Stander and Sterling Hayden are mentioned in dialogue. Mostly, the film feels the need (because it is so intent on distorting the big story while giving accurate detail) to have fictional characters stand in for the likes of driven-to-exile director Joseph Losey (Martin Scorsese as 'Joe Lesser'). McCarthy and Cohn are represented by Gailard Sartain (as 'Chairman Wood') and Tom Sizemore (as 'Ray Karlin'): the performances are chillingly apt, but neither of these high profile red-bashers was much concerned with Hollywood, which was left to lesser lights like J. Parnell Thomas. The big lie of the film, understandable given the need of Hollywood to feel important, is that the blacklist was exclusively or even mainly directed at the entertainment industry. *Guilty By Suspicion* makes a token gesture by having Merrill's wife (Annette Bening) be a teacher also dropped for political reasons, but all the breast-beating is about movie types.

Originally, when *Guilty By Suspicion* was to be directed by Bernard Tavernier, the idea was that the Merrill character would finally cave in, like the real-life Elia Kazan and Edward Dmytryk, who dealt with what they had done by making deeply ambivalent films about informing: *On the Waterfront* and *The Caine Mutiny*. However, original screenwriter Abraham Polonsky, who didn't direct between 1948 and *Tell Them Willie Boy is Here* twenty-one years later, didn't want to make a film about a rat, even though the position of informer was more commonplace (and, arguably, more interesting) than that of hold-out. Winkler, who took over as screenwriter and director, must have concurred: his film is designed to deliver in De Niro a straight-up hero the American public can cheer for.

The finale of *Guilty By Suspicion* perfectly recreates the chaos seen in *Point of Order* (and more relevantly

reenacted in *Citizen Cohn*), but unbelievably provides a Hollywood last stand in which, in defiance of historical fact, a movie star hero brings down McCarthy and the whole blacklist. On the stand, Merrill repeatedly addresses 'Wood' tearfully with "have you no shame?" as the gavel-pounding politico loses his rag and the audience turns against him. All very well, and this did actually happen, but the modest (in fact, very canny) hero of the hour was Joseph Welch, not a glamorous movie star but a lawyer representing an army dentist. The hearings were designed so the victims could never talk back defiantly at their persecutors, and Welch only got to deliver the *coup de grace* to McCarthy when the Senator was too far gone to be backed up by the anti-red colossus of the Establishment. By giving this bit of business to the fictional Merrill and removing it from its exact political context, *Guilty By Suspicion* renders it tritely meaningless.

The collapse in the 1990s of world Communism as a force for anything has rendered the anti-red hysteria of the fifties and beyond even more tragi-comic than it seemed at the time. There are those who supported the witch-hunts who now claim the credit for the overthrow of the Soviet Union, as if putting Zero Mostel out of work had any effect on the economic or political instabilities of a continent-sized country. And there are those, as with the Vietnam War (the overseas aspect of the political-social neurosis that led at home to the blacklist), who now admit too late their earlier mistakes.

Throughout this century, to be an American is to be afraid of something. The Communists of *I Married a Communist* are no more real Communists than the Indians of *Arrowhead* are real Indians or the aliens of *The War of the Worlds* are real aliens: they are a representation of a formless anxiety that has been felt by successive American governments and by succeeding generations of ordinary Americans. Insistently, these films claim America as the Greatest Thing on God's Earth but, in order to deal with the manifest wrongs inherent in the American Utopia, there has to be a snake in Eden. Without wishing to minimise the appalling effects of Stalinist or Maoist Communism throughout the world, no form of Marxist movement has ever posed a serious threat to the internal security of the United States. But insecurities gnaw from Washington to Santa Mira, from Beacon Street to Carroll Street, from Telegraph Hill to Beverly Hills. The message we should take away from the McCarthy movies remains pertinent: something is wrong with America. ∎

DON'T OVERACT WITH YOUR FINGERS!

THE MAKING OF BLOOD ON SATAN'S CLAW

BY DAVID TAYLOR

'Sorcery and sanctity... these are the only realities. Each is an ecstasy, a withdrawal from the common life.'
Arthur Machen, *The White People*

Attempting to chart the genesis of any film project when it has been twenty-five years since its inception is bound to be an imprecise science.

Even if you can track down surviving cast and crew members, you then fall prey to vested interests, defective memories and, worse, sheer lack of interest. I was lucky in this respect. Everyone I spoke with who had been involved in the making of *Blood on Satan's Claw*, whether on or off the record, was helpful, charming and candid.

Blood on Satan's Claw is by no means a perfect film. Its multitude of flaws will be scrutinised from

numerous perspectives over the next few pages. Yet, for all its faults, it is, perversely, one of the most perfect examples of British horror cinema. Its portrait of a creeping evil gradually infiltrating a community is the product of a peculiarly British point of view, a combination of lyricism and unease whose antecedents lie deep in our literary and artistic heritage. And, with typical British aloofness, we seem to have spent the last quarter of a century denying its existence.

The film has remained with me since I first saw it back in 1971, under the title *Satan's Skin*. I decided to take a trip back and see what remains that I could unearth about its creation. As Patrick Wymark remarks in the film: "It might merit further study..."

Blood on Satan's Claw is set in the mid-seventeenth century, just after the end of the Civil War, with Charles II in exile in France. A ploughman, Ralph Gower (Barry Andrews), unearths the decomposed skull of a 'fiend' in a field. He reports the discovery to his employer, Isobel Banham (Avice Landon), who is at the time entertaining a Royalist house guest, The Judge (Patrick Wymark). They investigate Gower's discovery, but the strange body has vanished in the interim.

Almost immediately, the youths of the local township begin to behave strangely. Precocious schoolgirl Angel Blake (Linda Hayden) finds a talon amongst the ploughed furrows of the field and undergoes a sinister personality change. Rosalind Barton (Tamara Ustinov), the fiancée of Peter Edmonton (Simon Williams), goes mad and one of her hands is transformed into a monstrous claw. Edmonton later severs his own hand, in the belief that he too has become infected. Departing for London, The Judge cautions: "I shall return when the time is ripe. But you must have patience even while people

die. Only thus can the whole evil be destroyed. You must let it grow."

And grow it certainly does. One by one, the children of the town fall prey to a mysterious infection. Those who do not immediately succumb to the illness itself, like the innocent Cathy Vespers (Wendy Padbury), are ritually murdered by the gang of delinquents which has formed under the authority of Angel Blake, who is communing with a strange hooded figure in a desecrated chapel in the woods. Ralph Gower rescues one of these followers, Margaret (Michele Dotrice), who is being tortured for being a witch and discovers a strange patch of fur — the "devil's skin" — growing on her thigh.

It transpires that each of the children is acting as host for a portion of the body of an ancient demon, which is being assembled patchwork-style by the members of Angel Blake's cult. Before the creature can be fully assembled, The Judge returns from London wielding a blessed sword and destroys it. The film comes to a close on an ambiguous close-up of The Judge's baleful eye, surrounded by flames — an explicit return to the image of the demon's eye as unearthed by the plough at the start of the film.

As can be seen from this outline, *Blood on Satan's Claw* was not typical of the British horror films of the late sixties and early seventies. It was not a cosy Gothic period piece coloured by lashings of Kensington Gore like the vast majority of the Hammer films of the period. Nor did it particularly cater for a 'swinging' youth audience, as most horror movies of the era were wont to do (not only in the UK, but also America and most of Europe). Quite apart from the plot having no distinct hero figure, it was further complicated by an exceedingly erratic narrative thread and an oppressive atmosphere of madness and decay. It also intertwined two of the cinema's greatest taboo subjects: the inherent evil of children and the overt sexuality of evil.

Moody, downbeat, thoughtful and, at times, both lyrical and overtly sadistic, *Blood on Satan's Claw* joined that small cartel of contemporaneous British horror films — including *Matthew Hopkins — Witchfinder General*, *Hands of the Ripper*, *Scream and Scream Again*, *Demons of the Mind* and *Blood from the Mummy's Tomb* — which occupy their own, very precise space at the outskirts of the genre.

The first furrow in the making of *Blood on Satan's Claw* was ploughed by writer Robert Wynne-Simmons early in 1970. As he explains: "I was just out of University and looking to find work in the film industry. So I didn't have any track record at all and I wrote the obligatory hundred letters. It was on the first of January that I got a reply — I remember it was the very beginning of the year — from a producer called Chris Neame, who was working, I think, for Tony Tenser at Tigon. He'd been collecting on behalf of the other producers — there were about four people involved here — a number of potential scripts from which to make a film."

Although jubilant at finally having made his first contact within the industry, the twenty-two-year-old Cambridge graduate then discovered the first stumbling block on the road to fame and fortune. To wit, the producers were already locked into a production schedule for the as-yet undeveloped project:

"They'd done a deal with Pinewood in advance, to get a low rate from the studio. It was booked for April 1

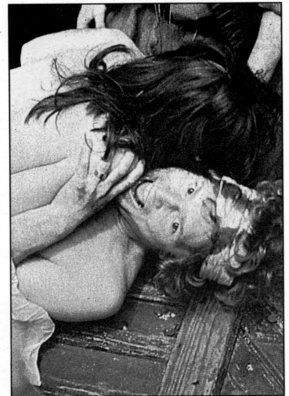

(Previous page) Linda Hayden, everyone's favourite hot teen nymphet, gets it on with Satan.

(Right) Sorted! Just one 'E' and Barry Andrews is possessed by the Devil.

If we can have Traci Lords pin-ups, I don't see why we can't have a full-pager of perky Patrick Wymark in an alluring little bedside number.

— which sort of seemed vaguely appropriate! The letter said we've got thirty possible outlines that we've been presented with and we notice that you've done some writing — I'd written some plays and things at university — do you have anything to offer us? Before I'd really got my head together, I rang them up and said yes, there was something really exciting coming and they said could they have it by next Thursday!"

Tigon were interested in doing a horror anthology along the lines of the Amicus movies *Dr Terror's House of Horrors* and *Torture Garden*, combining three or four stories with some sort of narrative device to link them together. Although Wynne-Simmons was less than happy with this format, he latched onto the fact that they were looking for tales "with a common theme". For inspiration, he turned to a set of unpublished short stories which he had written during his undergraduate days, eventually integrating two of them into the first draft of the screenplay:

"The first episode had to do with Simon Williams and Tamara Ustinov, and the whole idea of her going mad and being forced by the unpleasant aunt into the spare bedroom, where something nasty was lurking. That was the one which was loosely based on something I had written before. Then there was another story about a group of schoolchildren who found something nasty in a field."

In adapting these stories for the script, Wynne-Simmons began to develop the general mythology of the film — the gradual contamination of the community and the assembly of the demon. These concepts were not based on any existing folk tales or occult beliefs. "No, there was no precedent I know of," Wynne-Simmons admits, "just *Frankenstein*, I suppose. I was more interested in the ways that old religions has been supplanted and wiped out. That was, I suppose, a theme of the time, inasmuch as it was the New Age outlook on things and it seemed to address what had been out there before — the gargoyle on the church."

Wynne-Simmons was also aware that the script, to a certain extent, reflected his own generation's growing disenchantment. The transition from the sixties to the seventies had marked a crisis point in popular culture. The old ideologies of the sixties — sexual liberation, flower power, popular art in all its forms — were in the process of being redefined. Flashpoints like Altamont and the Tate/La Bianca murders had cast a shadow over the idealism of the sixties.

Wynne-Simmons drew on contemporary models,

like Charles Manson's Family, in creating the corrupted youth culture for his script: "Undoubtedly, the cults were not all purity and innocence. Michele Dotrice's character — her devotion against all the odds to what was happening — and the power that Linda Hayden's character held, has something to do with the really weird devotion that Manson's followers had to him. There was also, if you're looking for something that is dealing with the dark corners of the mind, another case of a child murderer called Mary Bell..."

The Mary Bell case was recently brought back into public consciousness by the murder of James Bulger by Robert Thompson and Jon Venables. In 1968, the eleven year-old Bell was found guilty of manslaughter on the grounds of diminished responsibility for the strangling of two children in Newcastle-Upon-Tyne. Although the crime in itself was appalling enough, the public was even more affected by Bell's apparent unconcern for either her victims or their relatives. As Wynne-Simmons recounts: "She would go up to the mothers of the children she'd murdered and virtually boast of it. She seemed to want to get herself caught and that horrifying idea of childhood innocence being totally evil was also a central theme of the movie."

In the script, Wynne-Simmons avoided making it explicit exactly what sort of demon the infected villagers were in the process of resurrecting. It was certainly not intended to be Satan himself, nor did the writer want to pigeonhole the pagan cult as being Satanists or witches: "It was deliberately ambiguous... Essentially it was a God-Devil. It was midway between what the God might have been and what the Devil, from the Christian point of view, was. The idea was that a God who demanded an unpleasant sacrificial type of worship was coming alive again. Also, there was this sort of feeling that evil though this creature might be, it was somehow more 'alive' than the Patrick Wymark character, whose viewpoint was essentially a dead one.

"The central theme of the whole film was the stamping out of the old religions. Not by Christianity, but by an atheistic belief that all sorts of things must be blocked out of the mind. So The Judge represents a dogged enlightenment, if you like, who is saying 'Don't let these things lurk in dark corners. Bring it out into the open and then get rid of it. When it becomes a fully fledged cult, it will show itself'."

To highlight this clash between pagan belief and establishment dogmatism, Wynne-Simmons originally set the film much later than the seventeenth century: "The original idea was much further away from the period of witch-hunts and that sort of thing. It was actually set during the Age of Steam, the early Victorian era. The idea was that the demon came from something that was obviously not in the folk memories of the people involved. It had come from somewhere way back and was not attached to any particular religion. There was to have been this image of The Judge arriving aboard a steam train, which was meant to be an image of him steamrollering the whole movement."

When the first draft of the screenplay was presented to Tigon, they were less than happy with this particular aspect of the script. "Tigon had just done *Witchfinder General* and it was in their mind that the real death of witchcraft — if you regard that as an ancient religion — occurred in the seventeenth century and that, therefore, the film should be set then."

Tigon were also somewhat unhappy with some of

What looks like a giant owl in a monk's cassock is actually the Devil himself — no wonder the Americans darkened the print...

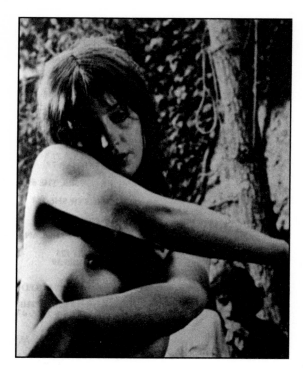

the deliberate ambiguity that Wynne-Simmons had built into the script, most notably in the climactic confrontation between The Judge and the corrupted townsfolk. In their eyes, it was just a straightforward showdown between good and evil: "In the original script, the last scene was probably more destructive than it was in the eventual film. Patrick Wymark had militiamen with him who actually gunned people down. There was a mass grave dug and that was the end. So it was really a very, very destructive thing. Rough justice, where he just obliterated this crowd of people."

Tigon also insisted on numerous other, smaller changes to the script. Although Wynne-Simmons was frustrated by their suggestions for the screenplay, he had little choice but to comply: "It was changed because there was a feeling that you had to introduce various clichés into these movies, otherwise they wouldn't be accepted. One of those clichés, which to my mind totally goes against the character of the man, was that he has a sword which just happens to be in the shape of a cross. Tigon wanted an *actual* cross. They said 'There's devil worship going on, so there has to be a cross'. Unfortunately, the person who is wielding the cross is usually the 'Van Helsing' force of good, and it was very difficult to reconcile the character of The Judge with the forces of good! This would have reduced his 'ethnic cleansing' to the minimum, sort of make him halfway acceptable." He laughs. "We eventually compromised on a sword that just looked a bit cross-like..."

Despite their most earnest efforts, Tigon ultimately failed to transform The Judge into the film's hero figure. "The close-up of his eye at the end rather suggests that he is now the devil himself," Wynne-Simmons acknowledges. "So it's rather a different outlook."

Wynne-Simmons was equally scornful of the other 'amendments' made at Tigon's behest. "There were certain other things which had to be added. One was this Book of Witches, which I thought was quite

dreadful... For heaven's sake, everyone's heard of witches! They don't really need to look them up in a book! The other addition was the witch-ducking scene. This had to be included because it had been so successful in *Witchfinder General*, so they wanted to repeat it. I didn't mind that so much, as it did show the incredible stupidity of people at the time."

One further sticking point for the screenplay was its title. Wynne-Simmons had originally titled his script *The Devil's Skin*, but Tigon had reservations. Literally dozens of alternatives were bounced back and forth, although executive producer Tony Tenser's particular favourite — *The Ghouls Are Amongst Us* — was, thankfully, rejected by everyone else involved. During filming, it was publicised as *The Devil's Touch*. By the end of the shooting this had been replaced by *Satan's Skin*, despite the fact that Satan didn't figure in the action at all. At the last moment, the film was retitled *Blood on Satan's Claw*, although it continued to be known as *Satan's Skin* in America and in most other English-speaking territories. To confuse matters further, Wynne-Simmons also believes that certain foreign prints went under the title of *The Claw*.

While Robert Wynne-Simmons was wrestling with revisions to the script, Tigon were actively seeking a director for the project. One name which came up was a young director called Piers Haggard, who had worked extensively in the theatre and on television. More importantly, he had just completed his first film, a melodrama entitled *Wedding Night*. Then just over thirty years old, Haggard was the great grand-nephew of the author H. Rider Haggard, whose novels included *She, Allan Quatermain* and *King Solomon's Mines*.

Wedding Night had been shot in Ireland in 1969, under the original title of *I Can't... I Can't*. The film starred Dennis Waterman, Tessa Wyatt and Alexandra Bastedo in the tale of a young Irishwoman who fears a repetition of her mother's death in childbirth and so refuses to consummate her recent marriage, thus forcing her husband into the arms of a former girlfriend. It was notable at the time for being one of the first films to directly confront the attitude of the Catholic Church towards contraception and caused much controversy when first screened in Cork. For whatever reason, the film was not given a general release in Britain until 1972, a year after *Blood on Satan's Claw*.

By this point in the proceedings, Christopher Neame was no longer involved with the project and had handed it over to another pair of producers, Peter

(Above left) Topless Satanic go-go dancing — three strikes and you're out for that kind of behaviour!

(Left) Michele Dotrice gets tortured.

Andrews and Malcolm Haysworth. "They were very young," Haggard recounts. "Peter Andrews was the financial man. He didn't come on the floor a lot. He liked the money side of the business — having the office and the blotting paper and talking to the financiers. Malcolm Haysworth was the hands-on chap. He would get his boots muddy and work in the field."

Although he was still in overall control of the film, Tony Tenser kept his distance, with the exception of a couple of brief visits to the set during shooting. Haggard quite warmed to Tenser: "He was quite an experience. He was one of those wonderful East End Jewish businessmen, who was sharp as a knife but rather warm with it. I rather liked him — despite the fact that he wasn't a particularly artistic or sensitive guy."

Haggard arranged a screening of *Wedding Night* for the producers: "They were at a little screening at the Bijou or one of those other little preview theatres in Wardour Street. I remember Malcolm and Peter were there — whether my agent had got them there I can't remember — and they said 'Very good, Piers. We'd like to talk to you about a project'."

To this day, Haggard doesn't know quite why he was selected to direct. At that point in his career, he had absolutely no experience whatsoever of working within the horror genre. "I don't think I'd ever been to a horror film," he says. "I was very arty. I'd worked at the National Theatre and in television, doing series like *Callan* and various BBC plays. I was quite arty farty really. So I couldn't have done a Hammer horror film... well, in the way that would have been accepted."

Despite all this, there was something about Wynne-Simmons' script that struck a chord with the director. Haggard puts it down to "the things in it — the lyrical, the poetic, the genuinely dark side of it. *They* caught my imagination."

One of the aspects of the screenplay which most appealed to Haggard was its bleak rural setting, which was very similar to the director's own youth, growing up on a farm in Scotland: "I was isolated until I went to university at seventeen, and those are the formative years. Your imagination is formed at that time. I had an absolutely passionate feeling for the countryside in a very Wordsworthian sense: the light on the bank; the feeling of beech trees in spring, so pale and green; the light on the river or the river at night; walking down the lane with no lights, guiding yourself by looking up at the stars. A very strong and vivid sense of country life."

Having agreed to direct the film, he set about preparing for the shoot by viewing some recent horror movies and getting a feel for the form: "I remember realising, at some point, that horror films are *great*. In horror, you can deal with big issues if you want to — life, death, resurrection, terror, nightmare — so long as you entertain. You can't deal with these issues in most commercial cinema. People just don't want to see it. It's also largely true that, in the commercial cinema, you're most likely to get things done if it is, in some sense, a genre."

Yet despite his enthusiasm for the project, Haggard shared with Robert Wynne-Simmons a suspicion about the screenplay's three-tiered structure. He voiced his reservations to Andrews and Haysworth: "They had this notion that it was cheaper to do three short films rather than one long single film, not reckoning on the fact that no one is ever interested in triple bills. I knew perfectly well from the theatre that no one had ever made any money on a triple bill. They're always a disaster."

Yet Haggard's reservations were not limited to the film's commercial viability. He was also concerned about its aesthetics from the audience's viewpoint. He argued that with an anthology film, "You don't get an experience. You get three small experiences. You don't get a *big* experience. A good, solid experience."

He continues: "At the time, I was saying this should be one story. I won't take all the credit, but I knew it would be better as one. All these stories were set in the same place, so it didn't seem impossible to combine them."

Robert Wynne-Simmons had, of course, already voiced his doubts about the film's structure. Faced with both director and scriptwriter mounting an effective blockade, Tigon took another look at the script. As Wynne-Simmons remembers it: "They looked at it and they said, 'This is really unfeasible, isn't it?' And I said, 'Yes, it is!'."

"And so," Haggard concludes, "we put poor Robert back to stitching them together, which he did as best he could."

Despite the unity of theme and setting, melding the three stories together was no simple task. "It was always a problem," says Wynne-Simmons, "and I still notice it in the script. The way it was written originally, there were certain characters who appeared in episode one, but who didn't appear in episodes two and three; some who appeared in two, but not in one and three. And so forth.

"The script wasn't really rewritten while the film was being shot. It was all there and ready and shot as planned, but right up until that time it was being adapted. I think if there had been a few more weeks to sit and think about it, it would have been possible to meld the three parts better. They look a bit strapped together. There are these characters that come in and just disappear, and that shouldn't have happened."

One of the most notable lapses in the film's

Linda Hayden puts the evil eye on Barry Andrews.

continuity is the sudden disappearance of the character of Isobel Banham after having her face clawed by Rosalind Barton. She disappears out of the farmhouse door and is never seen again. As Wynne-Simmons explains: "I wanted her to come back and, obviously, it would have been poignant because there was some sort of relationship between her and The Judge. In his process of obliterating everybody, he would have to, of course, obliterate her. That was a decision he would eventually have to take, having discovered she was participating in the rites by then."

As it was, such neat resolutions went by the board in the effort to get the screenplay ready for shooting. As Wynne-Simmons admitted: "What I regret, in a way, was that the script was kind of rushed. From the first of January and coming up with the idea to the first of April was not a long time. It was already mid-February by the time they had decided they would definitely adopt my idea. So we're talking about six weeks to have a script ready to shoot and then adapt the three parts into one."

Although a small sound stage at Pinewood had already been booked for the interiors, the script also stipulated numerous outdoor locations. Tigon were eager to keep the production at the studio to limit costs and suggested utilising the nearby Black Park for exteriors. Haggard, on the other hand, was "desperate to find a place to shoot that would have real magic and poetry."

Haggard was convinced that a sense of place was essential to the aesthetic success of the film, and that utilising such a familiar location as Black Park would only serve to highlight its artificiality. Haggard was trying "to get something real. Trying to attach it to something that feels real, so that the far-fetched story connects with experience, albeit in a hysterical and superstitious way."

The production team eventually found the perfect location at Bix Bottom, a small valley midway between the towns of Nettlebed and Henley-on-Thames in the Chiltern hills. The name Bix was a holdover from the days when the valley was used as a base for the Roman army — specifically the Roman century B IX. Robert Wynne-Simmons sets the scene: "It was one of those little valleys you get quite close to London, which is actually fairly unspoilt. That farmhouse had nothing but a track leading up to it. It's heath land for the most part. There's not much good pasture in that part of the world. It's mostly forest and heath. It was a good location — within reach of Pinewood, where we were based."

Haggard picks up the story: "The exterior of the farm was someone's house. When I saw it, I just fell for it. It had a barn, which was the garage. It didn't require much dressing. (Art director) Arnold Chapkis just put some doors on it and it was a barn again."

As luck would have it, Bix Bottom proved to have everything the team needed in the way of locations. About half a mile from the farmhouse, while they were scouting the area in search of suitable landmarks, the team came upon a small ruined chapel. Haggard realised they had found the ideal place for the children to practice their rituals: "When I saw the old chapel — I don't think the script said that they were in a ruined chapel or anything like that, they were just in the forest — I thought 'Wow!'. The other nice location is the chalk pit where Michele Dotrice is caught by the dogs. That was down by the Thames in the same area."

Despite the producers' reservations about spending

so much time and money away from Pinewood, Haggard held out for the Bix Bottom locations: "I did all a director can do — pleading, cajoling, swearing and stamping — to make sure we got them. It made a gigantic contribution to the film. You could start to feel you could believe it."

But there were other people, aside from the producers, who needed convincing. The valley had officially been designated a nature reserve and the production team had to assure the local authorities that they would behave responsibly during the shoot and not disrupt the land or the wildlife. As Haggard admits: "When we found (Bix), there were some very heart-aching days when we might not have got it. Otherwise there would have had to be some dreadful bodge. I just hung out for it."

Ironically, despite all of Haggard's efforts to avoid familiar locations, Black Park did finally figure in the finished film. "As it did in every film made at Pinewood at the time," laughs Wynne-Simmons. "The wood-chopping scene takes place at Black Park, but the bulk of the film was shot in the valley."

One of the great strengths of *Blood on Satan's Claw* is its sense of place. The landscape is so wild and untended, it could easily be the Yorkshire moors or some bleak outpost down in the West Country. Nor is there any sense of there being a motorway just over the nearest hillside or an electrical pylon just out of shot. The film manages to create — and maintain — a genuine illusion of seventeenth-century England.

Piers Haggard is particularly proud of the way the film captures its period setting: "That wildness was very important... When I look at the film now, there are lots of things I don't like about it. It's inconclusive and very partial. Bits work and other bits don't work at all. But the things that *do* work probably have to do with that."

Another aspect of filming which sets *Blood on Satan's Claw* apart from its contemporaries is the quality of the performances, particularly those of the minor, incidental characters. Rather than just deliver stock rustic performances, each and every member of

*Some genius on the **Shock** advisory board agitated for a caption with 'Bix Bottom' in here. Sorry, but this is a serious publication.*

the cast seems determined to make their character live and breathe, from Linda Hayden as the lascivious nymphet Angel Blake to Howard Goorney as the sceptical town doctor.

Tamara Ustinov, who was making her big screen début in the role of Rosalind Barton, puts that down to Haggard's preferred means of working: "Piers takes enormous trouble with everybody. He makes you feel at your ease and enables you to find things. I'm sure he was like that with everybody."

Simon Williams was particularly impressed with the amount of importance Haggard placed on preparing the actors for filming. Williams had just finished work on *The Breaking of Bumbo* — described by the actor as "another turkey" — and, after a pretty dismal

The only reasons for running this article.

experience making it, was pleasantly surprised that Haggard insisted on rehearsing with his cast prior to shooting.

As he explains: "We had the advantage of being rehearsed for a week or two before shooting, which is such a good thing to do. It gives the actor time to work, without the pressure of the camera crew waiting... It gave us the opportunity to become acquainted, to get used to Piers and let him get used to the sight and sound of us. So often you go on the set and you've only got the time it takes to line up the shot to really bring the whole thing alive."

Although the film was hardly a prestigious production, Haggard managed to attract a remarkable array of talent. Director of photography Dick Bush had recently left the BBC and was looking to establish a foothold in cinema, while Marc Wilkinson, whose haunting musical score adds immeasurably to the film's atmosphere, was, as Haggard describes him, "the composer of choice" at the National Theatre.

While most of the cast would have been familiar to audiences through their television or stage work, only Patrick Wymark could really be considered a household name, mainly due to his starring role in the popular TV series *The Power Game*, while Wendy Padbury would only really have been known to younger viewers for having played Dr Who's companion Zoë. During filming, the producers made the most of the youthful cast by pointing out how many of them came from notable artistic families. Aside from Piers Haggard's literary ancestry, they also trumpeted Tamara Ustinov as being the daughter of Peter Ustinov and the niece of Angela Lansbury, Michele Dotrice as being the daughter of actor Roy Dotrice, Simon Williams as being the son of actor Hugh Williams and Anthony Ainley being the son of actor Henry Ainley.

Blood on Satan's Claw was, as Haggard describes it, "a smallish production", budgeted at around £75,000, which eventually rose to approximately £82,000 by the time it was ready for release. This would be the equivalent of around £1,000,000 were it to be made today. The shooting schedule was, as Robert Wynne-Simmons remembers it, somewhere in the region of eight weeks.

Despite the cost overrun, filming went smoothly. "The overspend was quite modest," Haggard says. "Everyone felt good about the film. They felt it was going to be good. It was *happy*. It felt like something good to do." Wynne-Simmons agrees that it was one of the least traumatic productions he has ever been involved with, mainly due to both the cast and crew being relatively youthful and keen for the film to succeed.

Simon Williams found the script intriguing: "*Witchfinder General* was great. Then there was a spate of rather predictable horror films. This looked like having some sort of quirk to it that made it rather better." Despite his enthusiasm for the film and its director, he had some reservations about working with Tigon: "The whole thing had quite an 'iffy' feel about it. Rumours were going round about Tigon and we were all cashing our cheques quite quickly!"

Wynne-Simmons remained on-hand during much of the shooting. Haggard struck up a good relationship with the writer: "He had a wonderful imagination. A lot of the best things in the film were sequences which he dreamt up in the script and never got changed. He dreamt them up and there they were. Completely scary. One couldn't beat Robert for just inventing way out and terrifying sequences. The claw through the floorboards was a case in point. The way I shot it was not as good as it had been written, I'm sure."

Haggard also remembers that the rest of the cast were most bemused by Wynne-Simmons: "It was so funny. He was very young and pale faced, with big spectacles and a stammer. And he giggled a lot. He was the archetypal hesitant, stammering student at the time. Yet these lurid and murderous conceptions flowed from his brain. It was wonderfully paradoxical that this charming and shy boy had dreamed up these things."

The rest of the cast enjoyed working together on the film, to the extent that many remain in contact to this day. Actress Charlotte Mitchell, who played Ellen, even became godmother to Simon Williams' son, who was born just after the film was released.

One exception to the general *bonhomie* on the set, however, was Patrick Wymark. *Blood on Satan's Claw* was to mark one of his last film appearances; just after the film was completed, he announced that he would be appearing in a stage production of *Sleuth* in Australia and died there just before the play was due to open. Although the official coroner's report stipulated that he had succumbed to a heart attack, rumours persisted that he had actually died of a drug overdose. Of his work on *Blood on Satan's Claw*, Simon Williams says: "He was quite aloof and wasn't particularly warm or friendly."

Wymark's infamy as a heavy drinker was also a cause for concern. As Williams recounts: "That was a problem really. There was scene where he had to thump me one. Tamara had gone insane and I'd gone a bit hysterical, and he had to slap me to get me to pull myself together. We had a very good first assistant director on the film and he said, 'I promise you we'll get the scene in before lunch'. Sadly we couldn't get to it before lunch and we had to do it quite soon afterwards. He did actually hurt me quite a lot."

Tamara Ustinov also had more than her pride hurt in her scenes opposite Avice Landon, although she was more bemused by the incident than upset: "Avice had to give me a slapping and she did it for real. I was absolutely covered in bruises!"

Despite such incidents, Tamara found her first film acting experience highly enjoyable: "The atmosphere was very creative — things like the art direction. They obviously didn't have that much money, but the detail was terrific. Very thoughtfully done."

Of Haggard, she said: "Piers is a wonderful director and very good with actors. He's not one of those people who is purely technical at all. He's immensely empathic to actors. He brings things out of you in a marvellous way."

Piers Haggard places a lot of the film's aesthetic success down to the crew: "Dick Bush was the cameraman and he taught me something that I've used ever since. He said, 'You're shooting these wide shots in the woods, so you must have a dark foreground. Particularly in a horror film, where who knows what might be lurking in the foreground'. It taught me that it was terribly important to identify the highlight in each frame."

Haggard also made another intuitive leap during the making of the film: "I had this very strong feeling that the camera should be at blade of grass level a lot of the time. That the devil is in the ground. The infectious danger, the lethal force, is there in the ground. The best shots in the film, the most interesting shots, are the ones where the camera is absolutely at ground level."

One of the film's most powerful moments is the sequence where the recently infected Tamara Ustinov is brought down from the attic. As she passes by a distraught Simon Williams, she smiles spacily and he catches his first sight of her hand, now a furred claw, resting on the banister. Wynne-Simmons describes that moment as "Piers' best shot in the film. His use of the crane in the stairwell. The coming down and moving up with the crane in the stairwell has a very powerful effect. It seems to pull you in a direction you don't want to be pulled in."

Simon Williams remembers being very impressed with Tamara Ustinov in the scene: "She was unsettling in it. She was very good. She did a strange thing with her eyes. I remember that." Tamara Ustinov laughs at the memory: "It *is* an odd scene. When I started acting it was at Oxford University and I did a lot of 'mad' women there. And I've always enjoyed doing them. I guess I was able to draw on that."

Although generally pleased with Robert Wynne-Simmons work on the script, Haggard did make some substantial additions to the screenplay during the shoot, resulting in an 'additional material' credit. Although he was later to regret his decision, he made some amendments to the dialogue in certain sequences: "The last time I saw the film, one of the things that embarrassed me most was the language. There's a scene where Wendy Padbury is coming through the woods and it's all 'thees' and 'thous'. At the time, I'd thought that they ought to speak in period. Seeing it again, I realised I'd gone too far with the dialogue and it was just cluttered. Five years later, I would have known you just needed a bit of that and you'd be in it, but I was being very literal and trying to rewrite it."

The most notable change made by Haggard was the rape and murder of Cathy Vespers, played by Padbury. "In the original script," explains Wynne-Simmons, "I stopped short of an actual rape. You see Cathy Vespers being dragged off to some horrible ritual and then her body is found later. It was Piers who said, 'Well,

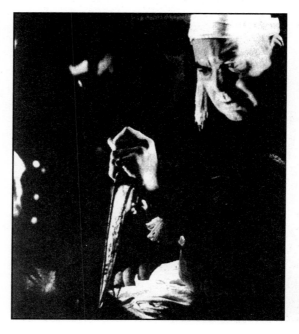

Patrick Wymark cracks open his last cask for a midnight taste.

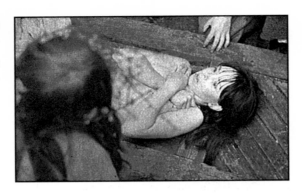

(Right) Wendy Padbury is 'processed'.

(Below) Michele Dotrice shows some skin.

obviously this is what's happening to her, the way it's all been set up' and decided to go through with it."

Haggard acknowledges that the entire sequence was down to him and that most of it was unplanned until the actual day of shooting: "I didn't have the idea of Wendy Padbury being beaten with May blossom — being processed and whipped with May blossom — until the morning of the shoot. It came to me as I went to the location. I noticed that the blossom was out and I cut some. I think it's one of the better ideas in the film. I was trying to devise some rituals that might seem meaningful for ignorant and superstitious people. It was an inversion of the stations of the cross in the Catholic Church. Likewise, the chant was written on the spot."

This chanting finally gave a name to the demon which the children were in the process of recreating. Although it had remained unnamed in the actual screenplay, Haggard christened it Behemoth.

"One was trying to pull together the ingredients," says Haggard, "(from) an imperfect script, not properly researched. Ideally, you'd have taken it away for three months and thought it through and structured it better, brought in real rituals. There was no time for that. It was composed under pressure. So one was grasping after things that might be fun and exciting and spook you in an unusual way."

Although this partially improvised method of composition adds an additional *frisson* to the rape sequence — what begins as a nasty incident of

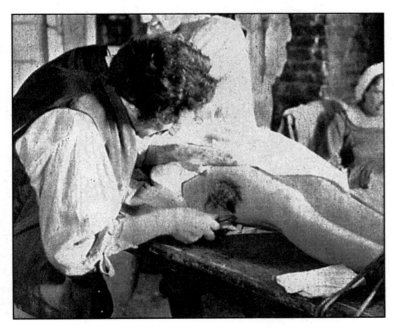

childish bullying abruptly escalates into something far more sinister — the actors were not wholly prepared for the outcome. As Tamara Ustinov recounts: "When they did the rape scene with Wendy Padbury, I remember she got very upset. I think Piers had said, 'Look, you've got to make this really realistic'. And word got out that she actually hadn't enjoyed it at all. I think that maybe it all went a bit far. But looking at what's done now, that's nothing... compared to what films are like now."

Nevertheless, the sequence still has the power to shock, even twenty-five years down the line. It isn't simply the callous eradication of one the film's few sympathetic characters that is so affecting, but rather the pleasure which the other children take in her murder. Watching as Vespers is stabbed, their faces take on an almost sexual anticipation of the event, a fact which is highlighted by their orgasmic chanting.

Although the film was considerably more explicit, in terms of nudity, sex and violence, than most other British horror films of the time, it was only the rape scene which caused the film-makers any censorship problems. John Trevelyan, then Secretary of the British Board of Film Censors, singled it out as a point of concern.

Haggard met with Trevelyan to hear his arguments: "John, with his white hair and his enthusiastic, housemasterly quality, came in and sat in the editing suite and he said, 'The thing is, Piers, it's sex *and* violence. You can have sex. That's alright. Violence is alright. But sex *and* violence... this is what we have to think carefully about. So if you took that out and cut that to that, it would still be quite good. It's just that thing with the pain and the sex.'"

Haggard felt Trevelyan's criticism was "very fair." Of Trevelyan he has this to say: "He liked the film and thought it was good. He did his best to suggest cuts which he could feel comfortable with but which wouldn't actually spoil the thing. I think there were six or eight seconds taken out. Nothing major."

Although Haggard followed Trevelyan's advice over reframing the sequence, Robert Wynne-Simmons still has his doubts about the scene: "It's always dogged me ever since and, even to this day, I don't know where I stand on it, because I do find it very disturbing to watch. Even now. It's very unpleasant to think that there might be people who get turned on by it. That has always worried me."

Nor does Wynne-Simmons think that the censors achieved their purpose in toning down the sequence. "They never insisted that the rape scene be removed, they simply asked that the amount of footage of the rape was cut down. The result of this is that the scene is very much more horrifying and more disturbing than it was originally. The result of the censor's intervention was to make the scene more censorable, in my mind. Because what you then have is a scene with a rape which is largely played out on the faces of the people watching it."

Beyond this sequence, the film sailed through the censors, complete with a surprisingly explicit sequence where the (supposedly) pubescent Angel Blake disrobes in an attempt to seduce Reverend Fallowfield. "Heaven and Earth had shifted," Haggard says. "The pendulum had swung. So much so that it wasn't a proper film unless some poor girl took her knickers off. Our nude scene was very much a token concession to the tastes of the time."

(According to reports, both Linda Hayden's full frontal nude scene and a sequence featuring a naked dancer at the end of the film were both apparently darkened to reduce their impact for the American print of *Satan's Skin*.)

Oddly enough, when the film was finally released, fewer people commented on the rape scene than the infinitely milder sequence where the doctor slices off the patch of furred skin from the thigh of Michele Dotrice. More surprisingly, even the staunchest horror fans condemned the film for its viciousness.

Haggard was taken slightly aback by the audience reaction: "I was new to all this at the time and it was interesting. I remember after screenings of the film, people would come out very shaky. It was, in a way, slightly stronger meat. Perhaps because of the lyrical side of it, or the fact that it purports to be real, it attempts to get under your skin. It's not just a sit-back-and-enjoy-it good old horror film... which possibly made it more disturbing."

Other viewers voiced dissatisfaction at the film's conclusion, unsure as to whether good or evil had emerged triumphant. Haggard only partially accepts such criticism: "I think if one had scripted it properly, one might have sorted that out. It's my instinct to make things ambiguous, which may be why the film didn't 'work' in the marketplace... Probably, if you were analysing it toughly, you'd have to say that the film is undecided. But it seemed better to me to be undecided than to be boring."

Simon Williams was surprised by the quality of the finished film and by the fact that it did not exactly conform to his expectations: "There was something slightly erotic about the whole thing. It was quite an erotic film. I can't remember being aware of that when we were shooting."

While the horror fans failed to support the film, critical response was, on the whole, favourable. Vincent Canby in the *New York Times* wrote '*Blood on Satan's Claw* is cinematic diabolism of some style and intelligence... a horror movie of more than routine interest.' Judith Crist remarked that it 'offers a satisfying sense of sunlight-and-terror.' Closer to home, *Films and Filming* magazine noted: 'For a pleasant variation on the usual unsubtle, corny examples of the current British horror genre, this is one for the collectors.' Sadly, this critical praise was not enough to transform the film into a hit at the box office.

"It slipped out a bit," says Piers Haggard of the finished film. "It didn't do as well as *Witchfinder General*. I think it fell between two stools. Although there was horror in it, it wasn't a slightly cynical, slightly campy, plenty-of-gore horror film. So people who went for that didn't get what they'd gone for. And although we put 'quality' into it, finally it was a fairly leaky structure and probably doesn't provide a completely convincing experience. So it didn't do very well. I guess it probably made its money back, because it sold around the world. It does keep popping up."

Nevertheless, Haggard does have a fondness for the film: "We did our best in the time that there was. Being rather young and quite inexperienced — I know so much more about the structure of scripts than I did then — but for me, whatever is good about it arises from that sense of emotional involvement in the world... For me, the film was poetic. One did one's best with the bits that were blatantly commercial, but there were all those other bits that were able to be haunting in a rich way."

He laughs: "It all sounds pretentious, because when I see the film now, I just see great holes in it. Things that seem fake and things that seem clumsy or slow or badly handled. But that is what we were striving for... Whether or not it worked, it was fresh."

Was Robert Wynne-Simmons happy with the way his script had translated to film? "On the whole, yes. I've worked on other things since where my work as a writer has been directed by someone else, where I definitely haven't felt happy about it... I can still get a *frisson* from watching the film, even now. Which is surprising, really."

Despite — or perhaps because of — its oddness and ambiguity, *Blood on Satan's Claw* has, after twenty-five years, finally established a small cult following. As Simon Williams says: "At worst, it doesn't quite know what it's doing in places... It's rather like one of those freak successes, like *Blow Up*, that becomes a success because of it actually being a mess."

Williams adds: "I always say that it's the film which has given me the title of my autobiography. There was a scene where I wake up and find my hand infected by the devil, with fur on it, and then I cut it off. They had a little insert shot of my hand reaching for the dagger and I was doing a lot of business of inching my fingers forward and twitching them. Piers said, 'Cut! Cut! Cut! Simon, don't overact with your fingers'. Which I thought would make a good title!" ∎

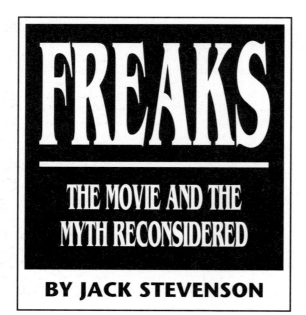

FREAKS

THE MOVIE AND THE MYTH RECONSIDERED

BY JACK STEVENSON

In the annals of Hollywood film-making, no movie bears a stranger legacy than the 1932 'monster' movie *Freaks*. Like its creaking circus wagons, *Freaks* rolled through the decades over bumpy ground, trundling on through the twilight and into the darkness — emerging in the morning light of a new day to be discovered once again, dragging along the horrified and fascinated in its wake.

It travelled alone, rejected by its creators, the mad script doctors, moguls and magic-makers of depression-era Hollywood. It travelled apart from any specific film genre or movement, simultaneously damned and blessed as a true freak of movie-making by the bewildered critics and crowds that witnessed its first mutant birth. It appeared and disappeared again, and each new generation watched it with the same astonishment as the previous one. It became more than a movie — it became a myth, a relic of long lost carney black magic, and around it swirled shards of stories and rumours, shattered careers and dashed dreams, as well as memories grown old yet still radiant.

First stop: 12 July 1882.

Charles Browning Jr is born in Louisville, Kentucky to Charles and Lydia Browning. Decent God-fearing folks.

At sixteen years of age, young Charles ran away from home with the travelling circus and took the nickname 'Tod'. Tod Browning, as he became known, worked a variety of carnival acts and scams over the next several years, everything from clown and escape artist to barker for a fake 'Wild Man of Borneo' — actually a Negro from Mississippi in outlandish make-up. Browning also worked as a 'living corpse.' This was a morbid bit of hokum pitched to rubes and gawkers who would pay to see a man buried six feet underground in a wooden casket. The casket was equipped with a hidden ventilation system to keep the 'corpse' alive and a tube-like optical device allowed customers to see the entombed man. Browning also worked the vaudeville circuit as a singer, dancer and comedian.

In 1913, at the age of thirty-one, Browning landed an acting role in a two-reel comedy called *Scenting a Terrible Crime*, shot at the Bronx-based Biograph studio. Soon after that he travelled to Hollywood, where he branched out into directing. In 1916 he worked as an assistant director on the D. W. Griffith classic *Intolerance*, and wrote the script for the cocaine cult-comedy classic *The Mystery of the Leaping Fish*, supervised by Griffith and starring Douglas Fairbanks Sr as the coke-snorting detective, Coke Enneyday. Browning later went on to direct a series of his own more-or-less routine adventures and melodramas for MGM. One of his more notable films during this period was the 1923 mystery thriller, *Drifting*, a tale of an American girl in China who doubles as an opium smuggler, starring Priscilla Dean, Wallace Beery and Anna May Wong: by this stage Browning had worked with some of the top acting talent of the silent era.

Shortly after *Drifting*, Browning began a two-year losing battle with the bottle that would see his film career grind to a halt. His fondness for Kentucky whiskey cost him his contract with Universal and put a serious strain on his marriage.

In 1925 he began work on his 'comeback picture,' *The Unholy Three*, with MGM. It was based on a thriller by popular period author Clarence 'Tod' Robbins, recounting the tale of three circus performers off on a crime spree — a milieu Browning was at home with. Lon 'The Man of a 1,000 Faces' Chaney was cast as the ventriloquist, while the midget was played by German-born dwarf Harry Earles, with Victor McLaglen weighing in as the Strong Man.

The Unholy Three was a stunning success, 'one of 1925's ten best pictures' declared *The New York Times*. Sweet vindication. Tod Browning's star was on the rise.

In 1930 Browning returned to Universal Studios to direct his most famous film, *Dracula*, under the watchful eye of production chief Carl Laemmle Jr. *Dracula* starred Hungarian-born stage actor Bela Lugosi, and despite its technical and artistic flaws became an enduring popular and financial success, confirming Browning's position in the top rank of Hollywood directors.

Universal already had another 'monster movie' in development, a thing called *Frankenstein* that James Whale was to direct. Boris Karloff would star. This monster stuff was coming on strong: audiences loved it, critics generally deplored it and the box-office boomed. A new genre was being born.

Noting the financial success of *Dracula*, MGM was more than happy to welcome Browning back into the fold. Browning promised to deliver the "ultimate horror picture," and production boss Irving Thalberg gave the go-ahead to what would become *Freaks*. The film had actually been in the works since November 1929, when MGM announced in the trade press that Browning's next film would be a 'sideshow' picture. The idea reportedly originated from a suggestion, by Browning's old friend Harry Earles, that he explore the possibilities of adapting the Tod Robbins story 'Spurs' for the screen.

In 1923, Francophile Robbins had published the short story in *Munsey's Magazine*. In 1929, MGM paid Robbins $8,000 for the film rights to 'Spurs.' Despite the tinkering of at least four script and dialogue writers (Willis Goldbeck, Leon Gordon, Edgar Allan Woolf and Al Boasberg) and the input of Browning himself, very strong similarities between the story and film remain, and a direct comparison is useful to understand the genesis of the movie.

'Spurs' is the tale of French circus dwarf Jacques Courbé, who falls in love with the voluptuous, daring bareback rider Jeanne Marie, a 'tall blonde of the Amazon type' who performs in tandem with the 'swarthy, Herculean' Simon Lafleur. At first glance 'Jeanne Marie's buxom charms, so generously revealed in tights and spangles, made Jacques flush and cast down his eyes.' The bodily acrobatic contact between Jeanne Marie and Simon make his 'blood boil.'

Jacque's act was a buffoonish parody of Jeanne Marie's: he too circled the ring bareback, yet his mount was no stallion but a large wolfish mongrel dog

(Above) *Tod Browning in a car.*

(Previous page) *Olga Baclanova uses the government-approved method of midget selection.*

(Above) Tod Browning.

(Below) You'd feel like Harry Earles if you knew you were going to appear in **The Terror of Tiny Town**.

named St Eustache... His nightly ritual of humiliation was greeted by waves of derisive laughter and flying banana peels rather than the cheers and applause sparked off by the derring-do of the two big people.

Suddenly left a fortune by a deceased relative, Jacques proposes marriage to Jeanne Marie since he can now keep her in grand style. Initially plunged into a paroxysm of hilarious disbelief, she composes herself and agrees: struck by the notion that dwarves die young, she would be able to leave the circus with Simon and live in luxury.

A wedding feast is held in the circus tent. The revelry soon degenerates into a grotesque drunken brawl between the egotistical freaks. Jeanne Marie's contempt for 'the little ape' explodes in torrents of abuse and ridicule. She perches the helplessly intoxicated Jacques atop her shoulders like a marmoset for the stroll back to the country estate, boasting that she could carry him 'from one end of France to the other.'

A year later, Jeanne Marie pays a surprise visit to Simon Lafleur, who doesn't recognise her. She's gaunt, haggard and shockingly aged. Jacques has kept her a virtual prisoner with the aid of St Eustache, riding her like a beast of burden with spurs on his boots, each day counting off the leagues that would constitute 'the width of France.'

At that very moment the dwarf and dog trot silently through the house to Simon's room. Nothing can be heard, but Jeanne Marie can sense it with growing terror. Suddenly Jacques and St Eustache enter the room and the jealous dwarf orders his vicious mount to attack the scoffing Strong Man. Jacques administers the fatal *coup-de-grâce* to Simon with a well placed thrust of his tiny sword and re-imprisons a doomed and defeated Jeanne Marie.

The movie *Freaks*, by contrast, is the story of Hans, a midget in Mme Tetrallini's travelling circus in France, who is engaged to Frieda, a midget bareback rider. But Hans is really infatuated with the beautiful Cleopatra, a sexy trapeze performer engaged in a love affair with the Strong Man, Hercules.

Cleopatra secretly ridicules the midget's amorous attentions, but after she learns he has inherited a fortune from a rich uncle, she plots to marry him, poison him and run away with Hercules and the money.

The broken-hearted Frieda confides her troubles to Phroso, the clown, and to Venus, the seal tamer. Despite their warnings to Hans, he marries Cleopatra.

The wedding feast is held in the circus tent. Cleopatra humiliates the quickly inebriated Hans by openly carrying on with Hercules. All the freaks are at the feast and in a jubilant mood. They vote to adopt Cleopatra as one of them since she is now the wife of a midget. The bizarre congregation of celebrants pass around a goblet of wine and chant "Gobble, gobble, we accept her, one of us..."

"Dirty slimy freaks! Make me want to puke!" she screams in revulsion and storms out.

Cleopatra subsequently secretly feeds Hans poison as he lies ill in bed, but is observed by the freaks who've discovered her plot. On a thundering, stormy, rain-swept night as the circus wagons travel to the next town, the freaks attack Cleopatra and Hercules, crawling and slithering through the rain and mud in one of the most amazing scenes of horror cinema. They mutilate Cleopatra (off camera), turning her into a squawking, legless, broken-nosed and partially blind chicken-like creature, and — according to the rarely seen original ending — castrate Hercules, who is shown singing in a high pitched voice.

The setting and plot similarities between story and film remain strong. The overtones of sexual frustration between Jacques and Jeanne Marie, and between Hans and Cleopatra, are very much out front in both versions.

The freaks too are attributed some type of almost supernatural power beyond the comprehension of 'normals'; in a somewhat similar fashion, Hollywood in the thirties and forties bestowed the power of secret malevolent knowledge beyond the grasp of Caucasians upon Chinese characters. Special power is attributed to Jacques Courbé and his dog, whom he raised after finding as a pup in a Paris gutter. Together in physical tandem they control Jeanne Marie. Similarly, *Freaks'* climatic scene shows them moving inexorably towards their doomed victims with a supernatural sense of purpose and unity, guided by something akin to magic. Something beyond our knowing.

A striking difference between film and story is that in 'Spurs' the freaks attack one another (at the wedding banquet) in a brawl that is both vicious and ridiculous, while in *Freaks* they are depicted as members of a secret social order, with their own codes of conduct, language and traditions. This idea of freaks as members of a closed fraternal order was very much in tune with the outlook of Browning and neatly dovetailed with Hollywood's hunger for myth-making.

Freaks lived apart from society, even other circus performers, Browning would explain upon release of the film, and "learning their customs, language and traditions is exceedingly difficult. When I was with the circus, years ago, I worked for months trying to gain their confidence, and even then I learned very little."

Over the centuries, Browning elaborated, "freaks developed a gibberish language of their own" (some of which was said to be included in the film). Midgets were particularly exotic in Browning's view. He claimed that most of them "come from the Carpathian mountains in Austria, where some climatic or other conditions seems to affect the ductless glands of the body in a way that arrests growth... there are whole villages of them in Austria, carrying on with all kinds of activities."

Today this type of talk sounds like naked exploitation, but in the context of the times it was just standard carney hokum, the usual expected stuff, not that far away from what Browning had spieled when he pitched the 'Wild Man of Borneo' in his younger days. *Freaks* was in fact pitched more like a freak show than a horror movie. The promotional hype weaved in and out of fact and fantasy in an effort to portray the freaks as exotic, fantastic and other-worldly.

The Making of *Freaks*

Freaks was shot from mid-October to December 1931. In the meantime disquiet grew within the censorship community about this new breed of 'horror' film. On 5 December 1931, Hollywood Production Code enforcer Jason S. Joy communicated his growing apprehension to boss Will Hays: 'Perhaps it would be wise to obtain an early estimate of the audience reaction and critical opinion concerning *Dracula* and *Frankenstein* by Universal (and) *Dr. Jekyll and Mr. Hyde* by Paramount... All of which are in distribution or about to be distributed. Paramount has another 'gruesome' picture about to be put into production, and Metro-Goldwyn-Mayer has *Freaks* which is about one-half shot. Is this the beginning of a cycle that ought to be retarded or killed? I am anxious to receive your advice.'

In casting *Freaks*, Browning sought out genuine freaks for many of the roles, employing the ultimate make-up man: God. Browning had often worked with the original make-up genius, Lon Chaney, and he very likely deemed this the only way possible to go 'beyond.' MGM was bombarded with hundreds of photos and résumés from hopeful side-show performers. The final cast would feature the most remarkable assemblage of freaks to appear in one movie.

There was Prince Randian, 'The Living Torso', a limbless Negro from British Guyana who rolls and lights a cigarette with his teeth. There was Pete Robinson ('The Living Skeleton') and Olga Roderick ('The Bearded Lady'), along with Martha Morris ('The Armless Beauty') and Joseph/Josephine, the half-man/half-woman. Five pinheads (microcephalics) appeared in the picture: Zip, Pip, Elvira Snow and sister Jenny Lee Snow, and the ever popular Schlitzie.

Many of the film's freaks would go on to various roles in other movies. German midgets Harry and Daisy ('The Midget Mae West') Earles would later be cast, along with their whole family, as Munchkins in the classic *The Wizard of Oz*. Harry Earles would also feature in the 1938 all-midget western, *The Terror of Tiny Town*. English-born Siamese twins Daisy and Violet Hilton would star in the 1950 exploitation film *Chained for Life*, while Johnny Eck, the charismatic 'half boy' born without a lower body, would play a hideous bird creature in the original *Tarzan the Ape Man* produced by MGM.

The most prolific actor from among the *Freaks* alumni was dwarf Angelo Rossitto, who later appeared in many of Monogram's low-budget forties thrillers, and also acted in such films as *Child Bride of the Ozarks*, *The Wizard of Oz*, *Mesa of Lost Women*, *Dementia*, *The Trip*, *Dracula vs Frankenstein* and *Brain of Blood*. Angelo stayed active throughout the seventies and into the eighties. His last substantial role was in *Mad Max Beyond the Thunderdome*, in which he added Tina Turner to a list of co-stars that included Bela Lugosi, Boris Karloff, Lon Chaney Jr and Vincent Price.

But despite a long list of post-1932 film credits, the freaks who starred in Tod Browning's production would first and foremost be ever-more identified with that movie.

Casting the 'normals' proved more difficult. Victor McLaglen was first choice to play Hercules, but was never signed. Irving Thalberg had originally wanted Myrna Loy for the role of Cleopatra, and Jean Harlow was first choice for the role of Venus, but both opted out.

Olga Baclanova, 'a fading silent screen vamp' and former member of the Moscow Art Theatre, was finally

(Below) The most frequently seen, but still effective, publicity shot from **Freaks**.

cast as Cleopatra. Baclanova liked the script but Browning wisely thought it best that she should meet the cast first. She was introduced to Harry Earles. Both spoke German and got on well. "Then he shows me a girl," Baclanova recalled, "that's like an orangutan... Then a man who has a head but no legs, no nothing, just a head and a body like an egg... He shows me little by little and I could not look, I wanted to faint. I wanted to cry."

Eventually Baclanova grew accepting: "It was very, very difficult first time... I couldn't look at them... It hurt me like a human being. How lucky I was. But after that I started to be used to them." All except one, though, "who was like a monkey. She goes crazy sometimes." (One account of the filming mentions a pinhead being "chained to his keeper.")

Strange encounters with the freaks on the set extended beyond cast and crew. Writer F. Scott Fitzgerald had been working on a script for MGM — he desperately needed the money to pay the costs of keeping his wife Zelda in a sanitarium. At a producer's

Joseph/Josephine in **Freaks**.

party, the intoxicated Fitzgerald made a fool of himself by singing an endless off-key song to the mortification of other guests. He realised he might well be fired: the studio was aware of his alcoholism and had hired him with hesitation. (He would, in fact, be let go within a week.) The following day Fitzgerald had lunch at the MGM commissary with screenwriter Dwight Taylor. Upon entering, Fitzgerald and Taylor found it to be full of freaks. "This must have added considerably to Scott's distraught frame of mind," Taylor would later recollect. "Scott and I had no sooner seated ourselves than the Hilton sisters, a pair of Siamese twins joined at the waist, entered and took a single seat at the same table. One of them picked up the menu and without even looking at the other, asked 'what are you going to have?' Scott turned pea-green and, putting his hand to his mouth, rushed for the great outdoors."

The production of *Freaks* was plagued by controversy in all quarters. Louis B. Mayer insisted the movie be filmed with a low profile and was reportedly incensed that Thalberg had even approved such a travesty. Producer Harry Rapf agitated to abort it, but director Jack Conway supported Thalberg (in a rather backhanded fashion): "Irving's right so often he's earned the right to be wrong."

As a compromise all the freaks except the Earles and the Hilton sisters were removed from the commissary to 'separate but equal' dining quarters closer to the set.

Film editor Basil Wrangell was another unhappy voice around the studio: "It was bad enough to see the freaks during the day when you'd go down on the set or have to go by their eating quarters, but when you had to look at it on the moviola for eighteen hours a day, it was enough to make you crawl up the walls."

Yet the shock and revulsion was all part and parcel of the horror movie that *Freaks* was conceived to be, and calls to mind the old adage: 'Be careful what you ask for — you might get it.' Thalberg himself, after reading an initial script treatment, had reportedly dropped his head in his hands and exclaimed, "I asked for something horrifying and I got it!"

Had the shooting script been faithfully followed, the film would have emerged with an even more caustic edge. Judging from a detailed synopsis of the script, certain scenes were later 'softened' during filming. The famous "Gooble gobble" wedding banquet scene, for example, was originally envisioned to include the freaks drooling into the loving cup of wine when it was passed around the table, to heighten the sense of nausea.

Freaks was completed and readied for distribution in early 1932. The finished product was a flawed masterpiece of the bizarre, couched, however, firmly in period genre stylisations. Its main drawback was the limited-to-non-existent acting ability of the freaks. Certain lines of the dialogue uttered by Prince Randian and Schlitzie are not only unconvincing but utterly incomprehensible. Baclanova's heavy Russian accent and the Earles' German accents further hampered the dramatic flow and contributed to a stilted effect.

Film historian David Skal speculates as to whether *Freaks* would have been more successful commercially and artistically 'as the silent film it was originally intended to be. The freaks' glaring deficiencies in reading dialogue would have been obviated, and the heightened stylisations of the silents, with the formality of intertitles and continual musical accompaniment, could have done so much to cushion viewer response.'

Yet the film overcomes these drawbacks with a

A MATCH FOR THE DEVIL HIMSELF
Directed by Tod Browning

strong storyline and bold, unflinching portrayals of the freaks themselves, which this writer views as a strength, not a weakness. Three scenes stand out in *Freaks* as classics of American sound cinema: the much discussed wedding banquet; the concluding storm scene where the freaks close in on Cleopatra and Hercules; and an early scene where Mme Tetrallini takes her 'children' for a romp in a sunny wooded glade. There is a sense of visual poetry to these scenes that attest to the talent of cinematographer Merritt B. Gerstad.

Freaks Unveiled

On initial release the film provoked an extreme response from critics — much of it damning. 'Mr Browning has always been an expert in pathological morbidity,' praised the *Herald Tribune* in backhanded fashion, 'but after seeing *Freaks*, his other films seem like whimsical nursery tales.' 'The difficulty,' chimed in the *New York Times*, 'is in telling whether it should be shown in the Rialto Theatre — where it opened yesterday — or in, say, the Medical Centre.' To the critic at *Harrison's Reports* it was 'so loathsome that I'm nauseated thinking about it.' At its San Diego première a woman literally ran screaming from the theatre.

Freaks and Universal's *Murders in the Rue Morgue* opened simultaneously in Washington D.C. in February 1932, prompting dire speculation from the *Washington Post* on the public's growing appetite for all things morbid: 'Those neurotic individuals who find agreeable occupation in following ambulances and pursuing fire engines find themselves, at the present moment, the beneficiaries of an era in the motion picture theatres dedicated largely to them and their quaint amusement tastes' (critic Nelson Bell).

Other critics praised the film, however ironically. 'Pure sensationalism, *Freaks* tops any picture yet produced,' wrote famous Hollywood gossip columnist Louella Parsons. 'I came into the Criterion Theatre from the gaiety of Mrs Gardner Sullivan's luncheon party and I felt as if I had suddenly fallen asleep and were having a weird nightmare... *Freaks* is a picture so different the public will want to see it.'

The *Motion Picture Herald* ran one of the earliest assessments of *Freaks* on 23 January 1932. 'That the production is bold and novel in conception and execution is unquestioned,' the trade paper contended, simultaneously expressing serious doubts about the 'taste that prompted it'.

And as for the even more important public response...

Variety weighed in after *Freaks* finally opened in New York in July: 'Planned by Metro to be one of the sensational pictures of the season, *Freaks* failed to qualify in the sure-fire category and has been shown in most parts of the country with astonishingly variable results. In spots it has been a clean-up. In others it was merely misery.'

Freaks encountered censorship problems as the new wave of 'horror' movies began to share the heat with the likes of sexy Mae West, then reddening the complexions of Production Code enforcers with films like *Night after Night*. The notoriously tough New York State censor board clipped nearly thirty minutes, and it was banned outright in a number of countries, including Britain where it wouldn't show until 1963. Baxter Phillips states in his book *Cut — The Unseen Cinema*, that *Freaks* was killed world-wide by censorship. This had to compound MGM's unhappiness since foreign receipts alone could make or break a picture.

Freaks was a money loser. Not only that, but it was an embarrassment to Mayer and other top brass at the studio who had disliked it from early on. *Freaks* had also been a gamble, and gambling was bad business for any studio in the midst of the Great Depression. Theatre attendance in general had gradually declined since 1930, and in 1932 it fell sharply. By the end of 1932, weekly attendance figures were off forty percent from 1929 and almost twenty percent of America's movie theatres had closed their doors. MGM remained solvent, but rumours of studio shut downs and massive layoffs abounded.

Freaks was yanked from distribution and banished to a purgatory few major studio films have ever known. At one point rumour had it that the film ceased to exist, the negative having been unceremoniously dumped into San Francisco Bay.

Popular wisdom says that *Freaks* destroyed Tod Browning's career and ruined him personally. This surely seems an over-dramatic reading of the facts, since Browning's alcohol problems were already well documented, plus he worked for eight more years, directing for MGM *Fast Workers*, *Mark of the Vampire*, *The Devil Doll* and his final film, *Miracles for Sale* in 1939. He did some scenario work for MGM, finally retiring to Malibu in 1942. Browning never officially spoke about *Freaks* after its release, but, at the very least, it must have been a massive disappointment for him. Upon his death, *The New York Times'* obituary didn't even mention *Freaks*...

It's Alive!

Freaks appeared to be stone cold dead, lying interred in a state of oblivion throughout the 1930s and well into the forties. But the coffin lid was slightly ajar and in 1948 America's most devious and demonic roadshow exploitationist, Dwain Esper, got his clutches on the cadaver and reanimated it with some of his patented carney voodoo — equal parts canned lightning and electrified press overkill. In the manner of Frankenstein's monster, *Freaks* rose from the grave, receiving a new face (via new ad campaigns and two new titles) and a sloppy organ transplant in the form of new footage of freaks, unrelated to the movie, that Esper reportedly 'dumped' in.

Born in 1893 (some accounts list 1899), Esper served in World War One and worked as a successful building contractor before starting out in movies by producing six-reel silent westerns. Esper's plunge into exploit-

Tod Browning's production

FREAKS

Do the Siamese Twins make love?

Can a full-grown woman truly love a midget?

Do the Pin-Heads think?

What sex is the Half-Man, Half-Woman?

THE BIG EXPLOITATION NOVELTY SENSATION of the Year!

YOUR CHANCE!

Frieda (Daisy Earles, Harry's sister) performs.

rapscallion like Esper, one must remember that this was long before TV, cable or video extended the life of a movie. Once a film had played itself out on the first-run theatrical circuit, in most cases it was history. A rare full-blown 'revival' or the exploitation circuits were the only options left to renew a film's financial viability. Esper had bought the rights to other films as well, including *The Good Earth*.

For the better part of a decade, Esper toured *Freaks* on the roadshow circuit, playing seedy vaudeville and burlesque theatres, sleazy skid row dives and any rural small town flea-trap that would have him. He also flogged it on the low-rent end of the new 'drive-in' movie circuit, where teenagers and hopeful perverts could watch a film encased in the anonymity of their automobiles.

Esper changed the name from *Freaks* to *Forbidden Love* and then *Nature's Mistakes*, designing an avalanche of sensationalistic posters and press that emphasised the sleazy and abnormal sexual element that the movie itself hardly warranted. *Freaks* was being pitched as a shameless come-on to winos, horny sailors, hot-blooded teenagers and unclassifiable degenerates now lured into theatres to catch glimpses of nudity contained nowhere in the film.

Exploitation movie producer and film historian, David F. Friedman, recalls meeting Esper in 1949 at an unpaved, backroad drive-in theatre outside Charlotte, North Carolina, where Esper was showing *Freaks* as *Forbidden Love*.

"Esper's ads guaranteed a plethora of prurience. An all-day downpour didn't deter carnality-crazed Carolinians from filling the muddy movie pen... Esper calmly averted a near riot in the mudhole that night. After seeing *Freaks/Forbidden Love*, and not seeing any skin, the audience of lusting degenerates began to demonstrate noisily.

'Here, put this on!' Esper commanded the projectionist, handing over his 'square-up' reel, a ten-minute nudist camp frolic that displayed extensive epidermis, both male and female — something for everybody. The sex fiends satisfied, they departed the drive-in harmoniously, leaving the property intact."

Esper used other approaches with the film, as Friedman goes on to describe: "Ever the evil-genius showman, Esper framed a combination 'movie-live' presentation, contracting a troupe of human oddities, headed by circus sideshow veteran, Sam 'The Man With No Face' Alexander, to travel with the picture. Esper sold and ran it like a tent show, hanging canvas banners on theatre fronts. The performers (freaks) worked from high stands in the lobbies, the floors of which Esper had covered with sawdust. He kept that unit on the road for five years. It worked like a charm."

Esper's conjure-job on *Freaks* hardly constituted a 'revival', however. It was more like a zombie death march. In urban areas the film played the sleaziest grindhouses double-billed with films like *Curucu, Beast of the Amazon*, *Hot Money Girl* or one of Esper's own grade-Z productions. On the roadshow circuit he flogged it through small country towns and outback hillbilly bergs, many in the deep south. The critics, scholars, students of cinema — they were not writing about *Freaks* — they likely didn't even know it was still being shown. It was playing to a whole separate, isolated demographic, hard to envision in a world of modern mass media where on any given day the whole country is watching the same TV episode. Had highbrow critics and cinéastes been made aware that

ation cinema came when he met and married a slight, blonde woman of German extraction named Hildegarde, who would faithfully assist him as a stage lecturer and scriptwriter throughout their long odyssey together. Hildegarde was no stranger herself to the seamy side of show business, having begun her career at the age of eight when she shilled as a snake charmer for an uncle who sold snake oil from the back of a horse-drawn wagon. She met Esper thirteen years later when he was working as a motorcycle stuntman and she was employed as a 'stringer' for the *L.A. Times*. A few years later, inspired by the death of her dope-addicted physician uncle, Hildegarde presented a script for a film called *Narcotic* to Dwain, suggesting they produce it themselves. They did, releasing *Narcotic* in 1932 to great success that followed it on the grindhouse and roadshow circuits into the fifties. At the peak of *Narcotic*'s popularity in the late thirties and early forties, Esper exhibited, as an added attraction, the embalmed body of 'Elmer the Dope Fiend'. Here was the perfect marriage between movies and the 'live' (or just as often 'dead') element of the circus sideshow that Esper would bring into play so successfully with *Freaks*.

In 1948 Esper leased the rights to *Freaks* from MGM for a reportedly paltry sum. If it seems unbelievable that a major studio would sell the rights so cheaply (if it hadn't been cheap he wouldn't have bought it) to a

Freaks was still being shown, they would have scoffed. It was as 'out', forgotten and buried as a movie could be.

In 1956, a wealthy San Francisco cinéaste, Mrs Willy Werby, was preparing a horror film retrospective to be screened as part of the Camera Obscura Film Society which she headed. The show was to be entitled 'History of the Macabre' and to consist of a programme of short compilation clips along with one yet-to-be-selected feature film. Friends of Werby's, local film aficionados Val and Claire Golding, referred her to the famous Satanist, Anton LaVey, who also lived in San Francisco and was at the time engaged in psychic research, ghost hunting and playing the organ at Morray's Point. LaVey had a highly specialised knowledge of (and personal interest in) esoteric horror films and saw this as an opportunity to unearth *Freaks* — a film Werby had never heard of — and give it its proper recognition in the context of classic horror cinema. Werby was fascinated by what LaVey told her and decided that *Freaks* should be selected as the feature film for History of the Macabre.

LaVey had always appreciated the satanic qualities of the film. He was himself part of the carney netherworld from which *Freaks* had come. It was a realm of hallucination where beauty and hideousness merged, then reformed and refocused into the component elements of horror and desire. The carnival was a cauldron of fear, pity, lust, repugnance, terror and laughter — base human emotions stirred and manipulated by horror show magicians who played to the bawling masses and mixed their tricks with the crowd's hysteria to produce magic. That the magicians could also be film editors, directors and cinematographers, LaVey was well aware. He saw film itself as basically an act, going back to the earliest movie projectors like the Kinetoscope and Vitascope — devices of awe and illusion, plain and simple. Film was something dangerously potent, a beam of light with a direct line to the psyche and the soul... A medium capable of magnificent heresy.

Cinema remains one of LaVey's great passions, especially early exploitation cinema which shared the milieu, techniques and aesthetics of the travelling carnival. *Freaks*, then, became to LaVey something of a sacred artefact. He had given the film his personal blessings and was acquainted with several of the freaks in the movie. To this day he retains an intense and not entirely decipherable connection to *Freaks*. On a recent visit to his famous all-black house in San Francisco's fog-shrouded Hill district, this writer saw him emerge from his basement, via a concealed stairway through a swing-out fireplace, lugging a complete set of 100 original studio stills, along with an armful of original one-sheet posters and a stack of yellowed press clippings documenting practically the entire life of the film.

Werby began to search for a print, but found nothing. By 1956-57 *Freaks* was truly a 'lost' film. Some people had heard rumours about it, most had never seen it. Werby called attorneys at MGM, who knew almost nothing about the film's present status and seemed to care less. They weren't sure where it was or who had the rights.

She recalls following "lots of false leads" in her efforts to locate it, including attempts to deal with Warwick Films — a non-existent company Dwain Esper had created as a dodge of some sort. Raymond Rohauer, a film distributor of notoriously shady repute, was also trying to locate the film and joined in

the wild goose chase. Werby found the address of a New York City theatre on the back of a *Freaks* still and they finally connected her with Dwain Esper. At last.

Werby bought the rights from Esper for a sum reportedly around $5,000. She remembers meeting Esper to seal the deal. He seemed somewhat 'desperate', down on his luck, like he'd seen better days. He made a transparent attempt to hide his enthusiasm at the sale. He was obviously eager, happy to get 5,000 smackers for a 'dead horse'. There was something of the smell of *Death of a Salesman* about him, Werby recalls.

Freaks had exhausted itself on the exploitation circuit. Esper hadn't shown it in years; finding a good print proved difficult. No attempts at proper preservation had been made (to say the least) and many of the 35mm nitrate prints had badly degraded. The search for a good print led to alleyway warehouses and the musty back rooms of decrepit movie palaces. Finally, a good print was found in the basement of Pete DeCenzie's El Rey Burlesque Theatre in Oakland, from which a negative was made.

Under Werby's guidance *Freaks* began occasional screenings at university, museum cinema and film society-type venues. This constituted the first step in its emergence from Esper's long whiskey-soaked night of exploitation roadshowing. The revival had quietly begun. Werby sold the rights to Raymond Rohauer shortly thereafter for $15,000 and he distributed the film, along with Myron Bresnick who had 'non-theatrical' rights, until rights reverted back to MGM. Rohauer specialised in unsuccessful revivals of older films, Werby recalls, though he later did well with some Buster Keaton material. Rohauer made bitter enemies with practically everyone with whom he ever had a single business transaction. Werby terms him "pathological" — "Rohauer would fight you in court every step of the way to avoid paying anything. He'd rather pay lawyers to fight you than to pay *you*. He was also a master of arguing both sides of a case —

whichever side fit his needs at the moment." Rohauer in fact refused to pay Werby until she had a sheriff go in person to a theatre and impound the ticket money during a showing of *Freaks*...

The Revival

The early sixties would witness the film's full rediscovery and recontextualisation. In October 1961, Dan Talbot, programmer for the New Yorker Film Society, booked a week long run of *Freaks* at the New Yorker Theatre on the corner of Broadway and West 88th in Manhattan. Diane Arbus, a fashion photographer whose photographic detours into the freakish and grotesque would become world renowned, attended the screenings night after night, transfixed.

The underground film movement, then taking shape in the East Village around venues like The Charles, Cinema 16 and The Living Theatre, would embrace *Freaks* in a special way.

The underground's use of unusual 'non actors' instead of glamorous, polished professionals found resonance in *Freaks*, whose major flaw, the critics had always complained, was the freaks' terrible acting. It was obvious they weren't actors, but 'real people' whose earnestness and vulnerability shines through as they grapple with their lines. It appears some of the freaks, especially the pinheads, have been led in front of the cameras simply to be themselves (in the same way that Jack Smith, Joe Dallesandro and Edie Sedgwick would be led out). The viewer realises he is seeing something genuinely abnormal shining through instead of the processed corn so often doled up by thirties Hollywood.

The underground would take this celebration of abnormal personalities to new levels. Andy Warhol

would have his screeching transvestite trio of Candy Darling, Jackie Curtis and Holly Woodlawn. Ron Rice unveiled his Negro 'fat lady' (and frequently naked) Winifred Bryant in *The Queen of Sheba Meets The Atom Man*, and John Waters would later introduce rotund female impersonator Divine, Negro fat lady Jean Hill and the indescribable 'egg lady' Edie Massey to the world. Loveable freaks all. In fact, most of the filmmakers themselves were social outcasts, and it was now high time to celebrate the fact.

In 1962, the Cannes Film Festival selected *Freaks* to represent their horror film category and the revival — in fact something closer to canonisation — was well under way in Europe, where cinéastes and scholars wrote about the movie in intellectual film journals using adjectives such as 'sensitive' and 'compassionate'. Ironically, 1962 was also the year of Tod Browning's death at eighty. He died on 6 October in Santa Monica, California at the house of friends who had taken him in. He spent his last years in relative isolation and poverty. He willed his 1941 Chrysler to his mailman. For years it had been rumoured he'd died in a car accident.

But *Freaks* had a life of its own now; if not nine lives then something close. In 1967 it made it to New York's Museum of Modern Art, and the same year David F. Friedman shot his own exploitation tribute called *She Freak*. Friedman had wanted Johnny Eck to star, but Johnny was having none of it and turned him down flat. Johnny would ever feel embittered over the tiny amount of money he received from *Freaks* from a deal cut by a dishonest agent, although he always spoke very highly of Tod Browning.

1967 was also the 'Summer of Love' in San Francisco. 'Freak' was now gaining widespread use among the hippies, many of whom considered themselves freaks — with pride.

Freaks would make yet another comeback during the Midnight Movie era of the 1970s, gaining exposure to a new generation. It would sometimes double-bill with other period rivals such as *Reefer Madness* or *The Terror of Tiny Town*. Often, however, it would play discombobulating double-bills with newer films such as *Pink Flamingos*, *Eraserhead* or *Night of the Living Dead* in the Midnight Movie craze of contextual integrity being subjugated to shock effect.

Jonathan Rosenbaum, in his 1983 book *Midnight Movies*, terms *Freaks* possibly the oldest of all midnight attractions and credits its transgressions against taboos involving sex and deformity for maintaining it as a singular exploitation item over the years.

The movie also claimed new, if unlikely, adherents in the seventies, including New York punk rock band The Ramones, who document their fealty in their 1981 biography entitled *Gabba Gabba, Hey*, their own skewed translation of the wedding banquet's famous "Gooble, Gabba..." chant.

"The 'Gabba Gabba Hey', 'We accept you, one of us' thing on (the song) 'Pinhead,'" explains Tommy Ramone, "we picked up from this silent (sic) thirties movie called *Freaks* by this guy, Tod Browning. When freaks admitted someone new into their ranks they carried signs saying 'Gabba Gabba Hey, we accept you...'".

"We were trying to find a chant," adds Joey Ramone. "We couldn't decide if they were saying, 'Gabba Gooble', or 'Gabba Gabba' or 'Gooble Gabba,' so we just used 'Gabba Gabba', but we found it's not

Angelo Rossitto, Daisy and Harry Earles.

'Gabba Gabba', its 'Gooble Gabba, Gabba Gooble!" "I saw that movie ten times," Joey Ramone testifies. "It's one of our biggest inspirations."

Concert scenes from the Ramones' cult movie, *Rock 'n' Roll High School*, show slam-dancing fans dressed as freaks, holding aloft 'Gabba Gabba Hey' signs during the song 'Pinhead.'

Cult film director John Waters first saw *Freaks* when he frequented the New York underground scene in the early to mid-sixties. In 1984, now an established director and celebrity in his own right, he was teaching film to hardened convicts at a Maryland penitentiary and showed *Freaks* to them. Their reaction? "They liked it..." he says, unable to suppress an evil chuckle at the memory.

In 1986, MGM-UA Home Video proudly released *Freaks* with elaborate packaging — the same film Louis B. Mayer had banished from distribution over a half century earlier. The video release gave the movie an instant mass circulation beyond any of its theatrical revivals, with some unintended results. Johnny Eck, living in poverty with twin brother Rob in the same North Milton Avenue rowhouse in which they'd been born, suddenly found himself harassed by a new and largely obnoxious breed of fan who'd come to the film via video. It was the last thing he wanted to talk about or deal with. These new 'fans' proved as menacing to his mental health as the criminals roaming the streets of his once-safe Highlandtown neighbourhood.

In December 1990, Johnny's plight was brought to the attention of MGM's Classics Division and they agreed to contribute free rental of a 35mm print of *Freaks* to screen at a benefit planned for Boston's Coolidge Corner Theatre. The benefit, slotted for early spring, with all proceeds to be sent to Johnny, never came off — the 4 February 1991 issue of *Variety* ran his obituary.

Johnny had died almost a month earlier, on 5 January. *Freaks*, which for years he had refused to discuss at all, remained a looming enigma in his life — the source of enduring bitterness as well as happy memories; private memories of a much different day. The carnivals, the packed crowds, the big tents and the sensationalistic hype of Johnny's heyday as a live performer in the twenties and thirties — that was all gone now, reduced to a stack of old photos and clippings. But the movie remained, continued and grew. The few brief minutes Johnny appeared in *Freaks* would increasingly come to define his life and career to new generations born long after the demise of the great carnivals.

Angelo Rossitto died blind and in depression in a Hollywood retirement home later that same year. He too refused to discuss *Freaks* and derived from it only memories.

A Shock for All Time

The fact that *Freaks* was such a unique film and impossible to pigeon-hole enabled it to be seen in the eye of the beholder, to be exploited, damned, praised, championed and contextualised from every possible angle: to be pitched by Browning as a revealing look at sideshow life, sold by MGM as a 'monster movie', exploited by Esper as an exposé on freakish and shocking sexuality, embraced by the early-sixties cinéastes as a compassionate and socialistic reading of society's outcasts, and championed by the Midnight Movie fanatics of the seventies as a weirdo-bizarro cult icon of the highest order.

Publicity shot of Johnny Eck.

The circus wagon rolled on. The 'weird nightmare' continued to illuminate the darkness. Today the movie is seen by some through the prism of political correctness, wherein the public display of freaks for profit or mere entertainment seems unforgivably insensitive, appallingly archaic. No studio would remotely consider such a film today. Freak shows had begun to go out of fashion in the fifties, largely due to more humanistic attitudes bearing on the 'handicapped' — ironically depriving many freaks of an independent means of livelihood. A dwarf became a 'disadvantaged person' in the sixties, becoming a 'vertically challenged' person today.

Yet the film's impact remains undiminished — has in fact sharpened over time — precisely because modern audiences have no familiarity with the milieu of the freak show that was a main component of thirties carnival culture. It retains power not because of its shocking depiction of real freaks, but because it is — despite the doctoring of a major Hollywood studio — a genuine human document with a universal emotional resonance. What are we but a motley collection of eternal outsiders, fatalists and dreamers who occasionally recognise the absurdity of our own existence? *We* form into clubs, gangs and tribes to 'belong', to battle the 'Big People' — 'society' or fill-in-the-blank... *We* forever feel desire for others we cannot have and *our* world is likewise full of borders we cannot cross or cannot imagine crossing.

Surely we see, albeit reluctantly, more of the truth of our world in this simple and weirdly archaic little Depression-era film about freaks than in a ton of gush, glow and glitter sparkling in Hollywood's mass-media mindscape peopled with perfect bodies and untested souls. ∎

THE PRESIDENT'S ANALYST

BY KIM NEWMAN

Acclaimed on its release as an important satire (in the *Monthly Film Bulletin*, Patrick Eason said it was better than *The Graduate*), Theodore J. Flicker's film has failed to attract a lasting cult. Because of James Coburn's star presence, it has tended to be lumped in

with the spy spoofs *Our Man Flint* and *In Like Flint* and dismissed as a minor offshoot of the already self-satirising sixties Bond boom. However, if you stumble over it late at night on TV (especially when Channel 4 remember to letterbox William Fraker's Panavision compositions), it emerges as one of the strangest artefacts of the late sixties collision of big studio money with vaguely counterculture thinking.

Dr Sidney Schaefer (Coburn), a chic Manhattan analyst who unwinds by beating a gong, is astonished when Don Masters (Cambridge), one of his patients, reveals in the course of a quite moving childhood reminiscence that he has worked out some of his deep-seated resentments by murdering an Albanian secret agent. "It explains your utter lack of hostility," Schaefer exclaims, "you can vent your feelings by actually killing someone." An employee of the Central Enquiries Agency, Masters has been checking out Schaefer for the post of analyst on call to the troubled President of the United States, which requires that he relocate to Washington and live in an electronic fishbowl from which he can be summoned at any moment. This reaches its absurd climax when a bowl of soup starts flashing a siren at him to signal that his presence is needed.

As the President unloads on Schaefer (with coincidental prescience, it turns out he's less worried about Russia and China than Libya), the shrink himself cracks up. Since he talks in his sleep, the Federal Board of Regulation insist his girlfriend (Delaney) move out to a hotel and Schaefer begins to suspect (correctly) that even she is spying on him. He makes his escape from the White House by latching on to a supposedly ordinary family, the Quantrills, and is pursued by agents of a dozen domestic and foreign agencies out to brainwash, deprogram or kill him.

Out in the world, Schaefer makes some disturbing discoveries about the nature of America. Wynn Quantrill (Daniels), at first a happy consumer boasting

about his 'total sound' system, turns out to be a gun-nut whose wife is into karate. Wynn rants that the liberals will only disarm when the right-wing extremists do and opines that his 'fascist' neighbours ought to be gassed. The hippies with whom Schaefer hides harbour a Beatles-style group called The Puddlians, who turn out to be Canadian secret agents ("you think it's fun being a silent bleedin' partner in North America?"). Then, in a dizzying finale which prefigures that strange Spanish short *La Cabina*, he is trapped in a rural phone booth which is collected and removed to the head office of The Phone Company. A smiling business suit android (Harrington) with a phone plug in his heel explains that the information Schaefer can give will enable TPC to blackmail the President into insisting that every American have a miniature phone installed in his or her skull before birth and that names be legally exchanged for numbers.

Masters, with his neurotic Soviet opposite number Kropotkin (Darden), stages a Bond-style assault on the high-tech fortress of TPC, and Schaefer, who has hitherto been an appalled pacifist in the middle of mass murder, discovers the joy of mowing down probably inhuman TPC thugs with a machine gun (a bit of business reprised in *Hot Shots, Part Deux*). In a downbeat 'Joy to the World' Christmas finale, all the principals are happily reconciled to a life of spying and being spied on and at The Phone Company ranks of androids sit in waiting.

The spoof side of the film owes a lot to *The Man from U.N.C.L.E.* and *Get Smart*; like Smart's Buck Henry (who was in Flicker's 1964 début feature *The Troublemaker*), Flicker came out of the Mike Nichols-Elaine May satirical stand-up tradition. But *The President's Analyst* goes beyond the cynical cool of the superspy series and tries for real paranoid dementia. One amusingly choreographed sequence has a blissfully unaware Coburn making out with hippie chick Snow White (Jill Banner, of *Spider Baby*) in a field while a fistful of multi-national agents murder each other all around them. In some specific nastiness, Walter Burke and Eduard Franz provide spiteful but not inaccurate parodies of the FBI's J. Edgar Hoover and the CIA's James Jesus Angleton. Though it's hard to imagine the unseen, but reputedly great, Prezz as Lyndon Johnson, this is a movie unusually rooted in the realities of the politics of '67, yet it also spins off into bizarre science fiction.

As the pervasive, insidious villainy of TPC becomes apparent ("that's one thing I learned from my patients, they all hate The Phone Company"), the film gets far closer (presumably accidentally) to the spirit of Philip K. Dick than *Blade Runner* or *Total Recall*, touching on such Dickian (*Dickoid? Ed...*) concerns as human-seeming robots, conspiracies inside conspiracies, mind-altering drugs, young hippie chicks, an absurd media landscape, the incipient fascism of the American state and the loss of personal identity in a welter of overlapping cover stories. There is even a trace of Borges in Schaefer's nightmare that literally everyone in a restaurant, including his dinner date, is a spy. This gag gets an emotional reprise when Delaney cries herself to sleep after betraying the hero, listening to their last telephone conversation on playback as she transmits it to her masters.

In a *Variety* editorial, Peter Bart (then a Paramount executive) revealed that among the people who took the satire seriously were the FBI and ATT (the American phone company), who tapped the phones of

Paramount brass for several years after the release of the movie. If one were really paranoid, one might conclude that some outside agency was responsible for the blacklisting of Flicker, who has subsequently made only a few, very marginal theatrical features (*Up in the Cellar*, *Last of the Good Guys*, *Soggy Bottom USA*) and been banished to lacklustre TV movies (*Playmates*, *Guess Who's Sleeping in My Bed?*, *Just a Little Inconvenience*, *Where the Ladies Go*) and series episodes (*Night Gallery*, *Banacek*, *Banyon*, *Streets of San Francisco*). It seems likely that Flicker will just have to go down in the books as one of the cinema's one hit wonders.

Among its many virtues, *Analyst* features one of the underrated Coburn's best performances (the precise nuances of paranoid twitchiness as he creeps out of the President's office are hilarious). Also, it deploys the full apparatus of 1960s chic, with a wonderfully overwrought Lalo Schifrin score that parodies his *Mission: Impossible* work and has some Swingle-sung weirdness. There is even (unless my eyes deceive me) an under-the-credits micro-cameo from Coburn's martial arts trainer, Bruce Lee. With distorted widescreen images that straddle the worlds of *Our Man Flint* and *The Trip*, this may well be the definitive 1967 movie and, over twenty-five years on, it has enough bite and anger to be worth rediscovering. ■

THE PRESIDENT'S ANALYST

US, 1967. Dir and Scr: Theodore J. Flicker. Prod: Stanley Rubin. Photography: William A. Fraker. Music: Lalo Schifrin. With: James Coburn, Godfrey Cambridge, Severn Darden, Joan Delaney, Pat Harrington, Barry McGuire, Jill Banner, Eduard Franz, Walter Burke, Will Geer, William Daniels, Joan Darling, Arte Johnson. Paramount/Panpiper.

(Previous page) James Coburn cunningly disguised as a counter-culture weirdo...

(Above) Inside every counter-culture weirdo there's a man with short hair and a gun just waiting to burst out...

SPAWN OF TARANTULA!

PART 3

BY DAVID McGILLIVRAY

THE STORY SO FAR:

Frightened as a boy by stills from the fifties science fiction film *Tarantula*, David has been drawn inextricably towards a career in horror and sleaze. After he is sacked from the British Film Institute in 1972, he writes screenplays for Ray Selfe, Pete Walker and Norman J. Warren. Before very long, he has artistic differences with his employers. 1975 dawns.

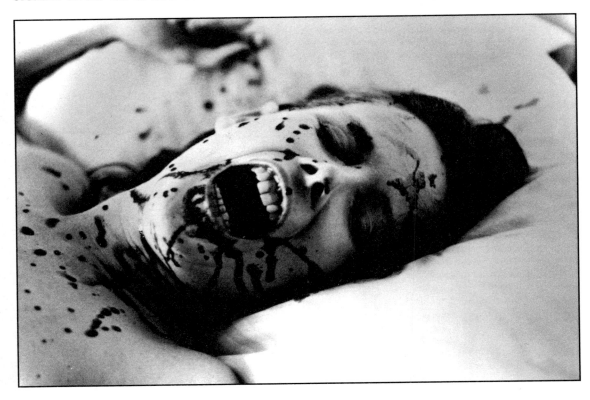

NOW READ ON!

It is very difficult to see where life is going while you are living it, but very easy to see where it is going after it has gone. While I was working for Pete Walker, Britain's foremost director of exploitation films in the 1970s, it seemed as though all we were doing was plodding dutifully from one sensational, sexy, bloody project to the next. Now, thumbing through my diaries for the period, I can see with blinding clarity how desperately he was trying and failing to climb from the exploitation rut, and equally how this frustration was bound to end in tears.

It appears now that, every few weeks during the mid-seventies, Walker was planning to try something completely different. First he said he would make a musical based on the 1948 British film *Miranda*, a comedy about a mermaid. At the end of 1974 he wanted me to rewrite Harry Alan Towers' script based on the Victorian erotic novel *My Secret Life*.

In the spring of 1975 he announced that he would direct a series of pop films for GTO, the company which made *Never Too Young to Rock* and *Side by Side* during the glam rock era. This unfulfilled scheme may have inspired his idea to remake *Svengali* as a musical with the sinister hypnotist as a has-been rock 'n' roll star (Alvin Stardust wanted to play the part). Thanks to a couple of jump starts, this old crock did get a little way down the road. Walker hired a print of the 1955 film for us to watch, and I completed a screenplay in June. By July, however, he was having "reservations". (*Svengali* was eventually updated, much as we planned, but as an American TV movie in 1983. Peter O'Toole was Svengali and Jodie Foster was Trilby).

Walker maintained his contacts in the music biz and, despite having little knowledge of pop culture, was still trying to crash the youth market long after I left him. In 1978 he was slated to direct *A Star Is Dead*, the Sex Pistols movie, from a screenplay by Michael Armstrong. The script was full of good ideas but, even if they hadn't split up, the Pistols, especially Sid, never would have been capable of giving the performances Armstrong expected of them.

In 1975 the media began to take notice of the bustling exploitation film industry. The BBC weighed in with a comprehensive survey of British low-budget sex and violence for the *Man Alive* series. It was directed by James Kenelm Clarke, who was so impressed by what he filmed that he soon left the BBC and began making sleaze of his own, notably three pictures with Fiona Richmond.

The *Man Alive* programme offered me my first major TV exposure and I was thrilled skinny. Walker, on the other hand, was deeply concerned that I would malign him as I had done (he felt) the previous year in *Films & Filming* magazine. I didn't, although I had every reason because of the chicken-feed he was paying me. Now I look back with amusement at the fees I received (£200 for *House of Whipcord*), but at the time I wasn't the only one who found them shameful. In *Man Alive*, both Clarke and interviewer John Pitman were keen to contrast Walker swanning around in his Rolls with me slaving away in my bedsit in north London. While he was setting up a shot, Clarke whispered to his cameraman, "Pan off the sink on to David."

I wrote part of *Svengali* in Walker's Mayfair office while he was visiting one of his properties in Portugal. Naturally I found a few papers I wasn't supposed to see. I learned that in 1971 Walker had paid Alfred Shaughnessy £1,000 to write the screenplay of *The Black Arrow*. The budget of *Frightmare* included an allocation of £2,500 for my screenplay. In fact, I'd been paid £400. 'I felt pretty glum by the end of the day,' I wrote on 30 May.

My memory is that all gloom was dispelled by another discovery, an old passport which provided irrefutable proof of Walker's closely guarded age. Ever conscious of his pulling power (prime targets being bits of fluff from page three of *The Sun*), Walker was claiming at this time to be anything from thirty-three to thirty-eight. The truth is that he was born in 1932, making his real age forty-three. The last time I saw him, at a convention in Manchester in 1992, he told me he'd just turned fifty. I think, what's more, that he really believed he had.

While I was writing *Svengali* and another abortive project, a children's television series about the Bengal Lancers, my sex comedy *I'm Not Feeling Myself Tonight!* went into production. 'This small piece of muck' (*Time Out*) had been instigated by boom swinger turned producer Laurie Barnett, who had formed a partnership with hard core porn supremo John Lindsay. Barnett had sold his idea for a film about a sonic aphrodisiac to distributor New Realm. When Lindsay was had up for making blue movies at a secondary school in Birmingham, the company removed his name from the credits.

The word came through that *I'm Not Feeling Myself Tonight!* would be directed by Joe McGrath. I could not have been more pleased. McGrath had worked with most of my comedy idols, notably Peter Sellers, Spike Milligan and Peter Cook, and the prospect of an association with this sacred pantheon made me go weak at the knees.

I should have heeded the warning bells. Prior to *I'm Not Feeling Myself Tonight!*, McGrath had co-written *Secrets of a Door-to-Door Salesman*, which I had dismissed as 'dismally slow and unfunny'. Sure enough, I was to discover that McGrath's own sense of humour was about on a level with *The Clitheroe Kid*. The geniuses with whom McGrath had worked probably would have been funny even if they'd been directed by the Archbishop of Canterbury.

Script development took a familiar course. The first I

(Previous page) Some victim or other.

(Below) The author is informed that scriptwriters sometimes work for more than luncheon vouchers... (All illustrations throughout from Schizo.)

heard from McGrath was that he thought my effort was 'very good'. Within days he'd suggested alterations, some of which were so stupid that I refused to make them. Consequently McGrath began re-writing the script himself. When I made a fuss, Barnett tried to pacify me that "ninety percent of the script is untouched." This wasn't true. Before shooting started, the coloured inserts outnumbered the original pages.

Still desperate to get in front of the camera, I demanded that I play a role in the orgy sequence, which looked to me as though it was going to be the most fun to shoot. My version of the orgy consisted of dozens of cut-aways at a disintegrating dinner party, but there was neither the time nor the money for that kind of extravagance. In McGrath's version, shot in the grounds of a house in Sheen, guests merely fell into the swimming pool and then chased each other round the lawn.

What I'd planned for myself was a joke I'd nicked from Jimmy Tarbuck ("I was at a dance and I said to this girl, 'Look out, love, your dress is coming off.' She said, 'Oh, I don't think so. Is it?' I said, 'Yes, I've made up my mind.'"). The actress chosen to have her dress torn off was gorgeous Monika Ringwald, the star of *Sexplorer*. I felt greatly honoured. I was also intrigued to find among the extras Michael Cox, who had sung 'Angela Jones', a Top Ten hit in 1960.

While I was waiting for my big moment, Laurie Barnett and I sat by the pool writing our next sex comedy, which was to be about a family of sex maniacs. It was called *Unzipper De Doo Dah* and the plan was to shoot it on video and then transfer it to film, a process still in its infancy. The project never progressed beyond a test sequence.

Occasionally Barnett and McGrath would be called away by the producer, Malcolm Fancey, and I could hear them arguing about the sexual content of *I'm Not Feeling Myself Tonight!* It was the same old problem. The director didn't like shooting sex scenes and the

actors didn't want to take their clothes off. Fancey was so determined to increase the flesh quota that he came over to me and told me to get my kit off. "You'll only be a blur in the background," he promised. "We won't see your bollocks." I knew that actors didn't strip unless it was an integral part of the script. I said no.

Eventually Fancey found a couple of extras willing to drop 'em for a few extra bob. Thus ensued the scene I have recounted a dozen times, but here it comes again. The couple lay down on the grass and pretended to have sexual intercourse. The man's name was Curtis Hall. During the shooting McGrath had his back to the set and turned round once to mutter, "Move your bum up and down a bit, Curtis." The stupidity of the situation so impressed me that I adapted it for a subsequent screenplay, *Terror*, and even called the male character Curtis.

I took two friends to the preview of *I'm Not Feeling Myself Tonight!* and wished I hadn't. By the end of the screening I was practically under the seat with embarrassment. All my lovingly crafted absurdist humour was gone, replaced with cornball gags that even Laurie Barnett's relatives didn't laugh at. My performance with the lovely Monika had also bitten the dust. I had delivered the lines so badly that the shot had been cut.

But Malcolm Fancey had got what he wanted — dozens and dozens of naked ladies, so many tits that it wouldn't have mattered if the dialogue had come out of a cracker. *I'm Not Feeling Myself Tonight!* was probably the most successful film I ever wrote. During its first week at London's Classic Moulin, it grossed £5,000, which may not sound a great deal by today's standards, but was enough twenty years ago to send the film straight into the box-office chart at number ten, a feat that Pete Walker's films were no longer able to match.

Walker's latest film, about a crazy old priest who murders his parishioners, was previewed while *I'm Not Feeling Myself Tonight!* was still in production. As with all my movies (with the exception of *Whipcord*), I haven't watched *The Confessional*, finally released as *House of Mortal Sin*, since it was made because I cannot bear to listen to the reams of dialogue. Even when I first heard it I thought it was silly. 'Many of the heavies' speeches are over the top,' I wrote. 'I cringed more than once.' But the film itself I liked. I thought Walker was continuing to improve as a director and I rated the performances of Susan Penhaligon and Stephanie Beacham as two of the best he'd had. 'The subject matter and Walker's treatment of it are the most distasteful yet,' I scribbled delightedly. 'I predict big outcries, big dramas and big box-office receipts.'

My predictions could not have been wider of the mark. The first blow came when Walker's distributor, Miracle, said that they weren't prepared to open the film at the London Pavilion unless Walker paid the rental. Walker was reduced to hawking his film up Wardour Street, something he hadn't had to do since the early years. Eventually he did a deal with Columbia-Warner, which put *House of Mortal Sin* into the Warner theatre with minimal publicity.

Far from finding the sins of Father Meldrum sacrilegious, critics were actually bored. 'A couple of sleeping pills should see you through it,' decided the *Daily Express*. Even the *Financial Times'* Nigel Andrews, one of the few who'd liked *Whipcord*, turned against us. 'A load of old rubbish,' he sneered. The film struggled on for four weeks. Months later it was sent

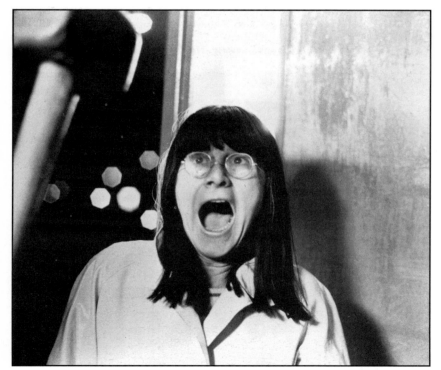

MPs' question time after Labour announces plans to legalise cannabis.

round the country on the bottom half of a double bill.

This chastening experience seemed to snap Walker back to reality. Suddenly the mermaids and the glitter rock and all the other flim-flam were things of the past and we had to buckle down to creating another blood feast with plenty of horrendous murders. One of the drawbacks was that I'd got too big for my boots. The exploitation industry was churning away quite merrily and I was being inundated with other offers. I could afford to be very indifferent with Walker and I was. We now argued most of the time.

Also Fringe theatre had reached its height in London. Everyone I bumped into was forming his own company and I did the same with my drama school buddy Walter Zerlin Jnr in order to produce some offbeat comedies. I saw a chance with Entertainment Machine for my pearls of wit to reach the public unpolished by hack directors. (I directed all our plays myself.) The move into live theatre was to prove a real lifeline. We didn't know it in 1975, but the British film industry was only five years away from collapse. The plays carried me very comfortably into middle age.

My relationship with Walker was strained still further by the fact that neither of us had a clue what we were going to do next. It would have been better under the circumstances to wait for another brainwave, but Walker couldn't afford to step off the treadmill. He had to get another movie into production now. Consequently he kept insisting that we adapt a screenplay by my predecessor, Murray Smith, that had been abandoned years previously.

Smith was a good writer. In fact, it was his screenplay for *Cool It Carol* that had alerted me to Walker's talents in the first place. But the reason *Schizo* had been put in a bottom drawer was that it was an utterly conventional whodunnit with, in my view, an easily guessable solution. This was not the kind of potboiler we would expect from the man who gave us *Frightmare*. But Walker saw it as his *Psycho*, a British nail-biter that would link him forever with his idol Hitchcock.

I fought tooth and nail to be relieved of this assignment and vented my spleen at the end of each day in a manner I reserved for the blank page. 'This latest project is really getting on my nerves,' I wrote on 17 September. 'I have no interest in it. I half wish he'd say forget it, but he's adamant that I write it. If he keeps nagging me about this fucking awful script I'll have a seizure.'

After we had spent many fruitless days and nights trying to pull *Schizo* into shape, Walker declared that he had other business to attend to and that we should take a break. While I waited for the next summons, I opened Entertainment Machine's first play at the Little theatre in St Martin's Lane (it's now Stringfellow's) and knocked off *Unzipper De Doo Dah*, whose quality can be gauged by the fact that I wrote the last twenty-four pages in one day.

Ironically, for someone who worked every day of his life to maintain the cool image necessary to impress starlets and bank managers alike, Walker was almost child-like in his deviousness with skivvies, particularly me. When he telephoned to say he was coming to see me in my humble flat, an unprecedented event, I knew something was up. This meeting confirmed the secret machinations I had uncovered earlier in the year and was to mark the beginning of the end of our relationship. The date was 9 November:

'P.W. announced that he was coming round this afternoon so I could sign a paper turning over the copyright of *House of Mortal Sin* to Columbia. He was eventually here for over six hours, the most extraordinary session in our career together. When he arrived I sensed something was wrong. He was too chatty, too friendly. There was much talk about how poor he was.

'The crunch came when he handed me the agreement already turned to the last page for my signature. I insisted I read the whole thing and was amazed to come across a line stating that I had been

(Above left) The wallpaper design finally proves too much for Lynne Frederick.

(Below) Our old favourite, the ping pong ball eye...

"'Allo, George? Yeah, well, I gotta little screenplay 'ere, name of Clitoris... A pony and it's yours — know what I mean? Yeah, same cubicle as last time..." Serious negotiations take place for a lost masterpiece of British docu-drama film-making...

paid £2,750 for the screenplay. Walker said he wanted Columbia to think the film was a major production and had therefore upped my fee. I was absolutely staggered. Of course I refused to sign a legal document that wasn't true. I was also deeply offended by this virtual admission that he felt so ashamed of the money he was paying me that he had to add £2,000 to it just to make it sound respectable!

'This led to me accusing him of exploiting me at which he returned to his usual defensive — that he paid me all he could afford and that he'd rather I didn't write the scripts if that's how I felt. After we'd been round in several circles, he still expected me to sign the paper plus, as a conciliation, a letter saying that I would receive a deferred payment of £2,000 when the film grossed $3,000,000 (impossible). This I refused to do as well. At any second I expected him to blow up, but he didn't. He packed away the papers and then returned to pleasant chat before leaving.' (The following day I signed the contract with the money clause crossed out.)

Under these circumstances, I didn't feel at all like returning to the dreaded *Schizo* and allowed myself to be wooed away by more exciting temptations. After months of delay, Norman J. Warren's *Satan's Slave* was finally due to start shooting and I'd written myself a part as a priest. I also agreed to meet director Georges Robin, whose only claim to infamy was *Mini Weekend*. Now he wanted to make the British *Emmanuelle*, but in one location for £25,000. I said that, for that kind of money, he was going to get another crappy sex film, but I was happy about this if he was. He was. The working title for this masterpiece was *Clitoris* and I still have Robin's handwritten contract to prove it.

At the pre-shoot party for *Satan's Slave* I met the stars, Candace Glendenning ('I must admit I wasn't knocked out by her'") and Martin Potter, who'd

worked with Fellini and was now on the skids ('He's one of these actors who invents life histories for the people he plays. I felt like saying, "Don't worry. It's only a cheapjack horror film."'). On the second day of shooting I turned up at the country house location (used four years earlier for *Virgin Witch*) and provided my cameo. There I was sharing a scene with the great Michael Gough and I had all the lines. As always I was rubbish.

I forced myself back to the typewriter and laboured over *Schizo* without the slightest enthusiasm. Halfway through, I saw the first British screening of *The Texas Chain Saw Massacre* at the London Film Festival and saw in a flash the future of the horror film. With *Frightmare* we had helped pave the way for it, and this was the sort of film Walker and I should now be making! Walker rang me up to check on my progress. "How's it going?" he demanded. "It's not *The Texas Chain Saw Massacre*," I said with a regret I know he registered.

After eleven days labour I turned in *Schizo*, all sixty-seven pages of it. It was at least twenty-five pages too short, but the murders were truly horrendous and I planned to protest that the plethora of action would fill out the running time. I didn't get the chance. Walker hated it. "It's awful!" he screamed down the telephone. "Dreadful! I don't know what to do with it!" I knew what I didn't want to do with it and that was to rewrite it. I visited him in his office on 15 December, hoping against hope that we weren't going to have to start work all over again:

'Walker was in a bad mood. "I can't shoot this script. You can't believe in the characters. It's a fifty-nine minute film. I want quality. (etc, etc.)" I put up a bit of a fight. I said that it was grossly unfair to say that it didn't work because you couldn't believe in the characters. If it didn't work then it was because it was a lousy story. His belief in its wonderfulness, however, was unwavering. I kept dreading that he would say that we had to work on it further. But he didn't. He said he may work on it himself, he may get another writer in. He won't do either. There were curt farewells and I walked out of his office with a sense of the greatest relief. No rewrites! Christmas free of worries! I won't mind if I never hear from him again. I want to move on.'

I got my wish to move on two days later. I started writing *Clitoris*, not exactly the great leap forward I thought my career deserved, but it made a change from being shouted at. *Clitoris* is another screenplay I have managed to expunge almost totally from my memory. I'm pretty sure it had something to do with people having sex in a country house. Georges Robin's original outline included a helicopter crash. He noticed my look of cynical disbelief. "We'll just hear it crash," he assured me. I wrote the screenplay in thirteen days, handed it over to Robin and never heard from him again. The film wasn't made. Robin disappeared. Years later I heard what had become of him, but now I've forgotten.

In the first weeks of 1976 Walker re-established contact to tell me that he'd hired Frances Megahy and Bernie Cooper to rewrite *Schizo*. All they'd done previously was a film called *The Freelance*, which had been put on the shelf for five years. Later they were to break through with the TV movie *Dirty Money*. Walker said he didn't like what they had written for him. I asked to see this new version and Walker wouldn't show it to me. I still don't believe it existed. It was a ploy to demonstrate that I was not indispensable. It proved to me that I was and so I agreed to rewrite *Schizo*.

Over the next few weeks I behaved as though I were William Goldman. I held out for more money. Walker said the cheque was in the post. It wasn't and so I didn't write anything. Eventually I screwed the grand total of £850 out of him. I still didn't start writing. Thanks mainly to the money I had made out of *The Adventures of the Bengal Lancers*, I had bought a flat and was having it renovated. Walker phoned up in a rage. "There won't be a next time!" he threatened. He then fired off a three page letter detailing his grievances. I thought I'd better earn my money and effected a complete rewrite in ten days. 'All that can be said for this new version is that it's the right length,' I wrote on 3 March. 'I like it no more than the first. It's undoubtedly the dullest thing I've ever written and contains some of my worst dialogue. I can't imagine what Walker will say.'

Walker was an ominously long time in coming back to me. In the interim I did another day on *Satan's Slave*: 'I was supposed to drop spiders and snakes over a naked Gloria Walker. But the spider man never showed. I did some other things instead. First I played Michael Gough's hands fiddling at a black magic altar; then I was Martin Potter's right hand, stabbing Gloria; then I dragged Gloria across the floor; then Norman and I were robed, masked loonies; then I was Gough in a goat's head mask; and finally I even dubbed Gough's voice incanting something for the prologue. I found it all great fun.'

To my astonishment Walker accepted the second draft of *Schizo* with hardly a word of criticism. I was given only one short scene to rewrite. There was no mention of the previous unpleasantness and, before I left his office, Walker offered me old chairs, desks and a coffee table for my new flat. From then onwards he referred to *Schizo* as his best film to date. I couldn't understand it.

The plot we ended up with involved an ice skater being terrorised by a dark stranger who may already have killed her mother. This was the first Walker film to include a supernatural element: at a seance, a medium speaks with a dead man's voice to accuse his murderer. The killings — most of which were censored from the subsequent video release — included one that came to me in a rare burst of inspiration. Ray Selfe's wife was turning out her wardrobe for props I could use for one of my plays and came across her knitting. I picked up one of the needles and thought — 'Wow! That could be driven into somebody's ear!'

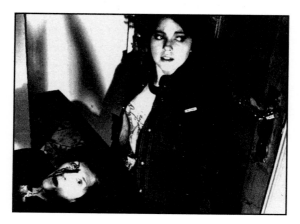

As always with a Walker production, the great names supposedly interested in the script — on this occasion Richard Attenborough, David McCallum and Patrick Mower — soon faded into the background. Even Bill Maynard turned down the role of the stranger and we were stuck with Jack Watson. The damsel in distress was Lynne Frederick, who'd done a couple of juve leads.

I shared a scene with her at the seance and rated her 'intelligent but not very interesting.' She was later furious when nude pics grabbed of her on the *Schizo* set turned up in print. She initiated legal proceedings, something that later became second nature to her. (She successfully sued the producers of *The Trail of the Pink Panther* for using without her permission material featuring her late husband Peter Sellers.)

Norman J. Warren's friend, a Polish émigré called Andrzej Jasiewicz, came sniffing round me for a quick screenplay. As with Georges Robin, he had one shady sex film in his past, in his case *To Rio For Love*, abandoned in 1970 when the unpaid British crew walked off the set in Brazil. Now he claimed to have found £50,000 for a movie called *Dead Centre* which, if memory serves me, was a complete rip-off of a novel called *The Dice Man*. (I do have a copy of *Dead Centre*, but I would have teeth pulled rather than read it.) By now I could smell failure. 'This script will not be filmed,' I wrote on 17 March. But Jasiewicz was playing a bit part in one of my plays and I thought that he might walk out if I refused to write his screenplay. I began it under sufferance.

Months after it was 'completed', *Satan's Slave* was dragged back in front of the camera because more filth and nudity were required to ensure a sale. I got a call from Norman J. Warren, who summoned me to a house in Cuffley, Herts, and told me to bring two friends. I chose Jasiewicz and my writing partner

(Above) Lynne Frederick before discovering that legal proceedings can be more lucrative than appearing in B-movies...

(Below left) Never tell your kids they can't stay out late rollerskating.

Zerlin. They spent a morning torturing two naked women (one of whom was Monika Ringwald), and then I was dressed up as a witchfinder and we all branded and whipped another naked woman. We had a jolly good time and got £10 each. It didn't seem to matter to anyone that I was already in the film, playing a completely different part. Those were the days.

The scripting of *Dead Centre* dragged on and on as Jasiewicz demanded more and more rewrites. He kept setting the most impossible deadlines until, at one point, I had to pretend I'd been rushed to hospital. In reality, I was staying at another flat trying to complete yet another draft. Jasiewicz claimed that Edward Fox had committed to the lead, but when he read the script, he was obviously so appalled that he tried to wriggle out of the deal by demanding £10,000 instead of the £4,000 agreed. The whole thing went up in smoke shortly afterwards. Andrzej Jasiewicz went the way of Georges Robin. He owed money not only to me but several members of Pete Walker's crew, who had begun pre-production.

When I received a final demand from the Inland Revenue, I decided I needed a scripting job that paid big bucks in a hurry. There were vague offers from Kevin Francis and David Grant, but neither of the erratic producers could be pinned down. I was therefore highly susceptible when Pete Walker telephoned, eager to get started on a new script. He'd just seen *Lipstick* and wanted to do something erotic. He was thinking about under-age sex as a theme. He sent me a mediocre synopsis, which I told him I loved.

Then everything changed for me. My theatre company took a play to the Edinburgh Festival and we became the smash hit of the 1976 Fringe, winning ecstatic reviews and an award from *The Scotsman*.

When I got back to London, one of the interviews I did was for BBC Radio London's Mike Sparrow, who then offered me a job on his new daily arts programme *Look Stop Listen*. I said yes. A few days later I said no to under-age sex. Eventually this film was made. It became *Home Before Midnight*, written by Murray Smith.

Schizo opened on 18 November 1976 to even worse reviews than *House of Mortal Sin*. 'Quite awful,' declared *The Guardian*. 'God help the British film industry if this sort of farrago becomes its staple diet.' Later TV's Barry Norman rubbed salt in Walker's wounds by declaring that *Schizo* was "after Hitchcock, but so far after that it couldn't catch up if it were on Concorde." The box-office takings were disastrous. At Bayswater the film managed only £500 in its first week, the cinema's lowest take of the year. *The Texas Chain Saw Massacre* opened the same day to sensational business.

Thus ended my formative years at the feet of the king of exploitation. I had no further contact with Pete Walker until 1982, when I attempted to interview him and ended up having yet another row. He has driven me up the wall virtually from the day we met and I still cannot believe my good fortune in being able to work for him. His meanness is infuriating and yet he has been unstintingly generous, never once allowing me to buy so much as a cup of coffee, let alone the slap-up meals of which there have been countless. The films we made together were terrible. The critics hated them and the public wouldn't go to see them. But they were cults even in the seventies, and the reason they are back on video this year is that they're great. But enough of trying to prove that Pete Walker was a man of contrasts...

(To be continued.) ■

The 'amended' **Schizo** *poster — see colour section for the original...*

SHOOTING THE LIGHT (AND DARK) FANTASTIC

THE CAREER OF GARY GRAVER

BY JULIAN GRAINGER

"Most of the time, making a film is more fun than actually sitting down and watching it."

There are some careers which seem to defy categorisation, some people who just don't fit into any obvious mould: the object of this piece has worked for directors as diverse as Orson Welles, Al Adamson, Steven Spielberg, Fred Olen Ray, Ron Howard, Hikmet 'Howard' Avedis, Charles Martin Smith, David L. Hewitt, Allan Arkush, Anthony Cardoza, Paul Bartel and many more besides. Gary Graver shoots movies — but he also directs, writes, produces, edits and

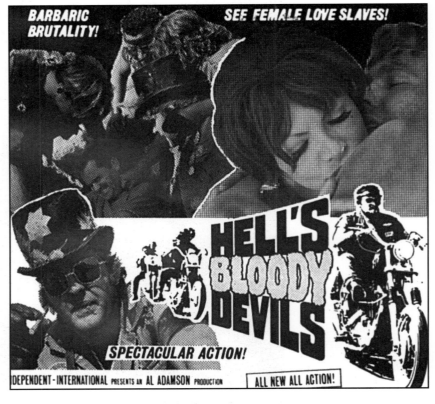

BARBARIC BRUTALITY!

SEE FEMALE LOVE SLAVES!

HELL'S BLOODY DEVILS

SPECTACULAR ACTION!

INDEPENDENT-INTERNATIONAL PRESENTS AN AL ADAMSON PRODUCTION

ALL NEW ALL ACTION!

acts. He's been making movies since the early sixties, and in the thirty-plus years since then has clocked up a phenomenal number of credits. This man really likes to work and he's extremely fast.

"It's not just like making one or two films a year; I made eight films last year. They only shoot for about a week or something, sometimes two."

He is a quiet, diffident man who assiduously avoids the limelight. Watching him work on the set of Fred Olen Ray's *Haunting Fear*, it was clear that here was someone who knew just what they wanted, treating his co-workers politely but firmly and achieving a great deal in a short space of time.

That many of the directors with whom Graver has worked ask for him again and again is a testament to his skills, and whether it was Welles or Ray, Adamson or Spielberg, they seem to like the same things about him — not only is he good, he's also fast. In 1986, Graver shot no less than twelve adult features, directed and shot a teen high-jinx flick named *Party Camp*, oversaw the technical aspects of the Armand Mastroianni slasher *Distortions* and still found time to shoot a big budget, TV movie remake of *Stagecoach*.

Graver has a small office in a nondescript building on Santa Monica Boulevard — it contains what you'd expect: a moviola, piles of film cans — and there's a screening theatre just across the hallway. But what takes your breath away as you enter is a huge photo — no publicity still — of Graver with Orson Welles and John Huston, working on Welles' (as yet unreleased) *The Other Side of the Wind*, in which Huston starred and Graver worked as director of photography. He saw me staring at it and said, "Three greats... Well, two down and one to go, huh?" laughing with only a slight trace of bitterness. The man himself is in his mid-forties, a paradigm of Californian fitness, still brimming with ideas for any number of projects. However, he did comment:

"You've caught me at a time that is very frustrating. I would like to be doing a lot better — especially when you're as obsessed with film-making as I am. It's all I want to do, but it's tough to get a picture, to get the better projects, but I work a lot so I guess I'm lucky."

To complicate matters further, Graver has an alter-ego, a man named Robert McCallum, who is one of America's most sought-after creators of adult films. He has won a number of awards for this work, but is seldom seen at ceremonies.

"I come from Portland, Oregon, and as a director I work a lot with the actors because that's how I started out, as a little kid doing theatre. I studied with Jeff Corey, Lucille Ball and Lee J. Cobb.

"I made some shorts in 16mm and then a short in 35mm called *Seeking* — it played in a theatre in Beverly Hills alongside a Buñuel film. I decided to put the money I made into a picture called *The Great Dream* — later changed to *The Embracers* and released as an exploitation picture. It showed at the Cork Film Festival in Ireland. I'm remaking it right now — I'm going to cut out all the stuff that I don't like (the cans of film were by his left knee). I'm the star of it so I'm going to grow a beard, put mud in my hair and become a bum on Hollywood Boulevard, sitting there with a little dog, who is approached by a TV crew and is interviewed about his experiences. Then I'm going to flashback to the old black and white footage — which I shot very inexpensively — and put more sound effects on it. I think the idea of seeing one person age twenty-three years in a movie will be interesting. I'm going to change the name to *Going Hollywood* and put an eight minute travelogue on the front of it containing all the crazy, goofy things in Hollywood. It's something like we did on *Eating Raoul*.

"I got drafted into the service to go to Vietnam. I wasn't a cameraman, just a director of one short and one feature and I hadn't been hired by anybody. I said I'd like to be a cameraman, but I didn't know anything about it so I ran over to the various rental houses around Hollywood asking, 'How do you work a light meter?', that sort of thing. I photographed everything for the Combat Camera Group and they sent me to Vietnam, to Japan and even San Diego. I

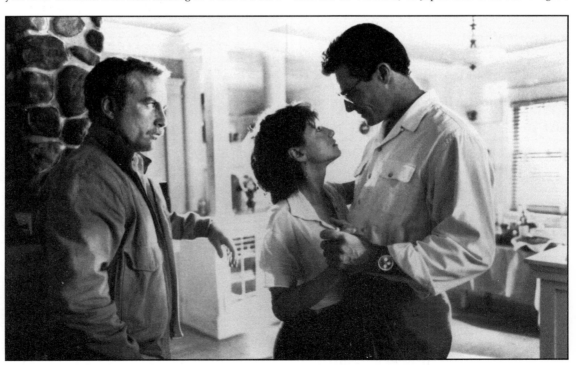

(Above) Raucous! Hysterical! Unbearable...

(Right) The most exciting scene in **Always.**

filmed every day.

"My preference when I came out of the army was to direct pictures, but I found out that there are a lot of directors around and they all need a cameraman! So it was easy — the phone kept ringing — and I had to do what I had learned. The easiest things to do [as a director] were nudie pictures — and they were fun. They gave you a chance to experiment a lot with the camera and the lighting. It was a great learning ground and a lot of guys did it, like Laszlo Kovacs and Vilmos Zsigmond. I was shooting and directing — I did documentaries for a year — and then I got a job on a picture with Al Adamson called *Fakers*, which started out under the title *Operation M*. One of the co-producers of *Fakers* was a theatre manager who had a ranch up in Roosevelt, Utah, above Salt Lake City, and part of the deal was that we had to go up there and film. I was in the movie too. I said, 'Jawohl, mein Herr' as a Nazi goon sitting whittling wood. They had already shot [some of] it and I went to Utah to work as second assistant cameraman, which meant loading the film so I hardly got near the set. It was started by Laszlo Kovacs, then Frank Ruttencutter took over and then they stopped — Al would do that — and after they were finished he said, 'Do you want to shoot it?' and I said, 'Sure'. I shot a little bit of it to finish it... And then we finished it again as *Hell's Bloody Devils* with some biker footage."

This was because of the runaway success of *Satan's Sadists* which, as opposed to Roger Corman's pictures, painted the bikers as drug-addicted, psychopathic animals.

"After Al's picture I hung around a place called the Hollywood Stage and I met Dave Hewitt, who was making a motorcycle picture called *The Girls from Thunder Strip* with Jody McCrea, Jack Starrett and Casey Kasem [later a famous disc jockey]. It was shot in Techniscope, which they don't have any more, in a Salvation Army camp in a park outside LA. Next I shot Al's *Satan's Sadists* out in the desert in a place called Indio down below Palm Springs, which took three weeks."

What about *The Kill*, which you directed, wrote and photographed?

"It was a picture for the nudie market... Awful. I shot it silent in two days, then added all the voices later myself — except for the girls. It's been re-released on video as *Blood Hunger*. I was anxious to take any job, anything that was offered, whether it was gaffing, sound, key grip or whatever."

You also edited *Satan's Sadists*...

"I learned editing from a guy called Bud Molin, who helped me on *The Embracers*. He was a friend of my stepfather's and had edited Orson Welles' *Fountain of Youth* and all of the *I Love Lucy* and *Dick Van Dyke* TV shows. [He now edits Carl Reiner's pictures]. He was extremely fast and I liked that — I like to work fast."

What about *The Blood Seekers*?

"That became *Dracula vs Frankenstein*. I shot that in Hollywood, but just after we finished they went back East with it and filmed five or six minutes in New York out in the woods somewhere."

Why?

"They took the picture back to Sam and he said, 'Put a new ending on it.' Invariably..."

Was some of that shot at The Hollywood Stages?

"Al had an office and shot everything there. We used the corridors for the police department in *Dracula vs Frankenstein* and it had a big castle set [where

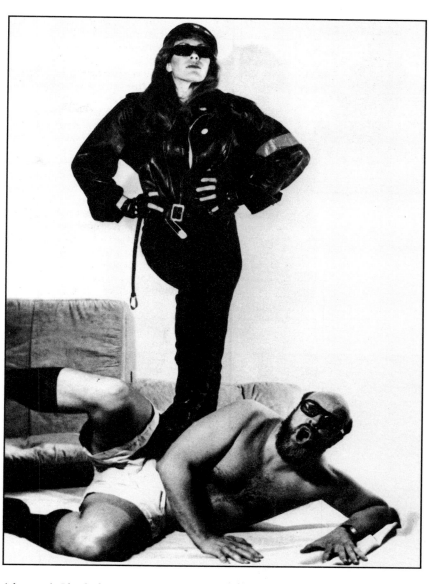

Adamson's *Blood of Dracula's Castle* was made]. During the day I was editing *The Fabulous Bastard from Chicago* and at night I would edit *Satan's Sadists*, even though it was too much work. Al didn't care... It was awful, everyone else was having fun and going out to nice dinners."

How would you characterise Al's shooting style?

"One of the good things about working with Al — and this is often true of low budget pictures — was the ability to exercise my creativity, to do a lot myself. My suggestions were usually taken. It's fun with Fred [Olen Ray] too. Doing Japanese commercials is not a lot of fun, because they are absolutely storyboarded and rigid and you can't vary from them."

What was *Hard Trail*?

"Well, I left that one — I didn't complete that one... There was a lot of stuff..."

In the late sixties and early seventies Graver worked on a large number of 'nudie-cuties' as they were called then. *The Fabulous Bastard from Chicago* and *Diamond Stud* were made for David F. Friedman, while *Wanda, the Sadistic Hypnotist*, *Wild, Free and Hungry* and Graver's own *Erika's Hot Summer* were made for Harry Novak's Box Office Pictures International. With many of these films being re-released on video, some pundits

A **Sight and Sound** *editorial meeting, modelled on* **Eating Raoul**...

now believe this period was the 'golden age' of American soft porn, when movies had at least some budget to speak of, were shot on film, usually included some semblance of a plot and tackled subjects now considered too unsavoury. Graver also made *One Million Years AC/DC* for the great Ed DePriest and *Excited* under the alcoholic pseudonym 'Akdov Telmig'. However, Graver would work on anything going, and if you pick up any piece of early seventies US sleaze you may well find him credited in some capacity or other.

"I was doing all these pictures and they were fun (and lucrative — I had bought a house in Laurel Canyon), but they were not very satisfying to me. I was also following Orson's [Welles] career and I knew that if he and I ever met we would get along — and that he needed someone like me. Sometime in 1971 I was standing in Schwabs Drug Store reading *Variety* and saw that he was staying at the Beverly Hills Hotel. I just called him up — out of the blue. They put me through and he answered the phone. I was scared but said I would like to work with him. He took my name and number, but he was about to leave for New York to make Henry Jaglom's *A Safe Place*. I thought that was that, but when I got home my phone was ringing

and it was Orson. He wanted an American cameraman and I was going to show him all the ways I knew of how to save money, how to get cheap lab work and how to get a crew fast and inexpensively. I wanted him to make a picture where he wouldn't have to kow tow to anybody because of the [lack of] money and I would be able to help him have complete freedom. I did, but little did I know that the first picture would take five years."

Welles was always in need of money for his own projects and would take almost anything he was offered. It was here that Graver's fast and efficient shooting style came in useful, and Welles would often bring Graver on board to shoot his scenes; a typical early job was six half-hour videos for the huge American department store chain Sears-Roebuck.

"When Orson returned from New York, we started making lots of tests. On the first day I forgot to bring the head of the tripod, then I forgot the lenses — I was so nervous it took me three or four days to get it together. He had this script he had been wanting to do for ages about a Hollywood director called Jake Hannaford — first we filmed Peter Bogdanovich, but later John Huston took over the role. We shot and shot and shot. Lots of people are in it: Dennis Hopper, Mercedes McCambridge, Lilli Palmer, Cameron Mitchell, Susan Strasberg, lots of people. We shot for four months and then just stopped. Next we went to Europe and did some stuff for Thames Television — the *Orson Welles' Great Mysteries* series on which I shot the opening, did the sound for his stuff — I did everything. We also made a PBS [Public Broadcasting Service] documentary series called *The Silent Years*. We made *F for Fake* practically with a one man crew, just Orson and myself. I was in it as an actor and Orson filmed me! We traipsed around Europe filming here and there, then came back to *The Other Side of the Wind* which we finished shooting in 1975. It's never been completed because of some legal problems."

Graver would work whenever Welles wanted, shooting guerrilla-style with a minimal crew. One of his more surprising credits was filming Welles' introduction to the 1975 compilation *Bugs Bunny Superstar*. Another example was *Filming the Trial*, which was to examine Welles' own 1962 version of the Kafka novel and was intended as a follow-up to *Filming Othello*. Graver filmed with Welles for just one day at the University of Southern California, but Welles lost interest in the project and it was never completed. Graver also wrote a screenplay with Welles called *Dead Giveaway*, based on a novel by Jim Thompson. It was to star Welles and Bud Cort but never entered production. Graver still has the script and intends to make it one day. "It's a good story but it's just so hard to raise money on."

Graver continued to work for Adamson and Sherman on pictures like *The Naughty Stewardesses* and *Girls for Rent*, while shooting projects as diverse as *Invasion of the Bee Girls* with William Smith, *Bummer* for David F. Friedman, Ron Howard's *Grand Theft Auto* and Richard Lang's unreleased horror opus *Blood, Black and White* starring Rory Calhoun. In 1975 he also began making adult films. Graver seemed embarrassed on my behalf when a trailer turned up for *V — The Hot One* on the end of his show reel; however, it was far superior to most of the other porn being made at the time. *V...* is beautifully-shot and displays Graver's characteristic flair for gynae-cological detail. It was also a great success and 'Robert

McCallum' kept making more and more films as the eighties approached. Many were made for Sidney Niekerk's successful Cal Vista outfit — *Dear Fanny, I Want to be...Bad* and *Garage Girls* amongst many; the latter even made it to these shores before the censor had his wicked way with it. Graver is extremely reticent about his adult work, so I was surprised to find that not only has he acted in other people's adult films (like Joe Sherman's *Ms. Magnificent*) but also makes amusing cameos in most of his own. Furthermore, when he was asked to shoot some extra footage to 'spice up' the Joan Collins' vehicle *Homework*, his Hollywood-by-night street scenes just happened to include shots of 'X' rated cinema marquees advertising Robert McCallum movies (some of this new footage featured a young Michelle Bauer). Other projects were the notorious *The Toolbox Murders* and actor Ross Hagen's violent *The Glove*.

Director Paul Hunt, with whom Graver also worked on *Wild, Free and Hungry*, *Machismo*, *The Clones* and *Twisted Nightmare*, decided to film a stage show featuring the musical talents of John, David, Keith and Robert Carradine, with Graver on camera. But this undoubtedly fascinating record of one of America's most eccentric acting families seems to have remained unshown.

After working with David Carradine on *Deathsport*, Graver filmed some material for the actor's epic *Mata Hari* starring his daughter Calista. The idea was to shoot for one week a year and trace the story of the infamous spy from her teenage years into adulthood.

"The shooting had a very laid back atmosphere — there was hardly any crew — with very nice results. He hasn't shot it for years."

When he made the horror movie *Trick or Treats* in 1981, Graver called in a number of favours, and while Welles served as 'special consultant', Carradine, Paul Bartel, Steve Railsback and Carrie Snodgress all appeared in the cast. Whatever his other work, Graver was always available when Welles wanted to work on projects — new or old — and in the eighties he shot black and white test footage for *King Lear* and material for *The Dreamers*, an adaptation of two stories by Isak Dinesen.

In 1980, Graver shot an extraneous ten-minute prologue to *Screamers*, the American version of Sergio Martino's *Island of the Mutations*, under the direction of the strangely named Miller Drake. James Cameron and Gale Ann Hurd were part of the crew and the new material contained lots of gloop and quite some gore.

"Miller Drake is a colleague who shared an office with me up at Jack Raben's building. He made *Cat Women of the Moon* and created all of Roger Corman's opticals. It was Corman's editing facility, and Joe Dante and Paul Bartel were also there. Miller was working for Corman and got a chance to put a ten minute sequence in this picture, so I shot it up at Bronson Canyon and down in Malibu with Cameron Mitchell and Mel Ferrer. We did it in three days, but the picture was all right as it was — a kind of Italian fantasy picture with fish men. Cameron [Mitchell] and I were sitting in the trailer and I gave him the script for *The Boys*, and he said he wanted to do it. He said, 'My son would be good to play my son'; I met him and so we cooked it up. We shot that picture in sequence, which was a luxury — just eight hours a day from ten till six in four weeks, which was something I had wanted to do for years. It helps the actors develop their characters. *The Boys* was a fairly heavy drama —

but my producer and the distributor re-edited it, shot some new stuff and made it into some sort of bad comedy. It was going to be a big thing for me, important, but they ruined it. It was re-titled *Texas Lightning*."

Texas Lightning was clearly an attempt at a serious drama, a study of southern-state America's attitudes to racism, sexism and the general bad behaviour of its male brethren as told through the relationship of redneck Cameron Mitchell with his sensitive son Channing. It was produced by Jim Sotos, who went on to make *Sweet 16* (a horror flick) and *Hot Moves* (a dreadful comedy). In its present form *Texas Lightning* is hardly a masterpiece, but a number of the scenes between father and son carry a strong dramatic punch. Graver makes a cameo appearance as the MC of a wet T-shirt competition.

Four years after he had last worked with Al Adamson on the wretched teen comedy *Sunset Cove*, Graver returned to the fold with the extraordinary *Doctor Dracula*.

"I think it started as a porno, but Al and Sam Sherman bought the rights and cut the sex out of it. We shot four days with Don 'Red' Barry and John Carradine at the Hollywood Stage and at some house up in the Hollywood hills. And then Don Barry shot and killed himself."

Doctor Dracula was a re-vamp of Paul Aratow's 1974 sex-with-the-devil flick *Lucifer's Women* starring Larry Hankin, a fine character actor seen in much expensive Hollywood fare. He was brought back for the new footage, along with an exhausted-looking John Carradine, who unfortunately gives one of his less inspired performances. The following year Graver worked with Adamson one last time on the drama *Lost* starring Sandra Dee, which appears to have had no English-language release whatsoever. A recent source claims Graver contributed second unit directing work to a number of bigger-budget or cult movies, namely *Enter the Dragon*, Cassavetes' *A Woman Under the Influence*, Walter Hill's *The Driver* and *The Warriors*, Dante's *The Howling*, Spielberg's *Raiders of the Lost Ark*

(Above) Thanks to some typical movie industry idiocy, heavy drama **The Boys** becomes a blockhead comedy...

(Below) Hard to imagine this objectionable little number even being made these days, let alone going out on a double bill with **Zombie Flesh Eaters**.

Another of Graver's movies
to suffer post-production
interference…

and Samuel Fuller's *White Dog*. I have been unable to confirm most of these credits and although Graver does receive a 'special thanks' credit on *The Howling*, he certainly isn't credited on *The Warriors* in any capacity.

The eighties saw Graver directing and shooting a phenomenal number of movies under his 'Robert McCallum' guise, most of which were designed primarily for the video market, since punters could now enjoy these movies at home rather than in some 42nd Street grindhouse. Nevertheless, the McCallum films did play theatrically abroad, usually in places like Holland. Graver also picked up a number of TV movie assignments, including *Through the Magic Pyramid* for Ron Howard and a trio of vehicles for *Diff'rent Strokes* star Gary Cole. The latter half of the decade saw Graver as busy as ever, working on at least thirteen films just for Fred Olen Ray, whose rapid production schedules seemed to suit Graver's penchant for guerrilla-style film-making.

In 1987 Graver attempted to remake an unfinished project of Welles' from 1969, known variously as *The Deep*, *Dead Reckoning* and *Direction Towards Death*. This had been based on a novel by Charles Williams about intrigue and murder in the confined space of a small yacht. Welles' version starred himself, Laurence Harvey and Jeanne Moreau; Graver brought in William Smith and John Phillip Law, but the best laid plans…

"If something is really attractive to me then I want to direct it. If it's just sort of blasé and unless I can really contribute something, I'd rather work as a cameraman.

"*Moon in Scorpio* was ruined. I've never seen it. I delivered a ninety-minute cut, but I had to go to Tokyo for a Welles retrospective and when I came back they had completely destroyed it. They [producers at Trans World Entertainment] brought in some cutters

from Israel and said, 'Go away'. They took the picture apart — put it back into little rolls of film — started all over again, remade the picture from scratch and made it stupid. I stayed with it as long as I could to save it — which was stupid — but eventually I had to walk away from it. It happens to everything and you have to accept it unless you own it — but it was such a good story."

Moon in Scorpio's extra material was shot by Fred Olen Ray… Australian director Phillip Noyce finally did justice to the story in 1989 when he made *Dead Calm* with Nicole Kidman and Sam Neill. Undeterred, Graver continued to direct various films: *Nerds of a Feather* was touted as starring David Carradine and John Phillip Law, but when it was shown there was no sign of either. *Variety* described it as a 'vanity production' for co-director and star Mario M. Milano, and it seems to have sunk without trace. More successful was *Crossing the Line*, a fairly decent-sized independent production made in South Africa (posing as Pennsylvania) with John Saxon, David Hasselhoff, Paul 'Bluto' Smith and Cameron Mitchell. Changes in the money laws in the late eighties meant that foreign producers could make movies where labour was cheap and locations attractive while writing off almost the entire cost of the film against tax. Independent Hollywood invaded South Africa for a short while and the results, which *Variety* dubbed 'Cape Town Quickies', were frequently anonymous and usually little-seen.

"*Crossing the Line* was classic showbusiness. I was just sitting at home one Sunday morning wondering what I was going to do next and the telephone rang: 'Would you like to go to South Africa and direct a picture?' I said, 'Yeah.' They said, 'Can you leave next week?' I said, 'Sure.' I spent the next week making the contracts and doing the casting, and the following week found myself in South Africa with a big office directing a movie — I was very happy with it and I got some good performances. We shot it for five weeks and I loved it down there. Not a lot of production facilities, but at the time it was booming, twelve or fifteen pictures going on at the same time so we didn't have much equipment. Once again they shot another ending and tagged it on to make a male-bonding type of picture, which wasn't intended but… that's what they do. It's dead there now. The money [laws] changed."

I asked Graver about a poster bearing his name for a movie entitled *Deadly Revenge*, which I've never heard of again.

"We did a twenty-minute promo and the advertising through a distributor named Norbert Meisel, but it never got made — couldn't raise the money on it. A lot of times people do that but they never make the movie. It was made by an actor named Eric Braeden who was on *The Young and the Restless* and just wanted to direct the thing." [Braeden was hiding under his real name of Hans Gudegast in the *Variety* ad.]

In 1988, Graver and Welles' long-time companion Oja Kodar made *Jaded*. Fred Olen Ray described this as being full of Graver's favourite subjects, namely midgets and transvestites. Shot in five weeks, it was made ostensibly to raise money to complete some of Welles' most cherished projects. Starring Charles Pierce (also a star of *Torch Song Trilogy*) and Fred Olen Ray's ex-wife, the sultry Dawn Wildsmith, it has yet to be released in any form in the United States.

In the late eighties Graver set up a company named

Grand Am Ltd with old Cal Vista pal Sidney Niekerk. Its output has been erratic but interesting: *Roots of Evil* was a sort of low-life cop thriller with nudity and cod-psychology thrown in for good measure. Alex Cord is not nearly as hard-boiled as he thinks he is but the wonderful Charles Dierkop scores highly as a detective. *Evil Spirits* was an all-star B-movie horror fest which those few who have been able to see it seem to like. Better was Graver's *Angel Eyes* for Fred Olen Ray's production company, American Independent, which has John Phillip Law fucking away like a dog on heat. Lost in the deluge of 'erotic thrillers', it deserved more attention than it received. As usual, Graver put in a cameo appearance as a cop who arrests a character named Wanda — an in-joke for those who knew something of his career. Grand Am's most recent release as of writing is Graver's documentary *Working with Orson Welles* which, typical of the way critics treat independent American product these days, was flatly ignored.

My time was up and Graver clearly had other things he needed to do — I got the impression that he doesn't really like to talk about his work and I often had to push him to get a response. I liked the man, admired his skills and am amazed that he has had the career he has. If he didn't get the breaks afforded contemporaries like Zsigmond and Kovacs, he clearly adored the years he spent working with Welles and he certainly hasn't given up. ∎

GARY GRAVER FILMOGRAPHY

1962: Seeking(s). Dir/prod/scr.
1963: The Embracers/Now (shooting title: The Great Dream). Dir/prod/scr, also act as The Boy. [Released 1966.]
1967: The Girls from Thunder Strip. Dir ph. Dir: David L. Hewitt.
    The Sadistic Hypnotist/Wanda, the Sadistic Hypnotist. Dir ph/ed. Dir: Greg Corarito.
1968: Faker$ (shooting title: Operation M). Second unit ph i.e. Co-dir ph/second asst cam, also act as Nazi goon. Dir: Al Adamson.
    The Kill/Blood Hunger. Dir/scr/ph.
1969: The Mighty Gorga. Dir ph, also act as Man at Zoo. Dir: David L. Hewitt.
    One Million Years AC/DC. Co-scr, credited as 'Akdov Telmig'. Dir: Ed DePriest
    Excited. Dir/scr, credited as 'Akdov Telmig'.
    Satan's Sadists. Dir ph/film ed. Dir: Al Adamson.
    The Fabulous Bastard from Chicago/The Fabulous Kid from Chicago/The Bastard Wench from Chicago/The Chicago Kid. Dir ph/ed [plus appearance in trailer]. Dir: Greg Corarito.
    Hell's Bloody Devils. Dir ph, new material. Dir: Al Adamson. [Re-edited version, with added footage, of *Faker$*.]
    Hard Trail/On the Hard Trail (shooting title: The Hard Bunch). Dir ph. Dir: Greg Corarito.
1969-85: The Magic Show. Dir ph. Dir: Orson Welles. [Unreleased.]
1970s: Don Quixote. Dir ph, new material. Dir: Orson Welles. [Unfinished.]
1970: Machismo (40 Graves for 40 Guns)/Forty Graves for Forty Guns/Revenge of the Wild Bunch. Act, as Tim Harris. Dir: Paul Hunt.
    The Affairs of Aphrodite. Dir ph. Dir:

Alain Patrick.
    The Making of Sandra/I am Sandra. Dir/co-scr/dir ph/ed.
    Blood Mania. Co-dir ph. Dir: Robert Vincent O'Neil.
    Diamond Stud. Dir ph. Dir: Greg Corarito.
    Erika's Hot Summer. Dir/co-prod/dir ph/co-ed.
    The Hard Road/The Hard Row. Dir/dir ph/ed.
    Dracula vs Frankenstein/Blood of Frankenstein. Co-dir ph new material, also act as [uncredited] guy on beach. Dir: Al Adamson. [Re-edited version, with added footage, of *Blood Seekers*, 1969.]
    Vampire Men of the Lost Planet. Act [uncredited], as a vampire. Dir: Al Adamson.
    Wild, Free and Hungry. Prod, also act, as Dave. Dir: 'H. P. Edwards', ie Paul Hunt.
1971: Moby Dick. Dir ph. Dir: Orson Welles. [Unfinished — 30 of 60 mins shot.]
1971-76: The Other Side of the Wind. Dir ph. Dir: Orson Welles. [Unreleased.]
1972: The Clones/The Cloning of Dr. Appleby/Clones/Dead Man Running (pre-shooting title: Mind-Sweepers, shooting title: The Cloning). Dir ph. Dir: Paul Hunt & Lamar Card.
    The Killing Kind/The Psychopath. Co-second unit dir ph. Dir: Curtis Harrington.
1973: There Was a Little Girl/And When She Was Bad. Dir/prod/scr.
    Bummer. Dir ph. Dir: William Allen Castleman.
    Blood, Black and White. Dir ph. Dir: Richard Lang. [Unreleased.]
    The Naughty Stewardesses. Dir ph. Dir: Al Adamson.
    Invasion of the Bee Girls/Graveyard Tramps. Dir ph. Dir: Denis Sanders.
1974: Girls for Rent/I Spit on Your Corpse/Day of the Maniac. Dir ph. Dir: Al Adamson.
1975: F for Fake/Verites et Mensonges/Nothing But the Truth. (Fr/Iran/WG) WG: *F wie Fälschung*. Co-ph of American & Toussaint material, plus act, as himself. Dir: Orson Welles. [Production completed in 1973.]
    Jessi's Girls/Wanted Women. Dir ph. Dir: Al Adamson.
    Moonshine County Express. Dir ph. Dir: Gus Trikonis.

(Above) The variously retitled Dracula vs Frankenstein.

(Below) Some mayhem from The Glove.

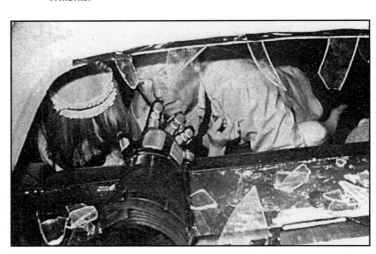

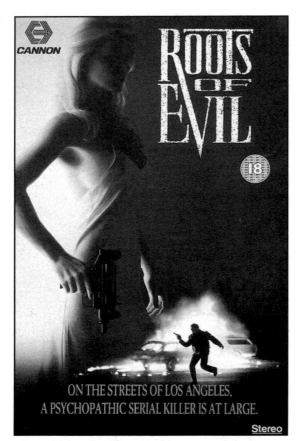

(Right) A Graver-directed sleaze actioner.

(Below) An Olen Ray-directed poop stain.

The Student Body. Dir ph. Dir: Gus Trikonis.

1976: F for Fake trailer. Act, as himself. Dir: Orson Welles.

Bugs Bunny Superstar. Dir ph of new material. Dir: Larry Jackson.

Black Heat/The Murder Gang/US Vice/Intrigue/Syndicate Vice (shooting title: Inside Straight). Dir ph. Dir: Al Adamson.

1977: Sunset Cove. Dir ph. Dir: Al Adamson.

Filming Othello. Dir ph. Dir: Orson Welles. [Production commenced in 1974.]

Grand Theft Auto. Dir ph. Dir: Ron Howard.

Death Dimension/Icy Death/Kill Factor/Black Eliminator/Freeze Bomb. Dir ph. Dir: Al Adamson.

Smokey and the Hotwire Gang (shooting title: Smokey and the Car Takers). Dir ph. Dir: Anthony Cardoza.

1977-1982: Mata Hari. Co-dir ph. Dir: David Carradine.

1978: The Toolbox Murders. Dir ph. Dir: Dennis Donnelly.

One Man Jury/Dead on Arrival/The Loner (shooting title: The Cop Who Played God). Co-dir ph. Dir: Charles Martin Smith.

Deathsport. Dir ph. Dir: 'Henry Suso', ie Nicholas Niciphor & Allan Arkush. [Production commenced in 1976.]

Orson Welles Solo. Dir ph. [Unreleased, possibly unfilmed.]

Feature length talk show pilot. Dir ph. Dir: Orson Welles. [Never shown.]

The Glove/Blood Mad. Dir ph. Dir: Ross Hagen. [Released in 1981.]

1978-85: The Dreamers. Dir ph. Dir: Orson Welles.

[Uncompleted.]

1979: Carradines in Concert. Dir ph. Dir: Paul Hunt. [Limited release.]

Sunnyside. Dir ph. Dir: Timothy Galfas.

The Attic. Dir ph. Dir: George Edwards.

Hollywood High Part II. Dir ph. Dir: Caruth C. Byrd & Lee Thornberg.

1980: Smokey Bites the Dust. Dir ph. Dir: Charles B. Griffith.

Scout's Honor (TVM). Dir ph. Dir: Henry Levin.

Screamers (pre-release: Something Waits in the Dark). Dir ph of new material. Dir: Miller Drake. [Re-edited version, with added footage, of *L'Isola degli Uomini Pesci/Island of the Mutations* (It), 1979. Dir: Sergio Martino.]

Texas Lightning/The Boys. Dir/scr/co-ph, also act [uncredited] as MC of wet T-shirt contest.

1981: The Howling. 'Special thanks'. Dir: Joe Dante.

Filming The Trial. Dir ph. Dir: Orson Welles. [Uncompleted.]

Doctor Dracula. Dir ph of new material. Dir: Al Adamson. [Re-edited version, with added footage, of *Lucifer's Women*, 1974. Dir: Paul Aratow.]

Through the Magic Pyramid (TVM). Dir ph. Dir: Ron Howard.

Child Bride of Short Creek (TVM). Dir ph. Dir: Robert Michael Lewis.

Mortuary/Embalmed. Dir ph. Dir: Howard Avedis.

Sweet Sixteen. Second unit dir ph. Dir: Jim Sotos.

1982: Homework (shooting title: Growing Pains). Second unit dir. Dir: James Beshears. [Production commenced in 1979.]

Trick or Treats. Co-dir/co-prod/scr/dir ph/ed.
The Kid with the Broken Halo (TV prod). Dir ph. Dir: Leslie Martinson.
Lost. Dir ph. Dir: Al Adamson.
Eating Raoul. Second unit dir ph. Dir: Paul Bartel.
The Kid with the 200 I.Q. (TV prod). Dir ph. Dir: Leslie Martinson.

1983: **They're Playing with Fire.** Dir ph. Dir: Howard Avedis.
The Fantastic World of D.C. Collins (TV prod). Dir ph. Dir: Leslie H. Martinson.

1984: **Chatanooga Choo Choo.** Dir ph. Dir: Bruce Bilson.

1985: **King Lear** (B&W video test). Dir ph. Dir: Orson Welles.

1986: **Party Camp.** Dir/dir ph.
Stagecoach (TVM). Dir ph. Dir: Ted Post.
Distortions. Technical supervisor. Dir: Armand Mastroanni.

1987: **Commando Squad.** Dir ph. Dir: Fred Olen Ray.
Moon in Scorpio. Dir/dir ph. [Uncredited dir, extra scenes: Fred Olen Ray.]
Twisted Nightmare. Co-dir ph. Dir: Paul Hunt.
Deep Space. Dir ph. Dir: Fred Olen Ray.
Deadly Revenge. Dir ph. Dir: 'Hans Gudegast', aka Eric Braeden. [Uncompleted promo.]
Beyond Fear (shooting title: Terminal Force). Dir ph. Dir: Fred Olen Ray. [uncompleted promo.]
Nerds of a Feather/Spies & Lovers in Beverly Hills. Co-dir/dir ph. Co-dir: 'Romeo M.', ie Mario R. Milano.
Hollywood Chainsaw Hookers/Hollywood Hookers (shooting title: Chainsaw Hook-ers). Second unit cam. Dir: Fred Olen Ray.

1988: **Terminal Force** (shooting title: Fatal Justice). 'Thanked', ie second unit cam/use of locations. Dir: Fred Olen Ray.
Real Bullets. Co-dir ph. Dir: Lance Lindsay.
Jaded. Co-p/dir ph. Dir: Oja Kodar.
Death House. Co-second unit dir ph. Dir: John Saxon & [uncredited] Fred Olen Ray.
B.O.R.N.. Dir ph. Dir: Ross Hagen.
Night Children. Dir ph. Dir: Norbert Meisel.
Beverly Hills Vamp. Second unit dir ph. Dir: Fred Olen Ray.

1989: **Alienator.** Dir ph. Dir: Fred Olen Ray.
L.A. Bounty. Dir ph. Dir: Worth Keeter.
Demon Wind. Add ph. Dir: Charles Phillip Moore.
Wizards of the Demon Sword (shooting title: Demon Sword). Dir ph, also act [uncredited], as desert soldier. Dir: Fred Olen Ray.
Click: the Calendar Girl Killer. Co-dir ph. Dir: John Stewart & Ross Hagen.
Crossing the Line (SA).
Always. Co-add ph. Dir: Steven Spielberg.
Bad Girls from Mars. Dir ph, also act, as director of photography. Dir: Fred Olen Ray.

1990: **Haunting Fear.** Dir ph. Dir: Fred Olen Ray.
Mob Boss. Dir ph. Dir: Fred Olen Ray.
Roots of Evil (shooting title: Naked Force). Dir/dir ph, also act [uncredited], as a cop who arrests 'Wanda' for the second time. *
The Revenger (shooting title: Saxman). Second unit dir ph. Dir: Cedric Sundström.
Spirits. Dir ph. Dir: Fred Olen Ray.
Evil Toons. Dir ph. Dir: Fred Olen Ray.

BEFORE YOUR FUNERAL...
BEFORE YOU ARE BURIED...
BEFORE YOU ARE COVERED WITH THE LAST SHOVELFUL OF DIRT...
BE SURE YOU ARE REALLY DEAD!

MORTUARY

...WHERE NOBODY RESTS IN PEACE

Evil Spirits. Dir/dir ph. *
The Channeler. Second camera. Dir: Grant Austin Waldman.
Ted and Venus (shooting title: Love in Venice). Second unit dir ph. Dir: Bud Cort.

1991: **Inner Sanctum.** Add camera. Dir: Fred Olen Ray.
Angel Eyes. Dir/dir ph/scr.
Teenage Exorcist. Second camera. Dir: Grant Austin Waldman.

1992: **Forever.** Dir ph. Dir: Thomas Palmer Jr.
October 32nd. Dir ph. Dir: Paul Hunt.
Mind Twisters. Dir ph. Dir: Fred Olen Ray.

1993: **Shootfighter.** Second unit dir ph. Dir: Patrick Allen.
It's All True (Fr/US). Dir ph, new material. Dir: Orson Welles.
Dinosaur Island. Dir ph. Dir: Fred Olen Ray & Jim Wynorski.
Working with Orson Welles. Dir/pc. *
Femme Fontaine: Killer Babe for the CIA. Dir ph/film editor. Dir: Margot Hope.
Rosabella La Storia Italiana di Orson Welles (It). Interviewee. Dir: Glanfranco Gagni.

1994: **Possessed By the Night/Dark is the Night/Night Eyes The Possession.** Dir ph. Dir: Fred Olen Ray.
Sorceress (shooting title: Temptress of the Dark). Dir ph. Dir: Jim Wynorski.
Bikini Drive-In. Dir ph. Dir: Fred Olen Ray.
Vrijema za... (Yug/It). Dir ph. Dir: Oja Kodar.

1995: **Night Eyes Fatal Passion.** Dir ph. Dir: Rodney McDonald.

The only smut we're 'allowed' to run! Write to your local MP!

Films marked * were produced by Grand Am Limited, a company set up and owned by Graver and Cal Vista's Sidney Niekerk

"Last night I watched *Peeping Tom*. I made that movie during a period of great rhythm in my life, when I was going to San Francisco about once a week to make movies — even though I didn't feel very sunny about the business. *Peeping Tom* was directed by 'Robert McCallum'. I usually don't get along with him, but that film was an exception. We respected each other's talent...

"Robert is a very attractive, sweet man with a shark-eyed face. One of my favourite directors, his shoots are free and unrestricted. He's like a rancher: he doesn't mind the stallions running around within the coral, because he knows the gates are locked.

"During sex scenes, Robert leaves his actors alone and does his own job: directing and camerawork. His camera always sought out the core of the scene and stayed with it, while most other directors are too mechanical, making you change positions every five minutes.

"Robert's doing legit movies now. Lisa even worked with him on a video for cable TV and found him to be nice, pleasant and respectful of her talent. In fact, she had no idea he had ever done adult-film work; Robert was that professional.

"Guys like Robert live in fear that the world will find out what he's doing. In fact, I promised him I wouldn't reveal his real name, and I always keep my word. Well, at least I try."

Jerry Butler (as told to Robert Rimmer and Catherine Tavel), *Raw Talent* (Prometheus Books, Buffalo, New York, 1990).

WORK CREDITED TO 'ROBERT McCALLUM'

1975: **3 AM.** Dir/prod/dir ph.
1978: **V — The Hot One.** Dir/dir ph.
Tangerine. Dir/dir ph.
1979: **Hot Rackets.** Dir/dir ph.
Ecstasy Girls. Dir/dir ph.
800 Fantasy Lane. Dir/dir ph.
Ms. Magnificent. Act, as the character Joe Sherman.
1980: **Garage Girls.** Dir/sc, also act [uncredited] as a painter.
Amanda By Night. Dir/dir ph.
Co-Ed Fever. Dir/dir ph.
1981: **Peaches and Cream.** Dir/dir ph.
Centerspread Girls. Dir/dir ph.
Indecent Exposure. Dir/dir ph.
1982: **Society Affair.** Dir/dir ph.
Satisfactions. Dir/dir ph.
1983: **Suzie Superstar.** Dir/dir ph.
Summer Camp Girls. Dir/dir ph.
Private Moments. Dir/co-sc/dir ph.
Private Teacher. Dir/dir ph — as 'Akdov Telmig'.
Coffee, Tea or Me. Dir/dir ph.
1984: **Trinity Brown.** Dir/dir ph.
I Want to Be... Bad. Dir/dir ph.
Sex Play. Dir/dir ph.
Unthinkable. Dir/dir ph.
Tower of Power. Dir/dir ph.
1985: **Beverly Hills Exposed.** Dir/dir ph.
Dear Fanny. Dir/dir ph.
Soaking Wet. Dir/dir ph.
Flesh for Fantasy. Dir/dir ph.

Perfect Partners. Dir/dir ph.
Suzie Superstar II. Dir/sc/dir ph.
1986: **Showgirls.** Dir/prod/dir ph.
Crazy with the Heat. Dir. [dir ph — as 'Bill Horny'?]
Ecstasy Girls II. Dir/dir ph, as 'Jim Reynolds'.
Joanna Storm on Fire. Dir/prod/dir ph.
Rated Sex. Dir/dir ph.
Peeping Tom. Dir/dir ph — as 'Jim Reynolds'.
Only the Best [Compilation — various clips from 'RM' films.]
Ten and a Half Weeks. Dir/dir ph.
Please Don't Stop. Dir/dir ph.
Doll Face. Dir/dir ph.
Erotic City. Dir/dir ph.
Hypatia Lee's Secret Dream. Dir.
1987: **Barbara the Barbarian.** Dir/dir ph.
Barbara Dare's Surf, Sand and Sex. Dir/dir ph.
Charmed and Dangerous. Dir/dir ph.
Spanish Fly. Dir/dir ph.
Two to Tango. Dir/prod.
Private Encounters. Dir/dir ph.
1990: **Dream Lover.** Dir.
1991: **Three Men and a Hooker.** Dir.
Purple Haze. Dir.
The Back Doors. Dir.
Decadent. Dir.
East L.A. Law. Dir.
The Erotic Adventures of Fannie Annie. Dir.
Victoria's Secret Life. Dir/prod.
Home But Not Alone. Dir.
Breathless. Dir.
The Stranger Beside Me. Dir/dir ph.
The Journey — Oral Majority: The Movie. Dir.
The Outlaw. Dir.
1992: **Black and White in Living Colour.** Dir.
Driving Miss Daisy Crazy #2/Driving Miss Daisy Crazy Again. Dir.
Shoot to Thrill. Dir.
Silence of the Buns. Dir.
Jugsy. Dir.
Cape Rear. Dir.
The Dragon Lady #3: Tales from the Bed #2. Dir/dir ph.

UNCONFIRMED CREDITS

1972: **The Artist.** Dir: Paul Hunt. [Production information on this uncompleted film gives GG as dir ph yet he does not recognise the title.]
1973: **Enter the Dragon** (US/HK) HK: Lung-cheng-hu Tou. Second unit dir. Dir: Robert Clouse.
A Woman Under the Influence. Second unit dir. Dir: John Cassavetes.
1978: **The Driver.** Second unit dir. Dir: Walter Hill.
1979: **The Warriors.** Second unit dir. Dir: Walter Hill. [Definitely uncredited].
1981: **Raiders of the Lost Ark.** Second unit dir. Dir: Steven Spielberg.
White Dog. Second unit dir. Dir: Sam Fuller.
1984: **Night Killing/Night Moon.** Dir ph? Dir: Norbert Meisel. [Ever completed/released?]
1987: **Swift Justice** (shooting title: Pop's Oasis). Dir: Harry Hope. [Although credited as co-dir ph when shooting, GG has no credit on the released film and states that he didn't work on it.]

With thanks to Fred Olen Ray.

INDEX OF FILM TITLES